Computer Integrated Manufacturing

The Data Management Strategy

Digital Press CIM Series

Series Editor: Olin H. Bray

Computer Integrated Manufacturing

The Data Management Strategy

Olin H. Bray

Digital Press

Printed in the United States of America.

9 8 7 6 5 4 3 2 1

Order number EY-6735E-DP

The Digital logo is a trademark of Digital Equipment Corporation.

Library of Congress Cataloging-in-Publication Data

Bray, Olin H.
    Computer integrated manufacturing.

    Bibliography: p.
    1. Computer integrated manufacturing systems.
I. Title.
TS155.6.B73   1988   670.42'7   88-3811
ISBN 1-55558-010-6

A BARD PRODUCTIONS BOOK
Editing: Alison Tartt
Jacket Design: Gayle Smith Advertising Design
Text Design: Mary Ann Noretto
Text Illustrations: Raymond Ojeda
Index: Linda Webster
Typesetting: Pamela C. Winsier
Production: The Composing Stick

Printed in the United States by Hamilton Printing Company

First Edition

Contents

CONTENTS

Part One. Manufacturing and a Framework for CIM

Part Two. Data Management

Part Three. Design and Manufacturing Functions

Part Four. Integration Issues

List of Figures and Tables

Figures

Tables

Preface

Today American manufacturing is an industry in trouble, rapidly losing its competitiveness. Four trends are changing the competitive environment and the way we do design and manufacturing. First, product life cycles are becoming shorter, requiring a faster development cycle. Second, products and manufacturing processes are becoming more complex. Third, customers want more customized rather than standard products. Fourth, there are simply not enough trained people, such as design and manufacturing engineers, draftsmen, and skilled machinists, for us to continue our inefficient, labor-intensive methods.

CIM can help us make more complex, customized, higher-quality products faster and cheaper. It can also provide the leverage to do this while making more effective use of our limited, trained people. (It should be noted that many different terms are used to describe the concepts discussed in this book. They include CAD [computer-aided design or computer-aided drafting], CAM [computer-aided manufacturing], CAE [computer-aided engineering], and more recently CIM [computer-integrated manufacturing]. While people can and will argue about the precise functions included in each term, this is a sterile debate. Therefore, throughout this book the generic term CIM is used.)

The design and manufacturing process involves many separate functions. Unfortunately, many products today concentrate on improving the productivity of only one or two functions. However, CIM must consider the entire design and manufacturing process as an integrated set of functions. The computer must be used to support and automate this overall process. It is not adequate to simply address each function independently. Therefore, this book addresses manufacturing from an integrated information management perspective.

The future of U.S. manufacturing depends on many factors, including many technologies. This book focuses on one of the most critical technologies—information management. It describes information management technology, specifically database management technology, and its key role in integrating the factory of the future. Without this critical technology all other improvements in manufacturing are simply improvements in individual pieces of the design and manufacturing process. Without more effective information management we will continue to develop isolated islands of automation. Effective information management is the key to integrating these existing islands of automation and in the long term designing and building integrated factories—factories in which managing and processing information is as important as processing materials. Without this technology we risk sitting on the sidelines, watching our foreign competitors build more productive, integrated factories of the future. A traditional, nonautomated manufacturing company simply cannot survive once its competitors have automated, a lesson we are beginning to see clearly in U.S. industry.

Furthermore, it is not enough simply to develop this new technology—something we are very good at. We must follow through and move it from the research labs to the shop floor.

This book provides a framework for such action by explaining this new information management technology and applying it specifically to manufacturing. The book consists of four parts. The first part sets the stage by providing an overview of manufacturing strategy, CAD/CAM/CIM, and the factory of the future. The second part describes data management technology and its role in integration. The third part describes specific design and manufacturing functions and identifies their information models. The fourth part discusses integration issues, including lessons from management information systems and CIM organizational issues.

This book was written for two groups—design and manufacturing engineers and their managers who must plan for, implement, and use CIM systems in their daily work as well as information systems people who must develop and support these systems. The book can also provide a common background for both groups and help begin the essential communications between them. It describes the design and manufacturing functions and shows the information flows among them. To do this, it explains why information management, the key to integration, is important in the factory of the future. In the university environment the book can be a key integrating text for an information systems course in manufacturing.

This book provides a valuable framework for corporate steering committees and task forces. There is frequently little common ground for such diverse groups of experts. As a starting point this book provides such a common background, and the methodology it describes provides a common approach so that the results of various studies can be quickly and easily integrated. The book describes the generic design and manufacturing functions. With these descriptions as a model, the experts on the task force can customize the analysis to describe the way the functions are actually done within their own company. It is easier to design a new part if you can begin with a similar existing design and modify it. These generic information models provide these initial templates. Every company does each of the design and manufacturing functions somewhat differently, but these models provide an easy starting point.

Olin H. Bray
West Hartford, Connecticut
May 1988

Acknowledgments

Computer integrated manufacturing is such a broad area that no one can completely understand it all. Therefore, a book like this depends on the comments, suggestions, and knowledge of many people too numerous to name. However, a few people stand out and should be thanked for the perspectives they provided and/or for reviewing earlier drafts. For the engineering and manufacturing perspective I am grateful to Charles Knox, Peter Patton, Robert Fulton, Glen Castore, Charles Blackburn, and at Combustion Engineering Donald Seccombe and Cameron McQuaid. For information modeling, NIAM, and database management the list includes Paul Thompson, Gail Vermilyea, John Zimmerman, Maurice Smith, and John Sharp. I also appreciate the many suggestions from those who reviewed the earlier drafts of the book.

I also thank my wife, Jan Bray, not only for accepting the time such a book takes, but also for editing each of the drafts. Her frequent "This doesn't make any sense, what are you trying to say?" has resulted in a much more understandable and readable book.

O. H. B.

Part One
Manufacturing and a
Framework for CIM

The three chapters in Part One provide the context for the rest of the book. It is important background information for those readers who are relatively new to manufacturing. Parts of Chapters 1 and 3 may also be new to those readers already experienced in CIM.

Chapter 1 describes the changing competitive environment and how it is affecting manufacturing. It also explains the critical importance of CIM for the survival of manufacturing companies and relates this technology to a corporate-wide manufacturing strategy. Chapter 2 identifies what CAD/CAM/CIM is and how it has evolved. Considering the speed of its development, it needs the broadest possible definition to include new technologies as they evolve. Chapter 3 introduces the concept of the factory of the future. The factory of the future is an information-hungry approach to manufacturing, so effective management of information is essential for its success.

1

Manufacturing Strategy and CIM

The New Competitive Environment
More Complex Products
Higher Quality
Increased Product Liability
More Customized Products
Shorter Product Life Cycle
Fewer Skilled Workers
Increased Competition

Manufacturing Strategy

Evaluation Criteria for Manufacturing
- cost/efficiency
- functionality
- quality
- customization
- volume flexibility
- product flexibility
- fast delivery
- valid delivery schedules

Components of Manufacturing Strategy

Relationship between Manufacturing Strategy and CIM Applications

Summary

 Manufacturing companies today have two options – "automate or evaporate." Companies must respond to their rapidly changing marketplace and to the new technologies being implemented by their competitors. Furthermore, manufacturing, which has been treated as an outcast by corporate planning and strategy, must become directly involved in these critical long-range decisions. Manufacturing can indeed be a "formidable competitive weapon," but only if we plan for it and provide the necessary tools and technologies.[1]

More complex products, a shorter product life cycle, and more customized products make manufacturing far more competitive today than in the past. These problems are especially severe for many U.S. manufacturers because they are not applying new manufacturing and information technologies as fast as many foreign companies can. This is especially frustrating because many of these new technologies were initially developed in the United States.

CIM will allow companies to respond better and faster in this more competitive environment. The first part of this chapter describes this changing competitive environment and how CIM will help companies respond to it. However, these technological and productivity improvements will not help unless we understand how they are related to, indeed should be driven by, an overall corporate strategy. The second part discusses criteria for evaluating manufacturing strategies and identifies the components of a manufacturing strategy. The third part of this chapter summarizes the relationship between manufacturing strategy and types of CAD/CAM/CIM applications.

The New Competitive Environment

Successful companies must respond effectively to the changing competitive environment. Their problems are more complicated today because many changes are occurring not only simultaneously but also more rapidly than in the past. Since some manufacturers have developed the strategy and technology to respond quickly to these changes, all companies must respond faster to remain competitive.

These changes are occurring in all sectors of manufacturing – consumer goods and capital equipment, with high technology and low technology products, and in the civilian and defense sectors. Specifically, these changes include:

- more complex products
- higher quality
- increased product liability
- more customized products
- shorter product life cycle
- fewer skilled workers
- increased competition

The impact of these changes and their relative importance vary among industries.

4

Even among different companies in the same industry their impact varies depending on the company's strategy. The rest of this section describes each of these changes and briefly suggests how CIM can help a company deal with them.

More Complex Products

Although many products are becoming easier to use, they are also becoming much more complex and difficult to design and manufacture. One example is the shift from vacuum tubes to computer chips, which—while cheaper and more powerful— are much harder to design and manufacture. Another example is the shift in our communications systems from relatively simple analog voice telephones to complex digital systems that are able to handle a mixture of voice, data, and video and use complex computerized switching and control systems. Even the automobile, once a relatively simple mechanical system, is becoming more complex with computer-controlled ignition, braking, and maintenance systems. Even consumer goods are becoming more complex with traditional magnetic tapes and records being replaced by sophisticated optical storage devices that were research projects only a few years ago.

There are three possible responses to this increasing complexity. First, we can slow down the product development cycle to allow more time to deal with this increased complexity. Second, we can continue to develop these more complex products with the same development cycle and sacrifice product quality. Third, we can develop new tools and technologies that will allow us to deal with this complexity without sacrificing time or quality. The last alternative is preferred. This approach requires improvements in design and manufacturing processes, in information management technology, and in the interfaces between them. Applications such as design, drafting, analysis, process planning, and shop-floor control support this third alternative.

Higher Quality

Customers are demanding higher-quality products. As prices increase, customers want their money's worth for the products they buy. This applies to both consumers and industrial customers. This improved product quality has two components— better design and better quality control in the manufacturing operation.

CIM applications assist in both of these areas. Design and analysis applications allow the designer to evaluate more alternatives and optimize the design. In the past we did less analysis, in some cases because we did not know how and in other cases because the analysis methods were too expensive. If a stress analysis was going to take several weeks or months, assuming it could be done at all, we frequently just overdesigned the part for the worst case. Today the same analysis might take several hours of an engineer's time and a few minutes on a computer. Even relatively small unit cost savings in manufacturing outweigh these low analysis costs. This improved analysis capability means that for the same cost we can design and build a higher-quality product. Alternately, the same quality can be provided at a lower cost.

Similarly, computer-assisted process planning permits more manufacturing options to be considered. This can lead to higher quality, lower costs, or both. Improvements are also possible simply by creating a better interface between the designer and the manufacturing engineer so that manufacturing considerations are included in the design trade-offs. Terms such as "design for manufacturing" and "manufacturing costs/design guidelines" indicate the growing awareness of the importance of this connection.

A second aspect of product quality involves the control of the manufacturing process. Improved machine tools and manufacturing processes can improve the results of the manufacturing operation. The use of numerical-control machine tools and test equipment on the shop floor leads to consistently higher-quality products. Real-time monitoring of the manufacturing processes can ensure the quality of the product. This is a dramatic change from our current approach to quality control: manufacture the product and then test it to find any defects. Monitoring promises greater customer satisfaction because the product always works — real zero defects. It also dramatically reduces scrap and rework costs. However, it requires better data capture and improved information management to integrate operations and relate the results of the monitoring to the appropriate standards.

Increased Product Liability
This trend is related to the demand for increased product quality. In the past, poor product quality simply meant loss of customers, a problem that was hard to quantify. Today, with the readiness to sue for damages caused by product failures, poor product quality can be very expensive. Product liability cases have been won for poor design and for manufacturing defects, even when the basic design was not in question. Therefore, there is a clear advantage to improving both types of product quality. This fact increases the importance of design audits and the ability to track design changes over the life of a product. New CIM applications addressing engineering change control and configuration management will be important in this area. Today these types of applications are used primarily for complex, high-quality products, such as aircraft and military systems. In the future this type of control will be used for a much wider variety of products. Concerns about product liability provide added justification for any CIM application that improves design or manufacturing quality.

More Customized Products
Another trend is toward more customized products. Customers are no longer satisfied with the basic product with no options. There is a competitive advantage in having a broad product line with many versions, or with a few basic models that can be customized. However, all of these variations have to be designed and manufac-

tured. CIM contributes to this customization by making it easier to find and modify designs so that every version does not have to be designed from scratch. Group technology, which was developed to optimize the production of similar parts, also supports customization because it improves manufacturing efficiency for producing related products.

Shorter Product Life Cycle

In the past, once a product was designed, it had a long life over which to recover its development costs. Today many products, especially high-technology products, have a relatively short life cycle. This change has two implications. First, companies must design products and get them to market faster. Second, a short product life provides less time over which to recover the development costs. At a recent meeting of Japanese and European manufacturers over 40 percent of them identified this shortened product life as one of their most critical problems.

Various CIM applications address this problem by compressing the development cycle so new products can get to market faster. This compression can occur in three ways. First, design, analysis, and process planning applications allow each of these functions to be done much faster, even when they are still considered as separate, independent functions. Second, an effective design retrieval application by itself speeds up the development cycle because it reduces the number of new parts that must be designed, analyzed, and routed. One study[2] found that for the typical new product 40 percent of the needed parts already existed in the company's inventory, another 40 percent required only minor modifications to existing parts, and only 20 percent were really new parts that had to be designed from scratch. Therefore, design retrieval alone has the potential to reduce development work by 40 to 80 percent. Group technology retrieval applications can provide similar benefits in manufacturing by quickly retrieving existing process plans for reuse or modification. Third, a dramatic shortening of the development cycle is possible when the design and manufacturing functions are more integrated. This improved information flow is especially important because of the iterative nature of the design, analysis, and manufacturing process.

Fewer Skilled Workers

Several demographic trends are seriously affecting manufacturing employment. The baby boom is over, so there are fewer entry-level workers. The education level and expectations of people are also changing. For many people expectations are rising, so fewer new workers are interested in manufacturing jobs, especially the unskilled and semiskilled ones. Even more critical is the lack of new employees for the skilled jobs that are essential for a factory. At the other extreme many people have such a poor educational background that they cannot qualify for these jobs. Finally, the number of engineers and technologists going into manufacturing is very low, so there is a growing shortage of both design and manufacturing engineers.

Furthermore, many of the engineers in the United States are absorbed by the defense sector. [3] Although there are spin-offs, this still represents a significant loss. As a result, there are simply not enough people with the required skills to continue to design and manufacture products the labor-intensive way we did in the past. These are much more serious problems than the usual complaint that labor is too expensive.

CIM systems are essential to make more productive use of the people we do have. Traditional CAD/CAM systems are allowing engineers and other functional experts to perform their jobs quicker and more effectively. The newer, more integrated systems are also improving the interaction among different types of experts. In the future, applications based on artifical intelligence and expert systems will address this skill problem even more effectively in two ways. First, since most of the expert's knowledge will be built into the system, many tasks can then be performed by less skilled people. Second, some companies are beginning to use artifical intelligence and expert system applications to capture the expertise of many senior technical people, both engineers and skilled workers, who are nearing retirement. This will help these companies preserve the experience they have built up over the years, especially with many skilled repair and maintenance people.

Increased Competition

Manufacturing companies are facing increased competition from two sources: from other manufacturers, especially those with a well-planned and consistent manufacturing strategy, and from new technology, which is developing many substitute products. For example, sheet metal is facing increased competition in the aircraft and automotive market from composite materials and plastics.

While each of the previously mentioned problems is bad enough, increased competition is making the situation even worse. All companies are facing these same problems, but some are responding much faster to introduce new products, incorporate new technologies, and lower their costs. This increased competition aggravates these problems and gives a company even less time to respond to them.

This section has described major changes and trends in the competitive environment faced by most manufacturing companies. How well a company does in this environment depends on how well the company perceives these changes, understands their underlying causes, and responds to them with a well-thought-out strategy. Without a clear corporate and manufacturing strategy a company cannot prioritize these problems and respond to them in a consistent way. The next section discusses manufacturing strategy and its role in CIM.

Manufacturing Strategy

Corporate strategy involves identifying what needs to be done: setting objectives and prioritizing them. It also requires a plan for meeting those objectives. Finally, there must be a clear, explicit set of criteria for evaluating progress toward those objectives.

A corporate strategy specifies the corporation's basic philosophy, identifies the markets in which it wants to compete, and specifies its approach to each market. A corporation's philosophy or culture may emphasize the latest technology, the lowest-cost production, or the best customer service. The company may focus on relatively narrow market niches for specific customers or products. Alternately, the company may support a broad product line or multiple product lines for different markets. In approaching each market the company can use any one of several competitive strategies—for example, be the lowest-cost producer, differentiate its product in some way to protect its market share and/or justify a premium price, or focus on a specific niche within the market.

A corporation's strategy has a major impact on its manufacturing operations. A corporate strategy must include a complementary and consistent manufacturing strategy. Different corporate strategies require different manufacturing capabilities, which the manufacturing strategy must ensure are either in place or being developed. The manufacturing strategy must also specify a way to evaluate manufacturing operations that is consistent with the requirements of the corporate strategy.

Most people evaluate manufacturing operations only by efficiency and unit costs. This is a serious mistake. Peter Drucker has repeatedly emphasized the difference between efficiency and effectiveness.[4] Effectiveness is doing the right things, whereas efficiency is simply doing things right. It does not matter how efficient a plant is if it is not doing the right things.

There are many criteria for evaluating manufacturing. Neither a company nor a factory can be good at everything.[5] If a company tries to be good at everything, it becomes good at nothing and vulnerable to competition from many directions.

A good manufacturing strategy identifies what a company must do well to survive and prosper. It also determines which design and manufacturing functions need to be improved and the order in which such improvements should be made. These areas are precisely the ones a company should focus on when it begins to automate and implement CIM. It may be nice to double or triple the productivity of the drafting department as some vendors suggest, but if drafting is not a critical factor in the company's success, then it should not have the highest priority. The resources could be better spent on more critical activities. Furthermore, early decisions in low-priority areas can unnecessarily constrain later decisions in more important areas. For example, the best drafting system may be incompatible with what the company needs in a more critical process planning or numerical-control programming system.

Evaluation Criteria for Manufacturing

This section identifies the criteria against which to evaluate manufacturing operations, discusses the components of a manufacturing strategy, and shows more explicitly how this strategy affects decisions about CIM planning and selection.

There are many criteria for evaluating manufacturing operations. They include:

- cost/efficiency
- functionality
- quality
- customization
- volume flexibility
- product flexibility
- fast delivery
- valid delivery schedules

Cost/efficiency—Unfortunately many people have assumed there is only one critical criterion—cost and efficiency. Other things being equal, it is clearly better to manufacture a product at a lower cost rather than a higher one. However, rarely are other things equal. When this criterion is used, it should be in conjunction with other criteria.

There are also many types of costs, and a company must make trade-offs among them. For example, long production runs tend to minimize the actual manufacturing costs; but they increase inventory costs for raw materials, work in process, and finished goods. Moreover, the cost structure of manufacturing is changing. The percentage of direct labor cost in products is declining in most products from automobiles to personal computers. This decline will continue as automation progresses. And there is an increase in the ratio of fixed costs to variable costs. These changes mean that even when cost is a major criterion, the problems and their solutions are different from what they were in the past.

Cost becomes the dominant factor only if the product is a commodity or if the company's strategy is to be the low-cost producer. If the corporate strategy is based on product quality, product customization, customer service, or rapid delivery, then cost should not be the dominant factor.

Functionality—Several important criteria relate more to the product being manufactured than to the manufacturing operation. Does the product have the necessary functionality for the marketplace? Every feature of the product increases the manufacturing cost. However, in many cases compromises are possible. Some design changes, such as a lower tolerance or a different shape of a feature, can dramatically improve the producibility of the product and reduce its manufacturing costs. These changes may make the product easier and cheaper to produce or reduce its reject rate. The important point is that these changes should not reduce the marketability of the product.

If the product is a commodity, there may be little to differentiate it in terms of functionality. However, in most cases a company must make a strategic decision about functionality. One company may provide a relatively narrow product line with a standard set of functions, while another company may decide to support

10

a broad product line with many optional bells and whistles. This decision affects the manufacturing operations because the two strategies lead to different-size production runs, different flexibility requirements, and different production scheduling and inventory problems. Over the life of the product line it also affects the production and management of spare parts. For example, a policy mandating the use of standard parts whenever possible would benefit both companies, but it would be more critical for the company with the broad product line.

Quality—Product quality is another important way to evaluate a manufacturing operation. Quality is a function of both design and manufacturing. CIM applications that support analysis and evaluation of more alternatives can lead to better design quality.

Manufacturing quality refers to how well the manufacturing process can build the product to the specifications. In manufacturing today an effective quality control operation prevents inferior goods from being shipped, although without 100 percent inspection this ideal is only approached, not actually obtained. In the future the emphasis will be on computer control and monitoring of the manufacturing process to ensure against defective parts. The quality of the manufacturing operation can be measured by the amount of scrap and rework, the cost of the quality control operation, the number of customer complaints about defective products, and the cost of warrantee repairs.

A company strategy based on quality has certain implications for manufacturing. It can mean more expensive machine tools with finer tolerances, more careful selection and monitoring of vendors, better training of shop-floor personnel, better feedback on production quality, and an incentive system based on quality, not simply volume and costs.

Customization—One of the trends today is for more and more product customizations. Each airline wants its own changes to its aircraft. Consumers want their own variations in everything from kitchens to cars. This trend affects some industries more than others. In some cases customization involves designing and building a new product from scratch, but this is rare. In other cases customization simply means allowing the customer to select from a predefined set of options. The automobile industry is a good example of this complexity. When a customer can select body style, color, interior, engine size, transmission, stereo, and other options, the number of possible combinations is huge. To bring all of the right parts together requires a very sophisticated production scheduling system and a complex materials handling system. In those industries and for those products where customization is important, the manufacturing operation should be evaluated in terms of how well it can support the necessary degree of customization. The fact that increased customization drives up the manufacturing cost is not an issue in evaluating manufacturing operations because in setting the product strategy the company has already made the trade-off between cost and the amount of customization to support.

Volume flexibility—Another important criterion in many industries involves

11

the flexibility of the production line. There are two distinct types of flexibility: volume and product. Volume flexibility is the ability of the production line to produce efficiently over a wide range of volumes. For example, when the demand for a product is seasonal or sporatic, a good production line should be able to adjust to the changing volume of production quickly and effectively. It is too expensive if the line has only one effective production rate that matches the average demand. Such a production line must operate at the same rate regardless of current demand. In slack periods it builds to inventory, and in peak periods — when production cannot keep up with demand — the inventory is drawn down. While this is one way to operate, it drives up the inventory cost and runs the risk of building up an obsolete inventory if the demand never recovers. Clearly it is more effective to have a production line that can operate over a wide range of production volumes.

Product flexibility — A production line can also be evaluated in terms of its ability to produce a wide range of products and the similarity of those products. If the demand for product X declines either temporarily or permanently, the more effective production line is the one that has the flexibility to begin producing product Y. The quicker a production line can be shifted, the greater its flexibility. Similarly, the greater the number of different products it can produce, the more flexible the line.

However, flexibility alone is not an adequate criterion. Its value depends on the industry and the product or products being produced. Product flexibility is not something to be desired if the product is essentially a commodity being mass-produced. The lower production costs and higher efficiency provided by hard automation are much more important than flexibililty for this type of product. On the other hand, if a company is producing hundreds of different parts in dozens of different part families or a highly customized product, then product flexibility is far more important than hard automation. In this situation a flexible manufacturing system (FMS) is desirable.

Fast delivery — In some cases rapidly delivery is critical. For example, an expensive piece of equipment may be down because a part is broken. The critical factor in this case is rapid delivery; cost and other factors are not important. Ideally these emergency orders can be filled from inventory, but in some cases the part must be made. Rapid delivery is essential if the company is building its reputation and competitive advantage on service.

CIM applications that support this fast delivery include flexible machining systems that allow individual small orders to be easily inserted in the schedule without major disruption. A scheduling system that tracks these special orders is also important.

Valid delivery schedules — Finally, valid delivery schedules can be important, especially for companies implementing just-in-time inventory management. If the promised materials are not delivered on schedule, a customer's own manufacturing operations may be disrupted. To perform well in this area, a company needs

12

a manufacturing and operations management system to track order status and provide an early warning for any potential problems.

Components of Manufacturing Strategy

There are several components of a manufacturing strategy. For an effective strategy all of these components must be consistent. If different components pull in different directions, there is confusion and ineffectiveness.

Skinner has identified five components or decision areas[6]: plant and equipment, production planning and control, labor and staffing, product design/engineering, and organization and management. Decisions in each of these areas should be evaluated in terms of the criteria identified above.[7] These decisions taken as a group should also be consistent.

Gunn also addresses manufacturing strategy, although in a different way.[8] Instead of the types of issues and decisions Skinner and Buffa discuss, Gunn emphasizes the objectives of manufacturing strategy that must be met if a company is to become a world-class manufacturer. These objectives include

- shorter product development lead times
- shorter manufacturing lead times
- higher quality
- more inventory turns
- more flexibility in the production process
- better customer service
- less waste
- higher return on assets

He states that for most companies three missing elements prevent them from becoming a world-class manufacturer. These three missing elements are vision, senior management leadership, and a process for translating the vision into reality. In addition to these missing elements world-class manufacturing also requires a commitment to quality, an educated and motivated work force, proven technology, and effective planning.

Gunn's manufacturing framework is described in more detail in Chapter 3 since it also provides a framework for the factory of the future.

Relationship between Manufacturing Strategy and CIM Applications

This section summarizes some of the links that have been described earlier between various manufacturing criteria and strategies and specific types of CIM applications. The need to make many design changes and models requires a CIM system to support the design process. The more complex the product and the more analysis it requires, the greater the benefits from this type of system.

If there are many product models and most design changes are variations of basic designs, then design retrieval is an important application. Group technology would also improve the manufacturing operations, especially if the strategy calls for quick response to customer orders.

If there are many design changes once a product is in production, then it is important to link the design and manufacturing applications. Otherwise, islands of automation may exist in design and manufacturing. Each group may be able to do its job more effectively, but the total design through manufacturing cycle may not be reduced. This product life cycle is critical if the strategy involves high competition or positions the company as a leader in product innovation.

Flexible manufacturing systems or workcells are a possibility if the production schedules vary extensively or if product quality is critical.

These explicit links between manufacturing strategy and types of CIM systems are important because a company cannot do everything at once. The overall manufacturing strategy, rather than individual departmental requirements, should drive the CIM selection and implementation process. This point is emphasized again in Chapter 19, which discusses system selection.

Summary

This chapter has provided the broad context for the following discussion of CIM. The competitive environment for manufacturing has become much more severe in recent years. Since no company and no factory can do everything well, it is important to focus on the key factors required to support the overall corporate strategy. A manufacturing strategy identifies the key decisions that must be made by manufacturing to support the overall corporate strategy. The chapter also identified the criteria against which to evaluate manufacturing strategies. The chapter concluded by relating various manufacturing strategy decisions to the CIM systems needed to support them.

Notes

1. Wickham Skinner, *Manufacturing: The Formidable Competitive Weapon* (New York: John Wiley and Sons, 1985).
2. George H. Schaffer, "Implementing CIM," *American Machinist* 125 (August 1981): 151–174.
3. William F. Hyde, *Improving Productivity by Classification, Coding, and Data Base Standardization: The Key to Maximizing CAD/CAM and Group Technology* (New York: Marcel Dekker, 1981).
4. Peter Drucker, *The Effective Executive* (New York: Harper and Row, 1966).
5. Wickham Skinner, "The Focused Factory." In Skinner, *Manufacturing*.
6. Skinner, *Manufacturing*.
7. Buffa has identified six components: positioning the production system, capacity-location, product and process technology, workforce and job design, operating decisions, and suppliers and vertical integration. See Elwood S. Buffa, *Meeting the Competitive Challenge: Manufacturing Strategies for U.S. Companies* (Homewood, Ill.: Dow Jones–Irwin, 1984).
8. Thomas G. Gunn, *Manufacturing for Competitive Advantage: Becoming a World-Class Manufacturer* (Cambridge, Mass.: Ballinger, 1987).

Further Reading

Buffa, Elwood S. *Meeting the Competitive Challenge: Manufacturing Strategies for U.S. Companies.* Homewood, Ill.: Dow Jones–Irwin, 1984.

Chiantella, Nathan A. (ed.). *Management Guide for CIM.* Dearborn, Mich.: CASA/SME, 1986.

Gerwin, Donald. "Dos and Don'ts of Computerized Manufacturing." *Harvard Business Review* 60 (Mar.-Apr. 1982): 107–116.

Gunn, Thomas G. *Manufacturing for Competitive Advantage: Becoming a World-Class Manufacturer.* Cambridge, Mass.: Ballinger, 1987.

Hales, H. Lee. "Productibility and Integration: A Winning Combination." *CIM Technology*, Aug. 1987, 14–18.

Martin, John M. "Developing a Strategy for Quality." *Manufacturing Engineering* 99 (Aug. 1987): 40-45.

Ohmae, Kenichi. *The Mind of the Strategist: Business Planning for Competitive Advantage.* New York: McGraw-Hill, 1982.

Porter, Michael E. *Competitive Strategy: Technique for Analyzing Industries and Competitors.* New York: The Free Press, 1980.

Skinner, Wickham. *Manufacturing: The Formidable Competitive Weapon.* New York: John Wiley and Sons, 1985.

2

What Is CAD/CAM and CIM?

Definition of CAD/CAM/CIM

CAD/CAM History

CAD/CAM/CIM Today

CIM Tomorrow

Solid Modeling
Feature-Based Design
Design Retrieval
Process Planning
Robotics
Real-Time Shop-Floor Control and Operations
Expert Systems

Summary

The previous chapter explained how a manufacturing strategy provides the context within which to plan for and implement CIM. It also identified how some types of CIM applications are related to specific competitive conditions and strategic decisions.

This chapter provides a more detailed overview of CAD/CAM/CIM. It explains how the term has evolved from its original narrow concept (i.e., CAD for computer-aided drafting) to its broader meaning, including the factory of the future, which is discussed in more detail in the next chapter.

Definition of CAD/CAM/CIM

Literally CAD/CAM is computer-aided design and computer-aided manufacturing. However, the real meaning of the term has changed dramatically since its inception. It will continue to change as more capabilities are added. Already the focus is shifting with the introduction of the new term CIM, computer-integrated manufacturing. The importance of the new term is that it recognizes explicitly that integration is the key. It is not enough simply to improve each of many separate, independent functions. This just intensifies the current problems with "islands of automation." People can, and probably will, continue to argue about precisely what functions are included in each of these terms, but this is a sterile debate. The real point is that more and more functions are being included in whatever the area will be called.

CAD/CAM History

Historically, CAD, as opposed to CAD/CIM, developed from the merging of three distinct areas: engineering analysis, computer graphics, and numerical control.

The first area of development was engineering analysis. Many of the earliest computer applications involved engineering analysis. Over time more complicated applications were developed for areas such as static and dynamic analysis of structural and thermal properties, aerodynamic analysis, and complex electronic circuit simulation.

In product design several types of analysis were often done in a specific sequence, with the output of one application becoming all or part of the input to the next application. Ideally applications would write their output to a magnetic tape or disk, which would then be read as the input by the next application. Unfortunately, because these applications were developed independently, each had its own input and output data formats, which were often incompatible with other applications.

Many of these applications were originally developed when most data was entered on punch cards—a laborious, time-consuming, expensive, and error-prone operation. As computer technology evolved, input and output changed from cards to on-line terminals, but many of these I/O problems remained. Some of these I/O problems were eased by developments in computer graphics. Much of the engineering analysis in CAD (sometimes called CAE, computer-aided engineering) is a direct outgrowth of these early developments. One of the problems is that we learned too well how to do these independent engineering applications. Developing an integrated set of CIM applications requires unlearning things that were once very successful.

The second area leading to CAD/CAM was computer graphics. In the 1950s

18

and 1960s the data for engineering analysis and numerical control programs were entered in alphanumeric form, usually as card images. This process, however, was an artifical and awkward method for entering what was frequently geometry. Output was even more difficult. The computer generated large volumes of numeric data, which the engineer had to analyze and interpret in terms of the previously encoded part geometry. Computer graphics and an interactive interface provided a major breakthrough. With interactive graphics the engineer could efficiently create a model of a part, view it, and rotate it to get different perspectives. The engineer could test a numerical control program by watching a simulated tool path as a part was being machined or could see a part flex or deform as various leads were placed on it. The real benefit of computer graphics for CAD/CAM was not that it allowed the computer to perform different or more complicated analyses, but that the human-to-machine interface was made friendlier and more efficient. As a result, more engineers were able and willing to use computers.

Numerical control (NC) was the third major area from which CAD/CAM evolved. Traditionally, machine tools were controlled manually by machinists working directly from engineering drawings and process plans or routings. Numerical control was introduced with Air Force support in the early 1950s in the aerospace industry. With numerical control a computer was programmed to control the machine tools. Numerically controlled machine tools allowed much greater precision and reliability than could be provided by a machinist. Different parts could be produced simply by loading a different program.

NC programming was, and still is, much more difficult than conventional programming. Even the use of high-level NC programming languages such as APT (Automatically Programmable Tool) required skilled engineers or technicians who knew both programming and the machine tools for which the programs were written. The NC programmer had to enter both the part geometry and the appropriate machine tool control commands, such as feed rates and speeds. When parts were designed manually (even if there was extensive computerized analysis), this was acceptable. However, with the advent of computer-aided design and drafting systems to capture the part geometry, much of this effort became redundant. The NC programmer had to reenter much of the data, especially the part geometry, that had been previously entered or created by the various engineering applications.

Today conventional numerical control has two major limitations. First, it is relatively static. It assumes that everything in a fairly complex process works correctly. Real-time feedback and processing is needed for the next step—adaptive control. Second, conventional numerical control focuses on a single machine tool. However, most parts require processing on many machine tools and may involve automated material handling systems and robots to move them between machine tools, such as in a work cell. Current work on programming the entire set of equipment in the work cell and, more generally, computer-aided process planning are logical outgrowths of this early NC work.

CAD/CAM/CIM Today

CAD/CAM/CIM is an outgrowth of these three areas, but in its original form it had a very limited scope, more accurately called computer-aided drafting and computer-aided machining. The earliest form of CAD used computer graphics to create and display an electronic version of the traditional engineering drawing. Although the engineering drawing is the standard form for design information, in reality it is simply a documentation tool, not a design tool. Although computerizing the engineering drawing is similar to word processing and provides many of the same benefits for engineering, it falls far short of the goal of computer-aided design.

Unfortunately, many people still think of CAD as essentially computer-aided drafting. One survey in 1985 suggested that between 85 and 95 percent of the existing CAD systems were still used exclusively for drafting rather than design in its broader context. A related figure on market penetration suggested that almost 95 percent of the draftsmen in the United States still did not have access to a CAD system. In its broader context CAD includes solid modeling and various engineering analyses that actually help the designer create, evaluate, and refine the design, not simply document. In this context CAD market penetration is even more limited, with one estimate that only a few hundred sites in the United States are actively using solid modeling in their design process in production.

The original scope of CAM was similarly restricted. It encompassed only machining in the form of numerical control applications. From the engineering perspective this is still the main scope of CAM today, regardless of marketing literature to the contrary. However, the number of types of machine tools and the specific tools covered by numerical control have increased dramatically. As in the 1950s, machine tools are still programmed one at a time and independently of each other. What is missing is the process plan, which must describe the coordinated activities on all of the machine tools required to produce the part. Some computer-aided process planning (CAPP) systems are now available and are being used to a limited extent. In fact, many of the expert system prototypes in CAD/CAM are in the process planning area. However, current CAPP products are still limited in their scope. In a related step the National Bureau of Standards' Automated Manufacturing Research Facility (AMRF) has a project to explore programming the entire work cell as a unit rather than independently programming each machine tool and robot within the cell.

The other major extension of CAM involves computer applications that support a wide range of traditional, business-oriented manufacturing management functions. Some would argue that since they are not engineering functions, they are not really CAM. However, they offer tremendous potential for improving manufacturing operations. These functions include bill of materials, material requirements planning (in its expanded form called manufacturing resource planning), production scheduling, purchasing, inventory control, order tracking, and shop-floor control. Taken as a group, these functions are today the most integrated part of CAD/CIM. In the future these systems will be linked more closely to the engineering and manufacturing applications that generate the data they use. For example, the process plan determines many of the parameters needed for production scheduling, such as which machine tools to use and how long the processing takes on each tool. The new term, CIM, emphasizes this linkage.

From its original limited scope, the meaning of CAD/CAM/CIM today has broadened to cover almost any area in which the computer can assist in the design and manufacture of a product. New applications are constantly expanding this scope. Examples include programming robots and flexible manufacturing systems, expert systems to support various aspects of design and manufacturing, and real-time data capture and monitoring for quality control and shop-floor control. Today most shop-floor control applications are essentially clerical ones dispatching and tracking manufacturing orders, but in the future they will be more directly involved with real-time control of operations and processes on the shop floor.

CIM Tomorrow

This section describes some important new CIM applications that promise dramatic productivity improvements. The specific areas include solid modeling, feature-based design, design retrieval, process planning, robotics, real-time shop-floor control, and expert systems. This section briefly describes each of these areas, which are discussed in much greater detail in Part Three.

Solid Modeling

Many of the more sophisticated companies in the aerospace, defense, and automotive industries are using solid modeling in the design process. A solid model provides a complete geometric representation of a part or assembly. It includes more information about the part than either a two-dimensional drawing or a three-dimensional wireframe model. An engineer can design either simple piece parts or complex assemblies with a solid model. A solid model can be generated quickly by engineers without highly specialized computer training and is easily understood by customers, marketing people, shop-floor personnel, and maintenance engineers.

Once the solid model is created, it can be used directly or indirectly in many other steps in the design and manufacturing process. Using it directly, the designer can determine whether the moving parts in a mechanism interfere with each other. Solid models of existing parts can be used to create the model for the new products or assemblies. Complex assemblies can be automatically exploded to provide clearer assembly and maintenance drawings. When it is used indirectly, translation programs can take the data in a solid model and automatically generate much of the data needed by other applications. The basic engineering drawing, including orthogonal views with automatic dimensioning, can also be generated from a solid model, although the annotation and comments have to be added later. (Many of these translators do not currently include automatic dimensioning; however, the necessary data is always in the solid model.) There are programs today that take a solid model and create the meshes for a finite element analysis or generate the NC program to fabricate the part.

Feature-Based Design

A new approach to CIM involves design based on features rather than geometry. This allows designers to design using their own engineering concepts rather than convert their designs into computer-based geometry. All of the CAD systems today allow the engineer to create a design by specifying the geometry and other characteristics of the part. The key aspect of their design definition is in the geometry they support. Depending on the sophistication of the system, it supports two-dimensional views of the geometry, three-dimensional wireframe geometry, or the more complete three-dimensional solid models. The distinction between these approaches is explained in Chapter 10.

With a traditional CAD system a designer must create a circle on a surface and then project the circle through the part. This defines a cylinder, which is then subtracted from the part. This is the low-level geometry-based way of doing design, which current systems require. What the designer really wants to do is create a hole in the part, which is closer to the way the part will be manufactured. With feature-based design the engineer specifies which features should go where on a part. The design is done in terms of features such as holes, threads, keyways, and chamfers. The CAD system would then automatically convert the feature information into the necessary geometry. When these systems become available, they will allow a much higher level of design. These features, not simply the geometry, are also needed by subsequent applications such as process planning.

Design Retrieval

An engineer has two ways in which to approach a design problem. The first and most common approach is to design the new part or product from scratch. The alternate approach is to begin with an existing set of parts and try to create the new product from these existing parts, modifying them if necessary, but creating new ones only as a last resort. Unfortunately, most designers today use the first approach, partly because that is the way they were trained but, more importantly, because it is difficult to find the appropriate existing part from which to begin. The necessary design retrieval systems rarely exist and definitely are not one of the major applications marketed by CIM vendors.

A CIM system that supports easy and quick retrieval of existing designs can dramatically reduce the time and cost of design, especially if the new product is similar to an existing product or if the company is planning an entire product family instead of a single product. A similar type of retrieval system using group technology codes for process plans will provide the same types of benefits for manufacturing engineers. These types of retrieval applications are very important for job shop manufacturing, where the ability to refine a design quickly and provide accurate estimates for bids is essential.

A classification and coding scheme is essential for these retrieval applications to be successful because a design retrieval system is only as good as the classification and coding scheme on which it is based. For design retrieval, parts can be classified by form, function, or both—that is, by their shape, their use, or some combination of these two factors. For other functions, such as process planning, there may be a completely different classification scheme. With the computer, however, multiple ways of classifying and retrieving parts is not a problem.

Process Planning

Until now, the manufacturing focus for CAD/CAM has been programming individual machine tools, although manufacturing involves far more than a single machine tool. Process planning (or manufacturing engineering) involves determining which manufacturing processes to use, the sequence in which they must be done, and which machine tools to use for each process. Only at this point does NC programming become an issue, and then only for those machine tools with that capability.

Now process planning is becoming a major focus to support all the functions of the manufacturing engineer. Variant process planning allows the manufacturing engineer to find and retrieve process plans for parts similar to the new one. The new process plan frequently requires only minor changes to an existing one. Generative process planning applications start with the part design, the company's current machine tool and raw materials inventory, and a machineability database. The application then generates a new process plan from scratch. This approach usually involves expert systems technology and is still very limited today.

Robotics

A robot is "a reprogrammable, multifunctional manipulator designed to move materials, parts, tools, or specialized devices, through variable programmed motions for the performance of a variety of tasks."[1] Robots are being widely used today in the automobile industry and by a few companies in many other industries. They are being used for welding, painting, assembly, and loading and unloading other machine tools. In a few cases they are part of flexible manufacturing systems or workcells, but in most cases they are used essentially as independent machine tools and with only modest use of their flexibility. In the future this will change.

Two developments will permit a much wider use of robots. First, the growing capability for off-line programming of robots will encourage using them for more tasks. Today's approach, which usually requires manually teaching robots already in place on the production line, makes reprogramming very expensive because it stops normal production. With better off-line programming only final testing is done on the production line. The second development, improved sensor technology, will also increase robot flexibility. This is because robots today are very accurate only in terms of repeatability, but not when directed to a specified position. Without sensors for improved positional accuracy, off-line programming will not be effective. Much of the current research in robotics focuses on vision and tactile sensors.

Real-Time Shop-Floor Control and Operations

Today in most manufacturing and operations management systems shop-floor control is essentially a clerical or business function—that is, dispatching and tracking manufacturing orders. However, in the future there will be more real-time control of actual shop processes. Automated workcells and flexible manufacturing systems are an indication of what is possible. However, this approach requires effective shop floor communications such as MAP (Manufacturing Automation Protocol) and sensor technology. Today in most cases computers download NC programs for individual machine tools, which run their own programs independently of anything else on the shop floor. Real-time shop-floor control requires a control system that can sense what is happening on the shop floor and change the instructions to the various machines, robots, and material-handling systems as necessary. This capability is being developed, but the technology transfer from the research labs to the factory is very low.

Expert Systems

One of the key new information technologies involves expert systems. (Information management and database management technology is not new. It is an existing technology that is just now being transferred to engineering and manufacturing.)

Expert systems allow the computer to store the complex set of rules needed for many heuristic tasks that are hard to define algorithmically. Today there are many expert-systems prototypes for process planning and equipment repair, with a few applications in production. Several vendors also provide expert-system shells. These shells allow companies to build expert systems relatively easily using their own rules for design and manufacturing. However, today most of these expert systems are stand-alone applications addressing only a small part of the overall problem. The real benefit of this technology will be realized when these individual expert systems can effectively communicate with each other and work in conjunction with the corporate engineering and manufacturing databases.

Summary

This chapter has provided an overview of CAD/CAM. It described the development of CAD/CAM from its origins in engineering analysis, graphics, and numerical control machining and summarized where it is today. Finally, it identified some of the key areas of future CIM development. These areas include solid modeling, feature-based design, design retrieval, process planning, robotics, real-time shop-floor control, and expert systems.

Note

1. Joseph F. Engelberger, *Robotics in Practice: Management and Applications of Industrial Robots* (London: Kogan Page, 1980).

Further Reading

Groover, Mikell P. *Automation, Production Systems, and Computer-Aided Manufacturing.* Englewood Cliffs, N.J.: Prentice-Hall, 1980.

Groover, Mikell P., and Emory W. Zimmers, Jr. *CAD/CIM: Computer-Aided Design and Manufacturing.* Englewood Cliffs, N.J.: Prentice-Hall, 1984.

Stover, Richard. *An Analysis of CAD/CAM Applications with an Introduction to CIM.* Englewood Cliffs, N.J.: Prentice-Hall, 1984.

3

The Factory of the Future

What Is the Factory of the Future?

Benefits of the Factory of the Future

Impact of the Factory of the Future

Framework for World-Class Manufacturing

Role of Information in the Factory of the Future

Summary

This chapter provides an introduction to the concept of the factory of the future. It explains the concept, identifies the benefits of the factory of the future, and describes its impact. The chapter also describes Gunn's framework for world-class manufacturing. This framework, while not directly addressing the factory of the future, identifies most of the functions that would be integrated in such a factory. Finally, it explains the role of information in integrating the factory of the future as well as the use of this book in providing a foundation for such integration.

27

What Is the Factory of the Future?

The factory of the future is an ideal or a goal to work toward rather than a specific, real thing. It is a moving target always based on state-of-the-art technology. Because technology is constantly changing, even the most up-to-date factory will never achieve the status of being the "factory of the future" in every respect, but it will still be a very good factory if it pursues this aim.

Today the factory of the future is a tightly integrated, highly automated facility. Design is done on a CAD system, perhaps using a solid modeling system. The designs are passed electronically to other departments for analysis and process planning. Numerical control programs are created for the machine tools and robots on the shop floor. Given a set of production requirements, the computer can schedule the production. This includes determining which machine tools are needed to produce which parts, scheduling production on those machine tools, determining what additional materials (raw material, workpieces, tools, and fixtures) are needed where and when, and controlling an automated material-handling system to deliver those materials to the appropriate places when they are needed. The appropriate control programs are also downloaded to various NC machine tools and robots to directly drive the production processes.

Obviously, this is an ideal example, but it is an ideal that many companies in the United States, Japan, and Europe are striving for. In the United States companies such as IBM, Apple, and Deere have designed, built, and are now using factories of the future. People still work in these factories doing some of the more complex assembly jobs that are too difficult to automate yet. But the scheduling, material flow, and many of the manufacturing operations are automated. Today there are only a few fully automated, "lights out" operations, in which people are there primarily to repair equipment, not to actively participate in production. In the long term even many of these maintenance operations may be automated.

Benefits of the Factory of the Future

Since these factories are complex to design and expensive to build, what are their benefits over current facilities? There are three major benefits: greater flexibility, higher and more consistent quality, and lower labor cost. The first two benefits are the most important because labor is a rapidly declining cost component in many products today.

These benefits relate directly to the ways in which the competitive environment is changing. People want more customized products. One aspect of flexibility is the ability to produce efficiently a wide range of products and product models instead of a single model. Scheduling flexibility allows a manufacturer to produce this variety of goods cheaply by rapidly responding to changing orders rather than maintaining large, expensive inventories. This flexibility also allows the manufacturer to introduce design changes and new products quickly, another critical factor given the shortening product life cycle.

Another benefit is improved product quality and consistency because many of the operations are done by NC machine tools and robots. This reduces scrap, rework, and warranty repair costs. In many cases automated testing is built into the production at individual machines or at separate test stations. In most cases every part, not just a sample, is tested.

While both U.S. and Japanese manufacturers are moving toward the factory of the future, the driving force is often different. Although the quality of Japanese products is already high, improved quality is one of the major forces driving the Japanese to this approach. In the United States reduced labor cost is often the driving force. This partly explains why General Motors began scaling back its new Saturn facility after the decline in the dollar reduced the cost differential between U.S. and Japanese labor costs.

Impact of the Factory of the Future

The factory of the future cannot exist in isolation as a production facility. It needs to be supported upstream by the design process. This means a focus on the entire design and manufacturing process in the factory of the future, not simply on the production facilities. Unless manufacturers consider the entire process, they may be automating poor designs, inefficiency, and confusion.

"Design for produceability" is becoming a new buzzword. It simply means that manufacturing considerations are integrated in the design process. This is important because most major product cost decisions are made early in the design phases, not later when manufacturing engineers are deciding how to manufacture the product.

Design for produceability will improve nonautomated operations, but it is essential with automated operations such as the factory of the future. For example, IBM built a fifty-robot assembly plant in Charlotte, North Carolina, for the Proprinter. At the same time the company specifically designed the product for that type of production. This resulted in only 60 parts to assemble instead of the previous 150. The resulting savings would be significant no matter how the product was assembled.

Framework for World-Class Manufacturing

This section describes Gunn's framework for world-class manufacturing.[1] This framework identifies the types of functions that must be integrated in a factory of the future. The framework is based on three supporting pillars—CIM, TQC (Total Quality Control), and JIT (Just-in-Time). Each of these supporting pillars is described in more detail below.

Gunn uses the same four basic functional areas to discuss the three pillars.

These functional areas—product and process design, manufacturing planning and control, information technology, and production processes—are shown in Figure 3.1. This framework has evolved from his earlier work with the A. D. Little CIM framework, which had the following components:

- information technology
- CAD
- group technology
- manufacturing planning and control
- automated material handling
- CAM
- robotics

First, there is the CIM pillar. For product and process design CIM includes computer-aided design, group technology, configuration management and engineering change control, computer-aided process planning, and workcell device programming. The CIM manufacturing planning and control functions include MRP II, schedule simulation and optimization, preventive maintenance, and cost management. The production process part of CIM includes numerical control (including DNC and CNC), group-technology–based workcells, computer-aided testing and vision, quality control and statistical process control, robotics, automated material handling systems, and automated guided vehicles.

All of these functions are important, and many manufacturers are doing one or more of these functions. However, few companies are doing more than a hand-

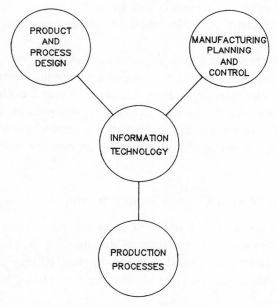

Figure 3.1   Gunn's framework

ful of the functions. Among those companies that are, virtually none have fully automated, closed-loop interfaces between all of the functions. But it is the linkage between these functions, not the functions themselves, that is essential for the factory of the future. As a company adds functions and improves the integration among them, it moves closer to the factory of the future ideal.

The information technology area is the final CIM component that is needed to provide this integration. The key elements of the information technology are database management, network communications, applications (both traditional algorithmic applications and artificial intelligence/expert-system–based applications), decision support system tools, application development and software engineering tools, and the hardware to support this software.

These CIM components are the basic tools from which the factory of the future will be built. However, it needs additional management and administrative components. These additional components involve TQC and JIT.

The total quality control pillar also includes product and process design, manufacturing planning and control, and production processes. Product and process design includes design standards, the Taguchi analysis method, and quality function deployment. (The latter two areas are described in Chapter 14.) Manufacturing planning and control includes the planning and control of the quality functions, whereas the previous function involved designing the quality mechanisms and integrating them with various aspects of the design process. This planning and control function involves planning quality control at both the factory and at the suppliers. Finally, in the production process TQC emphasizes employee involvement, such as quality circles and other small group activity.

JIT is the final pillar in the world-class manufacturing framework for the factory of the future. In product and process design JIT implies concurrent product and process engineering and design for manufactureability with trade-offs being made between engineering and manufacturing. JIT manufacturing planning and control includes more precise planning with highly visible feedback on operation status and close supplier involvement. Production processes for JIT includes employee involvement and cross-training, workplace reorganization, and standardization. It also includes a focus on minimizing setup times and small batch runs. Efficiency in JIT comes from rapid setup rather than long production runs, which build up unneeded inventory.

These three pillars (CIM, TQC, and JIT) identify the tools and management approach necessary for the factory of the future and a world-class manufacturing operation.

Role of Information in the Factory of the Future

A key to the factory of the future is information. Without effective information management the necessary level of automation and control would not be possible.

The factory of the future requires a much more disciplined manufacturing environment. Information to both monitor and control operations is essential to ensure this discipline.

Each factory of the future requires a unique information model. However, there is an underlying commonality in these models. This book describes the type of information models that are needed to drive the factory of the future. It looks at generic design and manufacturing functions and identifies the information models they require. Common objects appear in many different models and provide the links needed to integrate various operations, whether for the factory of the future or for one built on a less ambitious scale.

In addition to information models the factory of the future also needs a communications network to pass data among the users, applications, and equipment that need them. As an example, one of the newer General Motors truck plants is using dual MAP networks to drive the entire plant. This includes downloading robot and NC programs and collecting work center, machine tool, and order status information for reporting and control.

The details for factory communications are beyond the scope of this book, which focuses on the type of information that must be communicated, not on the actual communication mechanism. However, three communications requirements are obvious. First, the network must have an adequate bandwidth for the anticipated load, which can include large NC and robot programs, not just short status messages. Second, the network needs to interface to a wide variety of computers and factory equipment made by many vendors. Third, the communications system must be fault tolerant—a communications failure must not shut down the factory.

Summary

In summary, the factory of the future is a concept to work toward—a moving target. This book explains the data management tools and information models needed to integrate manufacturing and move toward the factory of the future.

Note

1. Thomas G. Gunn, *Manufacturing for Competitive Advantage: Becoming a World-Class Manufacturer* (Cambridge, Mass.: Ballinger Publishing, 1987).

Further Reading

Bairstow, Jeffery. "GM's Automation Protocol: Helping Machines Communicate." *High Technology* 6 (Oct. 1986): 38–42.

Richardson, Douglas. "Implementing MAP for Factory Control." *Manufacturing Engineering* 100 (Jan. 1988): 79–82.

Part Two
Data Management

This part provides an introduction to data management concepts and relates them specifically to design and manufacturing. Chapter 4 describes the evolving role of data management technology in CIM. Databases are now providing directory support for existing applications, but in the future full engineering databases will become more common. This chapter explains the importance of information management technology and ways in which it will benefit manufacturing. Chapter 5 provides an introduction to database management concepts, especially for CIM personnel who have not been exposed to this technology. Chapter 6 emphasizes database design. It explains the importance of information modeling and logical database design in obtaining the expected benefits of data management. It also explains NIAM (Nijssen Information Analysis Methodology), the information modeling and database design methodology used throughout Part Three. It explains the concepts of the methodology and uses manufacturing examples.

4

The Role of
Database Management in
Design and Manufacturing

No Role—The Current Approach

Use of a Database as a Directory

Database and File-Oriented Applications

Full Database Management Systems

Migration Strategy

Summary

This chapter sets the stage for Part Two, and for the rest of the book, by explaining several ways in which a database management system can be used to integrate design and manufacturing functions in CIM. It identifies four roles for a DBMS—ranging from minimal use to a full engineering database. (These roles are discussed in more detail in Chapter 8, which includes some database designs to support some of these roles.) The remainder of the chapter describes a migration path for a company that wants to increase its use of database management as its understanding of the technology increases.

These four roles are as follows:

1. No role for a DBMS
2. Use of a database as a directory
3. Use of a database to store data and continued use of file-oriented applications
4. Full use of data management technology for both data storage and application development and maintenance

In the first role, still the most common today, a database plays little or no part because the applications are all file-oriented. In the second case the database plays a directory role on top of existing file-oriented systems. This is a simple, easy way to introduce this new technology into a large file-oriented environment. In the third role the database is used to store data. This approach does not require converting existing applications, but it does allow new applications to benefit from the data sharing and improved productivity provided by data management technology. The fourth role involves a full engineering database environment, in which the data are stored in a database and the applications are developed and maintained using data management technology. For large, existing systems this role will be the longest in coming because of the conversion problems. However, some new vendors are starting from scratch in building CIM systems in this environment.

No Role—The Current Approach

The current approach in CAD/CAM is not to use database management systems at all. There are only two exceptions. The first exception involves a few of the most advanced systems in the traditional CAD/CAM areas, such as design, analysis, and process planning. In a few cases these systems are provided by relatively new vendors, such as Automation Technology Products (ATP). In many cases, however, they are in-house enhancements and applications written by some of the larger manufacturers, such as General Dynamics, Deere, Ingersoll, and Boeing. The second exception involves the many business-oriented manufacturing management packages, such as those provided by COMSERV and some of the DBMS vendors such as Cullinet. These systems, which came out of the business rather than the engineering area, have been using database management for years.

Otherwise, virtually all of the CIM applications are designed and written using conventional file management techniques. The physical format and structure of the files are optimized for the specific applications that use them, and there is little concern for other applications that could use the data. Each application is treated separately with its own input and output file formats. Furthermore, all of the information about these data files is buried in the application programs that use them rather than being widely available. Translators are usually needed to convert the output files for one application into the input files for another application. These applications are not integrated, and the translators simply provide an interface between them.

This process is shown in Figure 4.1. Using a solid modeling application and perhaps a library of standard parts, an engineer creates the initial design for a new part. The solid model is the main output of this application. Additional outputs may include one or more shaded images or pictures of the part from various viewpoints and some basic analysis results, such as center of mass and moments of inertia. The next step in the process is to create an engineering drawing. A translator converts the solid model into a two-dimensional view in the proper file format for the design/drafting application. Dimensions, tolerances, annotations, and other information are added. The design/drafting application stores the data in its own file format and can produce a hard copy of the engineering drawing. The design may then need to be analyzed using an application such as ANSYS or NASTRAN. Another translator is used to convert the solid model design into the format expected by these applications. Similar translations would be required to move the design to another application to generate an NC program. This process involves translation between different CIM applications rather than database management technology, which can integrate applications.

There is, however, another type of translator that is also important, especially for many large companies. These are translators between products from different vendors that perform the same function (e.g., between two different drafting systems). Different divisions of large companies may have different CAD systems. This creates a problem when designs must be shared across divisions. Clearly, individual translators can be written to convert data between any two CAD systems. This, however, creates several problems. First, it requires many translators. If there are N CAD systems, then $N*(N-1)/2$ translators are needed. Second, any time one vendor changes a file format, all of the translators into and out of this system must be modified.

The ideal translation approach is to have a standard into which and out of which all the vendors translate. The difference in these two approaches is shown in Figure 4.2. This preferred approach is the one addressed by IGES (Initial Graphics Exchange Specification) and its successor PDES (Product Definition Exchange Specification).

The next three sections describe three ways in which current DBMSs can be used to improve data sharing and the productivity of both individual applications and the overall design and manufacturing process.

Use of a Database as a Directory

Large manufacturing companies must keep track of thousands or tens of thousands of designs. This design proliferation exists even without CIM. Drawing administration is hard enough, but it becomes even more difficult with the addition of configuration management. The information management problem is even more complicated because each part has many different types of design documentation:

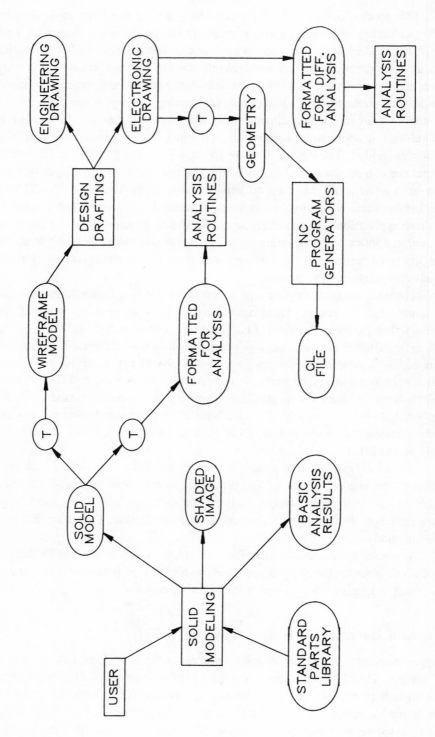

Figure 4.1 Translator approach to application interface

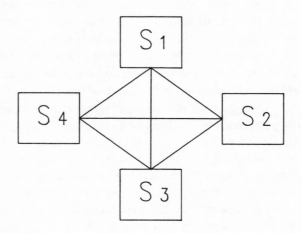

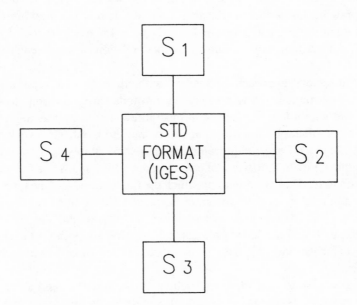

Figure 4.2   Alternate translation strategies

engineering drawings, bills of materials, analysis models and results, process plans, and designs for special tooling needed to manufacture the part.

The same problem exists when these companies convert to CIM systems. Instead of keeping track of hard copies of engineering drawings and other documents, the company now must track all of the various design files. To further complicate the problem, many of these companies have multiple CIM systems, often of different types. Engineers on one system may need a design stored on another system. If there are multiple copies of design data, they must be kept consistent when a change is made. An additional complication is that much of the design and manufacturing data, especially for older parts, is still on paper rather than in a computer system.

The directory approach uses a database to keep track of this design information, whether in computer files or on paper. This approach can be used on any of several levels of complexity. In its simplest form it is simply an administrative tool for the engineer. It allows the engineer to ask for design documents without having to remember the file name. The engineer can ask for the drawing for Part 1234 without having to remember whether it corresponds to File ABC on System 3 or is still a paper drawing stored in Drawer X. In this limited approach the database structure maps engineering document names into file names and locations.

A more sophisticated approach extends the database to include most of the traditional librarian functions. In this case the structure is extended to track who has a document or file, when it was checked out, and where it is now. The database can also maintain a change history—when was the file modified and by whom. Finally, it can track the relationships among various files. For example, File 1 is the solid model for Part X, and File 2 is the shaded image for the part. File 3 is the drawing for version 1 of Part X, while File 4 is the drawing for version 2. File 5 could be the cutter center line (CL) file for machine tool 1 and File 6 the CL file for machine tool 2. Maintaining these relationships is essential to integrate CIM.

The directory approach also helps with multiple CIM systems and in a distributed environment. Most turnkey systems today are minicomputer-based and are saturated with a few hundred or at most a few thousand drawings. Saturation involves a combination of storage capability and the number of workstations the system can support. Larger mainframe-based systems simply delay saturation; they do not eliminate it. In a distributed environment additional fields can be added to the database to indicate the system on which the file is stored and the type of system, since the company may have different types of CIM systems.

Since all engineers must access this directory to find the files or design documents, it should be stored on a central machine accessible to everyone. The directory database does not have to be stored on the same machine as the files themselves.

An extension to this approach includes procedures to send a copy of a file from the computer where it is stored to the engineer on another computer. If the engineer wants only to review the design, the system sends only a copy of the file.

However, if the design is to modified, then the file needs to be locked so that other users cannot simultaneously modify it. This control is already done manually in drawing libraries to ensure design consistency and change control. For better data control, some companies are centralizing both the directory database and the data files. Other organizations are centralizing only the directory but allowing copies of the files to remain at the locations where they are used. Even in these cases, however, a backup copy is usually stored at the central site.

This directory approach helps the CIM user find and manage the company's design and manufacturing data, whether in manual or computerized form. However, the computer is managing engineering data files, not the individual fields and records as it normally does in database management.

This approach is easy to implement because neither the file formats nor the applications are changed. The user needs only to design and load the relatively simple directory database. Furthermore, the directory application and its data structures are so simple that almost any DBMS can support them. The hardest part of the implementation is developing the necessary support procedures so that most functions are transparent to the users. Examples of these procedures include transferring files, invoking the desired applications, and ensuring that only files in the proper format are passed to each application. Ideally, the user on an Intergraph system should be able to request the drawing for version 2 of Part X and have the system automatically obtain the proper file, whether it is stored on the same or another Intergraph system, and then invoke the desired application. In an even simpler implementation the system informs the user of the file name and the system it is on. The user then transfers the file and invokes the desired application. While this is not the ideal approach, it does provide some benefits and could be done as a first step, with the more transparent support procedures added later.

This approach is also applicable in a heterogeneous environment, if the necessary translators are available. In this case the system must know the file format, the type of system on which the file was created, and the type of system with the application. Then, in addition to transferring the file, the system could automatically invoke the necessary translator. Because of the translation time involved, the system should first inform the user that a translation is necessary. If the user approves, then the translator is invoked.

As described above, this directory approach does a minimal amount for the user. The engineer must still specify the type of document (e.g., drawing, solid model, or NC program) and the part. However, with the proliferation of designs, determining which part is often the hardest step. The directory approach can be still further enhanced to make it a very powerful design retrieval tool. The main difference is in the design and structure of the directory database. This additional functionality requires some additional fields and some additional application logic.

These additional fields describe the characteristics on which the design can be retrieved. Design retrieval is discussed in more detail in Chapter 8, so at this point let us assume that only two additional fields are needed: a form and function classification code and a group technology code. Figure 4.3 shows the information model for a directory database.

The basic object in this figure is a part. A part is uniquely identified by a combination of a part number and a version number. Parts are related by a bill of materials structure. A part has a designer, a release status (which has a release date), and many forms of design documentation. Examples or subtypes of these design documents include drawings, solid models, shaded images, analysis models (possibly several different types), and analysis results. For this analysis assume that each design document is stored in a file, one document per file. (A complete analysis would also include noncomputerized design documentation, which could also be managed by this type of directory system.)

For each file there is the application that created it and the appliction or applications that can read it. In addition, the file has a format. Each application also has an acceptable input and output file format. Some of these applications are translators whose sole purpose is to map files from one format to another.

This data structure is adequate for implementing a basic directory database. A user can choose to run a specific application against a certain type of design documentation for a part (e.g., to make some drafting changes on the drawing for Part 123, version 2). The user simply specifies the part and the application, and the system then selects the proper file, determines whether it is in the correct format for the application, and if necessary invokes the translator to convert it.

Additional functions are possible if the data structure is extended. For example, to add some of the librarian functions, additional attributes are related to each file. Each file has a status to indicate whether it is available or checked out (i.e., locked). Each time the file is checked out, the time and the identification of the user is stored. A multisystem environment would include the location of the person and the current location of the file, since it could be transferred to another node. The system could record only the current locking status or a complete history of who had locked the file.

Database and File-Oriented Applications

This approach is an intermediate stage between use of the database as a directory and the full DBMS approach. The former approach involves no conversion, while the latter approach requires extensive conversion. As a compromise this approach only involves converting the data.

Since the applications are not converted, they will not benefit from the database approach, but if they are relatively stable, this is not a serious problem. However, since the data have been converted and stored in a database, new applications can use this new technology.

Existing applications continue to read and write their own file formats. When the application is set up, the needed data are extracted from the database and

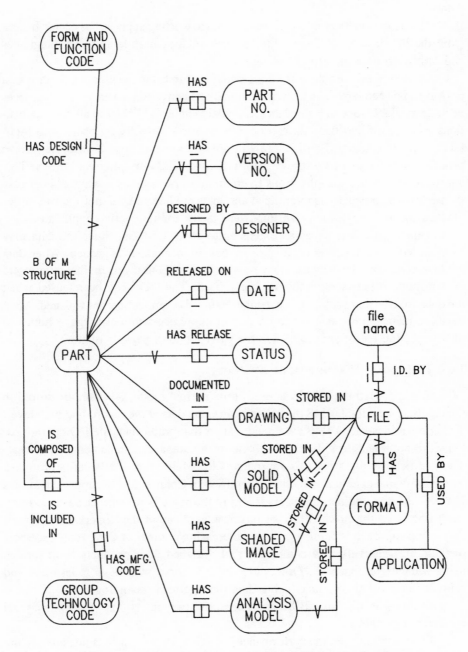

Figure 4.3   Information model for a directory database

converted to the input file format. The application then runs as it always did. When the application finishes, the output file is converted and the data are stored in the database.

The main penalty of this approach is that the existing applications cannot benefit from the database technology, with features such as high-level query languages and improved data integrity.

Offsetting this problem are three benefits. First, the existing applications do not have to be converted, or they can gradually be converted whenever the resources become available. Second, the data are available under a DBMS so all new applications can benefit and the data can now be accessed directly by users with high-level query languages. Third, there will always be some applications that are so process-intensive that they cannot afford the overhead imposed by a DBMS. This approach allows those applications to continue to run as they always did because the performance penalty is minimized and incurred before and after the run rather than during the application—an important factor for interactive applications.

This approach requires an extension to some DBMSs. Since the data may be modified by the existing application, a locking mechanism is needed. When data are extracted from the database, they must be checked out to ensure that other users do not modify them while they are being used. The locks can be released when the data are checked back into the database after the application has finished. Most database management systems today do not allow users to lock large volumes of data (e.g., the entire solid model for a part) for long periods of time.

Full Database Management Systems

With this approach the DBMS is used in its normal mode. All data are stored in the database, and the DBMS directly manages the data at the record and item level. The applications use DBMS commands rather than traditional file I/O operations. Only this approach provides the full benefits of database management technology. The justification for using this approach is to obtain all of the benefits promised by database management, which are identified in Chapter 5. This approach allows CAD/CAM and engineering users to enjoy the same benefits that have dramatically improved the productivity of business application developers and users.

This approach is being used by an increasing number of CIM vendors. Some of them are relatively new companies that designed their products from scratch using a database approach. Others are older vendors who have redesigned and reimplemented their products using data management technology.

Skeptics of this full DBMS approach raise two objections—peformance and conversion problems.

First, let's consider the performance objection. Performance is just one evaluation criterion. Given a choice between machine efficiency and personnel effectiveness, the trade-off should be toward greater functionality and personnel effectiveness rather than simply faster performance.

The real question is how to weigh performance against other criteria, such as ease of use, development time and costs, and maintenance time and costs. The implication of the performance criticism is that performance is the dominant criterion and all others are relatively minor. However, the more a system does in meeting other criteria, the more cycles it will take and the more it will affect pure application performance. In many cases the additional functions, such as integrity checking, involve having the DBMS do something that otherwise would have to be done by the application program. Therefore, these DBMS functions would not seriously affect the application unless the application ignored the function. However, there may be some performance degradation because more DBMS functions are generalized, whereas in a specific application they can be optimized. The trade-off is that it is frequently this optimization that increases application development and maintenance time and cost. This optimization also makes it difficult to share data among many applications.

Therefore, any performance penalty must be balanced against the benefits of easier application development and maintenance, improved data quality, and more effective use of the corporation's data resources because of easier integration of the design and manufacturing functions. The goal is not to optimize one specific function but the entire design and manufacturing process.

In fact, until the proper functionality is determined, performance is the wrong issue. It does not matter how fast the system can do the wrong thing or solve only part of the problem. Once the application requirements are defined and the functionality is determined, tuning the DBMS and the physical database design can lead to dramatic performance improvements. Consider the improvements in IPIP (the IPAD Information Processor, the multiuser engineering database management prototype developed by the IPAD program). In the original benchmarks certain geometric requests took over two minutes. Several years later after additional development and tuning, these same requests required less than three-tenths of a second. However, these improvements would never have occurred if the initial consideration had been performance. Functionality would have been eliminated to achieve the desired performance.

There are, however, some applications in which performance is the critical factor. In spite of the benefits, a few applications simply cannot afford the added overhead of a DBMS. For these applications there is compromise solution. In a preprocessing step all of the needed data can be extracted from the database and put into a file format optimized for the specific application. Once the application has been completed, a comparable postprocessing step can convert its output files and store the data back in the database. This compromise approach was discussed previously.

The second objection that is raised to a full DBMS approach is the conversion effort it would require. Most current CIM applications are not designed for this database approach and would have to be modified. For some well-designed applications these changes might be relatively minor, but for other, older applications these changes could be major and require a significant change in how the application manages its data.

Over time these application conversion problems will decline because current CIM products will be replaced or upgraded with a new generation of CIM software. These changes are occurring today with several vendors and many startup CIM companies. Several major vendors have also recently completed a major product upgrade and in some cases are now using database management technology. However, there will still be a data conversion problem in converting all of the existing data files into these databases. Much of this data will simply be archived and not converted until or unless it is going to be reused for a new product.

Migration Strategy

This section describes a migration strategy by which a company can progress from the simplest to the most sophisticated, integrated approach as it develops a greater understanding of data management.

A company at the starting point for this migration has little or no CIM. With the very small manufacturing companies there may be relatively little use of computers in any of its functions. However, most manufacturing companies of any size are already using computers for some functions, although perhaps only for business rather than CIM applications. Therefore, as a starting point let us assume a company with a small data processing department, primarily for business applications. It does a modest amount of in-house application development but uses a file rather than a database management approach. If it uses any CAD/CAM applications, they involve drafting, numerical control, and/or some limited analysis programs. These applications may be run on a separate engineering system, not the data processing one. The applications were bought as stand-alone packages, so any linkage among them is probably done by the vendor software or manually. Finally, while the data processing department writes some business applications, neither data processing nor the engineering department that owns the CAD/CAM system writes any CIM applications.

As a company's CAD/CAM systems and data management system evolve, some parallel changes may also occur in the company's business data processing. For the past fifteen years business data processing has increasingly recognized the benefits of data management over the conventional file-oriented approach. When this occurs in a manufacturing company, business data processing shifts to a database environment. This shift also occurs within CIM, but it can occur much faster in business data processing because the database approach is already widely accepted there. In fact, in most large companies and many medium-sized ones this change in business data processing has already occurred. Therefore, in most cases the business side of the organization already has the database expertise. If business data processing and the CIM systems groups talk to each other, most of the initial push toward data management will come from data processing.

The problem is that in most companies there is little contact between the two groups. (See Chapter 17 for a discussion of some of the lessons CIM can learn from management information systems.) This will have to change if design, manufacturing, and the supporting business functions are to become more integrated.

As these changes are occurring in business data processing, CIM information systems will also be evolving through six phases.

In phase one the company's CIM systems group will begin to write applications on top of or in addition to the existing turnkey applications. These new applications will be file-oriented because of the background of the CIM systems personnel and the file-oriented architecture of the turnkey applications. In some cases these in-house–developed applications will be simply macros or parameterized applications planned by the turnkey vendor. In the latter part of phase one these will be full-fledged applications, designed and implemented by the in-house CIM systems group.

Phase two occurs because of the proliferation of individual applications. Phase two is characterized by the development of translators to interface the applications that the company started to develop in phase one. At one level these translators will be relatively simple ones to provide interfaces between applications all written to extend a single vendor's product set. These translators will be simple because both the vendor-supplied turnkey product and the in-house–developed applications will use the same basic file structure and approach. More complex translators, such as IGES, will be vendor-supplied and will support translation across products of different vendors. In most cases the users will have to invoke these translators manually and keep track of the various file formats.

Phase three is the first phase that actually uses a database management system. This is the directory approach described earlier in this chapter. This is the first point at which the CIM systems group begins to use DBMS technology. Initially, it will involve a relatively simple database structure, but as additional functions are added to the directory system and as the group becomes more comfortable with the technology, more complex structures will be included.

Phase three can begin at different times—possibly as early as phase one. If the turnkey vendor provides a directory capability, then phases one and three may occur at the same time. However, this may delay, although not block, further movement into phase four. The company's in-house CIM group will not develop as much understanding of the underlying DBMS technology if the directory application is provided by the vendor. In some cases a company, especially a large sophisticated one, may choose to develop its own directory application even if one of its turnkey vendors provides one. For example, the company may have turnkey systems from several vendors and want a common set of directory functions.

Phase four occurs when the CIM group begins to design part of a CAD/CAM database and develop a few independent applications using it. (In a sense the phase three directory could be one of these applications; however, it is treated here as a separate step because it has much broader productivity implications beyond simply learning how to use the DBMS technology.) Phase four is the point at which the company begins to explore how to use database management in an engineering rather than the traditional business environment. Two types of learning occur in this phase. First, the organization must learn how to design large, complex databases using one of the formal database design methodologies. Second, the application programmers must begin to understand how to structure an application to benefit from the additional capabilities provided by a DBMS.

The changes that occur during phase four are the equivalent of those that occur within business data processing as it shifts from the file-oriented approach to the database management environment. Since this change normally occurs much earlier in the business application environment, the CIM group may be able to speed up phase four with closer contact and communications with the business data processing department. It is a waste for both parts of the company to learn the same painful lessons independently (see Chapter 17).

In phase four most of the CIM applications are still file-oriented. Only a few have been designed and implemented using a DBMS. Furthermore, these tend to be initially stand-alone applications with only limited links to the existing file-oriented applications.

Phase five is a transition in which most of the data are archived in a database, but many of the applications are still file-oriented. Starting in this phase, most new applications are designed and implemented using DBMS technology. In this phase the company has one or more major CIM databases, so new applications are designed to use these databases. When necesssary, the databases are extended to support additional applications. However, all of the company's applications have not been converted by this point. For the unconverted applications the required data are extracted from the database and put into the format required by the application. This is done as part of the job setup for the application. The application then runs normally using its existing input and output file formats. When the job is completed, the output file is converted and stored in the database. These data are then available for processing by other applications, most of which are database-oriented.

The NASA PRIDE (PRototype Integrated DEsign) system and its successor IMAT (Integrated Multidisciplinary Analysis Tools) are examples of this approach. Figure 4.4 shows the basic architecture of the PRIDE system. The user interfaces with the system through an executive that invokes the requested applications and controls the appropriate translators. For example, a user could enter AD/2000 (a design/drafting application) and define a structure to be analyzed. When the user saves the data, a translator converts the data from the AD/2000 internal file format into a relational database. If the user decides to run an analysis program such as SPAR or a structural optimization program, the data are extracted from the database

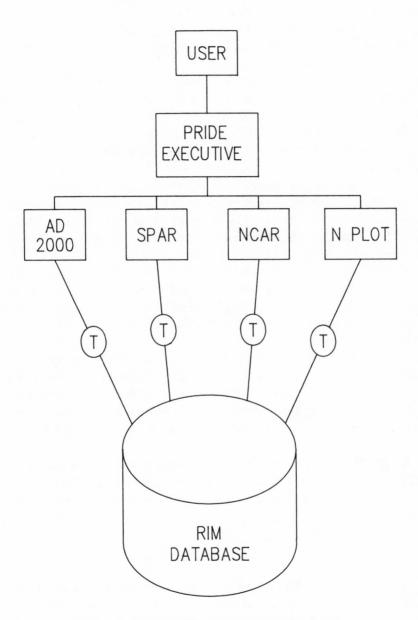

Figure 4.4   PRIDE system architecture

and converted into the appropriate file format and the application is invoked. Again when the user saves the data at the end of the job, another translator converts the data and stores them back in the database. All of these initial PRIDE applications are existing ones with their own file formats. However, because the data are stored in a database, new applications can written directly against the database without the need for a translator.

A company has two options with this archival database. With the first option the PRIDE database design is essentially a collection of the existing record formats that were defined using the database definition language. For a prototype this is adequate, and it makes some of the translators simpler than if the database were designed from scratch. However, this results in a poor database design and makes it harder to add new applications. Given the time savings in developing and verifying the design and analysis models, this approach is more than adequate to prove the benefits of the concept. Ideally, a company would use the second option: perform a careful information analysis to develop a good database design that would be more flexible as new applications were added. Over time, as a company's applications evolve, this phase will shift into phase six.

In phase six most of the data are routinely stored in one or more databases and most applications operate directly against these engineering databases. Translators and file-oriented applications would be used primarily for performance reasons—that is, when an application must have the data in a special optimized format for acceptable performance.

No company has reached phase six yet, and most organizations are somewhere in phase one or two. A few companies have implemented directory systems or prototypes of such systems, and several vendors have implemented such products. These include the Engineering Data Library from Control Data, the Drawing Management Control System from SDRC, and the Engineering Data Control System from DEC, Design Management System from Sherpa, and Product Data Manager from both Intergraph and Computervision. Both manufacturing companies and CIM vendors are working on phase four types of applications. Most of the vendor work today focuses on designing databases for either geometric data or for machineability data.

Summary

This chapter has described four roles for database management in CIM. These roles include (1) use of file-oriented applications with virtually no use of data management technology; (2) the use of a DBMS only to support a directory function to supplement the file approach; (3) continued use of file-oriented applications but use of a database to store the data; or (4) the use of a full CIM database environment for both data storage and applications development and maintenance. Only the latter approach provides the full set of benefits often used to justify the data

50

management approach. This chapter also described six phases of a migration path over which a company can move toward implementing the full CAD/CAM database approach.

Further Reading

Bray, Olin. "CAD/CAM Data Management." In *Proceedings of NASA Conference on Computer-Aided Geometric Modeling.* Washington, D.C.: NASA, 1983.

Encarnacao, J., and F. L. Krause. *File Structures and Data Bases for CAD.* New York: North-Holland, 1982.

Fulton, Robert E. (ed.). *Managing Engineering Data: The Competitive Edge.* Proceedings of the 1987 ASME International Computers in Engineering Conference. New York: ASME, 1987.

Hopwood, Norman W., Jr. "Managing Information as a Resource." *CIM Technology,* Aug. 1987, 33–36.

IPAD II: Advances in Distributed Data Base Management for CAD/CIM. Washington, D.C.: NASA, 1984.

Schumaker, Gerald. "Digital Product Models: A Must for CIM." *CIM Technology,* Aug. 1987, 27–30.

5

Database Management Concepts

This chapter provides an overview of database management system (DBMS) concepts. Information is now recognized as a critical corporate resource that must be managed. A DBMS is the essential computer tool for managing this information. This chapter explains why a DBMS is important, identifies its objectives and components, and shows how it works. It describes the evolution of database management and discusses the two major types of DBMSs—network and relational. The chapter also explains the concepts of database administration and data administration, which are key functions if an organization is to manage its information effectively. The focus of the chapter is on the user's perpective.

Why Database Management?

Many companies now recognize that information is a critical corporate resource. Like other corporate resources (such as money, material, equipment, and people), information must be managed and controlled if it is to be used effectively. This concept of information as a corporate resource is just now being recognized and accepted by engineering and manufacturing.

It is not enough simply to capture and store data. Users must be able to retrieve and modify the data quickly and easily. A DBMS is the key tool that makes this possible. In the past a computer program had to be written to access the data. To access or modify data in a different way required a new program or the modification of an existing program. Because early computers were slow and had little storage, programs were designed to optimize the use of these scarce and expensive computer resources. Application designers and programmers spent as much time trying to optimize the use of the computer as they did in understanding the problem. Designing and physically implementing the solution was a major effort given the limitations of early computers. This approach led to the long and painful system development process, for which data processing is so famous.

While there are many ways to describe the traditional system development cycle, the essential steps are these. First, the user identified a problem. Second, the systems analyst analyzed the problem and defined the precise requirements. Third, a system designer laid out a detailed design of what the computer had to do to solve the problem (i.e., the logical and physical implementation of the solution). Fourth, a programmer coded the design in a specific programming language. Fifth, the system was tested, ideally by the programmer, the user, and the computer operations staff. The program was then declared operational, and the user could begin to solve the original problem.

There are several assumptions built into this process: it assumes that the user's problem did not change during this long development process; it assumes that the analyst understood the user and correctly identified the requirements of the problem; it assumes that the designer understood the requirements and created a correct, consistent, and complete design; and it assumes that the programmer understood the design and implemented it correctly.

There are five major problems with this application development approach. First, it assumes that the computer resources are the most critical and expensive ones and emphasizes optimizing the physical design of the system. In the 1950s and 1960s and for part of the 1970s this was true. By the 1980s this had changed dramatically. Computer resources are far less expensive than personnel, and the gap is rapidly widening. Therefore, today we should be much more concerned with people efficiency and effectiveness rather than hardware efficiency and performance.

Second, the detailed design of the application is tightly bound to a specific set of hardware and software. The designer's expertise is in how to use the hardware and operating system to solve problems. Therefore, the resulting design is a tightly bound combination of logical and physical design decisions. This tight binding between the application logic and the specific system for which it is designed means that it is hard to evolve the application as the hardware and software change. It is also difficult to add new features as the requirements change over the life of the system.

Third, the users have little input in the design process once the initial requirements have been defined and accepted. As the user learns more about the problem and what is needed to solve it, he or she cannot feed this additional information into the design process. This was not a serious problem for the early, well-understood applications such as payroll, billing, or inventory. These early applications were automating relatively simple manual systems. This has become a serious problem, however, with newer, more complex applications such as CIM. The users do not completely understand many of these problems at the beginning of the development process. Detailed design of the application logic is a learning process for the users as well as for the information systems developers. Therefore, constant testing and feedback from the user is essential. This requires a prototyping environment in which new concepts and ideas can be quickly incorporated and tested during the development process.

A fourth problem is the long development time. A complex application can have a long development time during which the requirements can change dramatically. Some of these changes may occur because the users learn more about their problem and refine their requirements. In a dynamic environment, however, the problem itself can change during the development process. One organization spent two years on requirements definition and preliminary design for a reporting system, although the reporting requirements changed dramatically over an eighteen-month period. Another problem with a long development cycle involves schedule and budget estimates. The longer the development, the greater the uncertainty in these estimates.

The fifth problem is that each application is developed independently of all of the other related applications, both those that already exist and those that will be developed in future. This is the most serious problem in planning for integrated

CIM systems. An ICAM (Integrated Computer-Aided Manufacturing, a large multiyear Air Force program) report explicitly states that the most critical problem faced by large aerospace manufacturers is that "after years of developing individual applications to address selected parts of the overall requirement, they do not fit together as an integrated whole."

These are the general problems with early development methodologies which database management systems can help solve. A generalized database management system makes it much easier for both end users (e.g., technical, management, and clerical personnel) and application programmers to get the data they need, often without designing and writing a complex application program. Today good software engineering practice requires a clear separation of the logical design and the way in which it will be implemented physically. The DBMS insulates users and developers from the physical aspects of data management and allows them to deal with only the logical data structure and access paths. Finally, database management technology can support rapid prototyping. This allows the users to remain actively involve in the development process.

These early systems were file-oriented. File systems have two key characteristics that create serious problems. First, in a file system the logical and physical designs of the file are tightly bound together and are optimized for a particular application or small set of applications. Second, all the information about the file is included only in the application programs that use the file. Since the system knows little about the file, it cannot provide integrity checking to ensure the quality of the data. The application programs must do all of this checking. This leads to redundant development because many applications must do the same types of checking.

This lack of adequate integrity checking is the first major problem with file systems. The other two problems, consistency and maintainability, occur because some data must be shared by several applications. With the pure file approach there would be a separate file for each application. This means that shared data must be stored in each file. If some files were updated daily, some weekly, and some monthly, the data would become inconsistent. Retrieving the same data items would give different results, depending on which file was used. This is clearly a serious problem. The alternative is to eliminate multiple copies of the data by storing all of the related data in a single, much larger file. Then all of the applications needing the data would share this common file. The problem with this alternative is maintainability, for the file definition is buried within the applications using the file. Over time applications change and need new data. This means modifying the file structure for one of the applications. Once this happens, however, all the other applications must be modified because their definitions must conform to the new file format. DBMSs were developed to solve these problems.

In summary, a database management system has five major objectives:

1. Easier application development
2. Easier application maintenance

3. Direct user access to the data without programming
4. Improved data integrity
5. Improved data security

What Is a Database Management System?

A database management system is a set of system software to define, retrieve, and modify data stored in a database. It provides a way for the database administrator to define a database and allows both programmers and end users to retrieve and modify the data easily. It also controls access to the database so that many users can share the data without interfering with each other or destroying the integrity of the database. Access controls also prevent unauthorized access to the data.

A general trend is to incorporate common, well-understood operations that were originally part of application programs into system software, and in some cases eventually into hardware. For example, originally floating point operations were encoded in the application program. Since these were well-understood, widely used functions, they quickly became supported by the system software. Now all except the smallest machines do these operations in the hardware.

Database management systems are simply the extension of this trend to data management functions. This same migration trend occurred in input, output, and storage operations. Originally, application programs had to do the detailed control of various input, output, and storage devices. This created two problems: the application had to be changed when the hardware changed, and designers and programmers had to worry about these detailed control operations in addition to the application logic. By the early 1960s operating systems software had taken over much of this detailed hardware control activity. This freed the application designers and programmers to concentrate on the application logic and the data structures required to support the application.

In the late 1960s and early 1970s it became apparent that the same types of data structures and access methods were being used by many different types of applications. Similarly, most applications were doing the same types of data editing: making sure the data types were correct, ensuring that valid codes were used for various fields, and checking that new data were consistent with data already in the computer (e.g., verifying that a new account number is unique and not already being used).

Database management systems were developed to handle these functions at the system level rather than the application level. Today one or more DBMSs are available on all mainframes and minicomputers, most microcomputers, and many workstations. A few vendors, such as INGRES and ORACLE, provide essentially the same DBMS for all sizes of machines. Since the price of these DBMSs range from a few hundred to several hundred thousand dollars, there are major differences in the functions they support and in their performance. In spite of these differences, there is a common core of functions that most DBMSs support.

Today most database management systems support a common set of generic functions. The first and most common feature involves a separate database definition independent of the applications that use the data. Second, most DBMSs provide an interface for both end users (e.g., engineers, managers, and clerical personnel) and for programmers. The trend today is to provide the same high-level interface to both types of users. Third, most DBMSs allow multiple users of both types to access the database simultaneously without interfering with each other and without destroying the integrity of the data. Only a few of the smallest single-user systems do not provide this concurrent capabililty. Fourth, most DBMSs provide backup and recovery facilities.

DBMS Components

There are three major DBMS components: the database, the database definition, and the DBMS software. The database is the collection of all the data. The database definition provides a complete logical and physical definition of the data. It defines the data both as they are stored in the database and the way the various applications expect to see them. The DBMS software is the set of programs that controls access to the data and processes the requests. (A request is either a retrieval or an update generated by the user—either a person or an application program.) The rest of this section describes these components in more detail.

Database

The database contains all of the computerized data that the company has defined and stored under the DBMS. A company is interested in many different types of objects or entities—parts, customers, employees, suppliers, customer orders, purchase orders, shop floor orders, machine tools, and raw material.

Each type of entity has certain characteristics or attributes. A part may have a part number, description, cost, price, inventory level, and supplier. A customer has a customer number, name, address (possibly several addresses, such as a shipping and a billing address), a balance, and one or more orders. Some of these attributes are mandatory (i.e., they must exist for every entity of that type). Examples of mandatory attributes include part number, customer number, and address. These objects and their characteristics exist in the "real world." To keep track of them, a company designs a database to model that part of the real world.

Within the database these entities and their characteristics or attributes are modeled or represented by record types and data fields. In general there are one or more database record types or relations for each type of entity. The fields in each record contain the values of the attributes.

In the real world entities are related to each other in various ways. For example, customers generate customer orders for various parts. The company buys some of these parts from suppliers whereas it manufactures other parts starting with raw material and using various machine tools. Shop floor orders provide a link among parts, raw materials, and machine tools. Database design (see Chapter 6) is the process that identifies the various types of entities, their attributes, and the relationships among them.

Database Definition

The database definition provides the complete logical and physical definition of the database the way it is actually stored. It also provides a definition of the data the way each application and/or user expects them.

The earliest DBMSs combined all this information in a single definition. (Many of the current microcomputer-based and some of the workstation-based DBMSs still have this single combined form of the database definition.) In the early 1970s most mainframe and minicomputer DBMSs partitioned the definition into two parts: the schema and the subschema. Figure 5.1 shows this two-schema architecture. The schema was the complete logical and physical definition of the database as it was actually stored. The subschema defined the logical structure of the database as a specific application or user expected it. The subschema usually described a subset of the database. A database has one and only one schema, but it can have any number of subschemas, since each application must have a subschema. Several applications or users can use the same subschema if they need the same logical data structure. DBMS routines convert the data between the way they are defined

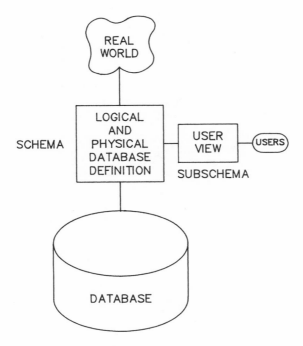

Figure 5.1   Two-schema architecture

in the schema and the subschema. This conversion is done automatically when data are retrieved or when the database is updated.

Today database management technology calls for a three schema architecture. This means that the database definition is divided into three parts: a conceptual schema, an internal schema, and one or more external schemas. Figure 5.2 shows the three major parts of the database definition and how they are related to each other and to the real world, which the database models. The top of the figure shows the real world and how various objects are related to each other, independent of any computer applications.

The conceptual schema describes the logical structure of the data in the relevant part of the real world. It identifies the types of entities, the attributes of each type, and the ways the various entity types are related to each other. The conceptual schema says nothing about how the database is physically implemented and stored or how any specific application views the data. The key point is that the conceptual schema models the real world, not the data structure required by a particular application. Therefore, in many cases when new applications are added, the conceptual schema does not have to be changed. In some cases changes are necessary, but if the conceptual schema has been designed correctly, it is necessary to add only new types of entities and new relationships. The existing entities and relationships rarely have to be modified.

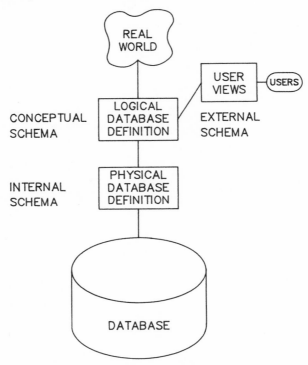

Figure 5.2   Three-schema architecture

The second part of the database definition is the internal schema. The internal schema defines exactly how the data are stored in the computer. It describes how various attributes are encoded, where they are stored in the record, which attributes are indexed, how to access each record type, and how the relationships among records are physically implemented. It also specifies how much space is allocated for each record type and how the records are clustered to improve the system's performance. The internal schema is defined by a database expert, the database administrator, and is invisible to the user.

The third part of the database definition is the external schema. This is the application or user view of the data. Each application or user must have an external schema. However, many applications can use the same external schema if they need the same view of the data.

If we compare Figure 5.1 and Figure 5.2, the difference between the two approaches is obvious: the schema has simply been split into separate logical and physical components in the conceptual and internal schemas.

The benefit of this three-schema architecture is data independence. The application (or the user) needs to know only its own external view of the database. The DBMS software automatically converts the data from the way they are stored in the database to the view defined for the application in its external schema. This means that if new data fields or record types are added to the database, the application sees no change as long as the DBMS can continue to convert the data from their new form into the view defined by the user's previous external schema. Thus the database can be modified and extended for many new applications without affecting most of the existing applications. In other words, most changes to the conceptual schema are transparent to the user. This ability to modify the logical structure (i.e., the conceptual schema) of the database without affecting the applications (i.e., the external schemas) that use the data is called *logical data independence*.

This logical data independence is absent when the conceptual schema was originally defined incorrectly and the correction is so drastic that the DBMS can no longer convert the data from the way they are stored to the way the application expects them. In these cases changes are needed in the application program and/or its external schema. This shows the importance of correct database design. Chapter 6 describes a methodology for designing such databases.

Even if the database design is logically correct, the way in which the database is accessed may change over time. This may require changing the way the data are stored or creating a new physical access path in the database. For faster access the records may also need to be clustered differently in the database, or the database may be shifted to new hardware devices for better performance. In all of these cases all that needs to be changed is the internal schema. The DBMS continues to convert the data between the conceptual and external schemas, neither of which have been changed, and between the conceptual and the new internal schema. Again, as long as the DBMS can continue to convert the data between the conceptual and internal schemas, the applications and users are independent of any changes in the way the database is physically stored. This is called *physical data independence*. This reduced maintenance is important because most data processing organizations spend over half of their resources on maintenance rather than on new application development.

DBMS Software

The DBMS is the system software that performs all of the DBMS functions. When the database is initially defined, the DBMS reads and checks the data definition language and creates the schema. At compile time and run time it interprets the DBMS requests to determine which routines to invoke to access the data and to perform the necessary conversions. It provides all of the update synchronization control to allow multiple users to retrieve and update the database without interfering with each other. The DBMS also ensures that all of the integrity and security constraints defined in the schema are enforced. Finally, it provides various reports and tools to support the database administration functions.

Database Management System Concepts

DBMS Functions

End users and programmers use two basic DBMS user functions: retrieving data from the database and updating data in the database.

The main reason for storing data in a database is to retrieve them. The user (or application) views only a part of the database through an external schema, and all user operations involving the database are in terms of this view. All DBMSs allow users to retrieve one or more attributes about one or more entities with a single request. Complex selection expression can be used to specify which entities to select. The data can also be sorted and summarized in various ways.

The other main operation is updating the database. There are three types of update operations: add, modify, and delete. The add operation adds a new record to the database. The modify operation changes some of the data fields in records that already exist in the database. A single command can result in changing data in one or more record. The same types of selection expressions used for retrieval can also be used for modifying. The delete operation deletes one or more records from the data. The same selection expressions used for retrieval and modification can also be used for deleting.

Types of DBMSs

There are many ways to classify database management systems, but the most important classification involves the data model they support. A data model consists of both a data structure and a set of operations on that data structure. The data model determines the type of DBMS. The two most common data models today are the network and the relational data models. Changes in the underlying data model determines different generations of DBMS products.

There are five generations of data management products:

1. File systems
2. Hierarchical DBMSs
3. Network DBMSs
4. Relational DBMSs
5. Object-oriented DBMSs

Although some companies and many applications are still in the first generation (i.e., no DBMS), most DBMS activity today involves third- and fourth-generation database management systems—network and relational types of systems.

The earliest DBMSs were all hierarchical. In 1971 the CODASYL Systems Committee published a report identifying the functional requirements for a network-based DBMS. Today almost all large (multigigabyte) production-oriented databases (for applications such as bill of materials, production scheduling, inventory control, purchasing, order entry, and accounts receivable) still use these network DBMSs. Data integrity and performance are the strengths of these network DBMSs. Although they are easier to use than the previous products, they are not as easy to use as the new relational systems. This network technology is mature, and little research is being done in this area. Much of the product development on these network systems concentrates on providing them with relational-like interfaces and on migrating them to the newer relational technology.

In the early 1980s production-quality relational DBMSs started to appear. The relational data model has two major benefits over the network model: it is based on a much stronger theoretical foundation—set theory; and it is much easier to understand and use.

A major difference is in how relationships are defined and implemented. The same real-world relationships can be modeled with either approach. A network DBMS requires that these relationships be predefined in the database definition. However, given the way most of the network DBMSs are implemented, there is tight binding between the way the relationships are defined and the way they are physically implemented, thus reducing their data independence. If a new application needs a new relationship, the network database often must be redefined and converted. This can be a lengthy process if the database is large.

On the other hand, with a relational DBMS a user can dynamically build new relationships by joining two relations with a common domain. This makes the relational approach much more flexible for unanticipated requests.

Today there are still very few large production-oriented databases using a relational DBMS. Although they are easier to use, they still do not have the performance and data integrity support of the network systems. However, this is beginning to change as relational products mature and their performance improves. This is occurring because most of the DBMS research today focuses on the relational model.

The fifth-generation, object-oriented database management systems are still primarily research topics. This technology involves a merging of database and expert systems. While this approach has much promise, especially for CIM and engineering, there are currently only two relatively new products in this category — V-Base by Ontologic and CIMPLEX by ATP. Therefore, except in special cases, this technology is not available to most organizations.

Many database-management-oriented organizations, however, do have both network and relational DBMSs because each has a different strength. Although network DBMSs are more difficult to use than relational DBMSs, their performance and data integrity checking are much better. Therefore, many organizations do their major production work on a network DBMS and download subsets of data to a relational database for easier end-user access and special reporting. This approach emphasizes the ease of use, friendliness, and development productivity of the relational DBMS.

Most production work remains on network DBMSs for two reasons — performance and integrity. Relational DBMSs still cannot compete with well-designed network databases in environments with high-transaction volumes against very large databases. However, this is changing as relational DBMSs mature and improve their performance. And relational DBMSs still do not support the level of data integrity routinely provided by all network systems. In fact, the standards committees are working on extending SQL (Structured Query Language), the industry standard relational query language, because today it cannot even express many of the integrity constraints that need to be included in the database definition. For example, in relational systems one can specify that a design's release code must have one of five specified values. But one cannot specify that NC programs only exist for released designs or that a project must exist before an employee to work on it. With relational DBMSs these constraints must still be checked by the application. As with performance, these referential integrity constraints are being added to relational systems. Therefore, in spite of these current problems, which are being corrected, industry is slowly converting to relational systems. The overriding factors are their ease of use and productivity benefits. The only long-term challenge to the relational DBMS lies in the future with object-oriented DBMS technology.

Network Data Model

In the network data model the data structures include records and sets. The network data model models the different types of objects and relationships in the real world. Each type of object is represented as a record type, with the attributes of the object being data fields in the record. For example, there would be record types of employees, departments, parts, machine tools, and orders. Attributes can be either mandatory or optional. Mandatory attributes are things like employee name, employee number, and part number. They must be included. Optional attributes may or may not be present for a specific record instance. The mandatory and optional specification is used to enforce data integrity. For example, the DBMS will not store a record if any mandatory attributes are missing.

Sets define the relationships among different types of objects. Departments "include" employees and parts "are made on" machine tools. These sets (e.g., "include" and "are made on") must be explicitly defined when the database is initially designed. Each set has an owner and a member record type. For example, department is the owner of the "include" set, and employee is the member record type. Network DBMSs implement sets using pointers, but in many cases the key attribute of the owner is also stored in the member record (e.g., the department number is also stored in the employee record). When this is done, a set can be defined as either manual or automatic. With manual sets the user must explicitly make the connection between the owner and member record instances. With automatic sets the DBMS automatically makes and maintains the connection. For example, if the "include" set is defined as automatic, when an employee is transferred (i.e., his or her department number is changed), the DBMS would automatically disconnect the employee record from the previous department record and reconnect it to the proper one. Maintaining the set relationships is one of the operations on a network data model.

The basic network operations involve retrieving and modifying data. Retrieval operation may get a single record of a certain type (e.g., the record for employee 1234). Other retrievals involve set processing. This involves retrieving one department record, such as the purchasing department, and then all of the member records (employees) for its "includes" set. Within a set additional operations include "get the next member" and "get the previous member."

Delete operations can delete either individual members or an entire set. Deleting the owner of the set results in deleting all of it members. There are also operations to create sets, add new owners for a set type (e.g., create a new department) or add new members to a set (as in hiring a new employee or transfer an employee from another department).

In general, anything that can be modeled in a network data model can also be modeled in a relational data model. There are network operations to perform the equivalent of all of the relational operations. In some cases the equivalent network operations are more difficult, but in other cases they are easier. In fact, some network operations cannot be performed by current relational systems, although this is more of an implementation problem than an inherent weakness of the relational data model.

Relational Data Model
In the relational data model the data structure involves relations, domains, and tuples, and the basic operations are selection, projection, and join. The relational data model

is easy to understand and use because it is built on the simple concept of a table with rows and columns of data. Table 5.1 summarizes these concepts and relates them to the corresponding network DBMS terms. The relational approach is used by many of the newer systems.

A *relation* is simply a table of data with rows and columns. The data about a specific type of entity are stored in one or more relations. For example, there would be relations for parts, suppliers, customers, employees, etc. For a relational DBMS the key database design problem is determining what relations or tables to store in the database and which attributes to store in which relations.

Each type of object has certain attributes or characteristics. For example, a part has a part number, a supplier, a type of material, a cost, and an inventory level. Employees have employee numbers, names, addresses, departments, and salaries. These attributes are stored in the columns of the relation and are called *domains*. A relation and its domains are the basic data structure in the relational data model. Each row in a relation, such as the part relation, represents a specific occurrence of that type of entity (e.g., Part 1234). This row is called a *tuple*.

The relational data model has three basic operations: selection, projection, and join. The first two operations involve a single relation type, while the third combines data from two relations.

Selection involves specifying one or more rows or tuples in the relation (e.g., requesting the data for certain parts). The part may be selected by specifying a

Table 5.1 Network and Relations Concepts

NETWORK CONCEPT	RELATIONAL CONCEPT
RECORD TYPE RECORD FIELD SET	RELATION TUPLE DOMAIN JOIN

unique identifier (such as part number) or by specifying certain attribute values, in which case all of the parts that qualify will be selected. The basic form of a selection request is as follows:

SELECT attributes FROM relation WHERE Boolean expression

This request can involve listing any or all of the domains in the relation (e.g., listing all of the data for Part 1234 or the data for released parts designed by Smith. Examples of selection requests are shown below:

1. SELECT ALL FROM part WHERE part_no = 1234
2. SELECT ALL FROM part WHERE
   status = released AND
   designer = Smith

A selection obtains data for one or more specified entities. Examples 1 and 2 retrieve all of the data from the part relation for the specified parts. Example 1 retrieves the data from a single tuple whereas example 2 obtains the data from all of the tuples that qualify—none, one, or many. In many cases, however, the application does not need all of the data. One application may need to know only who supplies part xyz, while another application may need to know only the type of material. This uses the *projection* operation. With each projection the user specifies which attributes or domains are needed, as in example 3 below. This allows the user to minimize the data retrieved from the database. Most queries involve a combination of selection and projection:

3. SELECT part_no description FROM part WHERE
   status = released AND
   designer = Smith AND
   material = steel

The most complicated operation is *join*. The join operation involves combining data from two different relations where there is at least one common domain. For example, consider the following two relations:

Part
part_no   material   weight   designer   status

Material_properties
material   density   strength   elasticity   expansion

To get the density of Part 1234, you must combine data from both relations. Conceptually, this is a two-step operation. First, you combine the two relations to create a third:

4. JOIN part WITH material_properties ON material FORMING x

This step would create a new temporary relation called x with all of the domains from both of the original relations. Then you would issue a request combining selection and projection:

> 5. SELECT part_no density FROM X WHERE part_no = 1234

With most DBMSs these two steps can be combined into a single command, but some of the simpler micro-based DBMSs require both steps. The single-command format would be:

> 6. SELECT part_no material density FROM part material_properties
>   WHERE part.material = material_properties. material AND part_no =
>   1234

The common join domains do not have to be the same, as they were in the above example. They need only to have the same set of values. The common domains could be salary in an employee relation and budget in a project relation. The join operation is meaningful only if salary and budget are in terms of a common value such as dollars. There would be a problem if one were in dollars and the other in francs. A more extreme example would be joining employee number and salary. Unfortunately, many DBMSs do not include adequate integrity checks to ensure that the requested joins are meaningful.

More sophisticated DBMSs support additional versions of the join operation. In some systems a join can combine more than two relations. In other cases the join condition does not have to be equality, as where the domain in one relation is less than or equal to the domain in the other relation.

The join operation is the key to the flexibility of the relational model. A join can be done at any time by a simple user request. Unlike with a network DBMS, all of the connections among the relations in the database definition do not have to be predefined. As long as there is a common domain between relations, a user can join them with a single SQL command. The trade-off is that the join operation is very expensive and time-consuming.

The last concept in the relational model is *normalization*. Normalization is the process of converting a relational data model into third normal form. Normalization is a process frequently used to design the logical structure of a relational database. Normalization is a top-down design approach, which was proposed by Codd. It begins by assuming that the designer knows approximately what the database design should be. The designer starts with a set of relations and the attributes identified for each relation. In many cases the initial relations are simply the record designs for the files the application currently uses or would use if it does not already exist. The logical design process consists of converting these relations into third normal form.

In first normal form a record can have no repeating groups. For example, the department record cannot include a list of employees. There would be a separate relation for employees. In second normal form all of the domains in the relation must be functionally dependent on the key domain. However, in second normal form a domain could also be functionally dependent on other domains in the relation. Finally, in third normal form all of the domains must be functionally dependent only on the key.

Example of DBMS Operation

Figure 5.3 shows the way a relational DBMS would process a sample query. Suppose an engineer wanted a list of all turned titanium parts that weigh less than one pound. The SQL query would be:

```
LIST part_number description FROM part
    WHERE material = titanium AND
          type = turned AND
          weight < 1.0
    ORDERED BY release_date
```

To process this request, the DBMS would go through the following seven steps:

1. The DBMS would check the syntax to ensure the query was expressed correctly.
2. The DBMS would then check the database definition to determine whether the user making the request is authorized to perform the requested operation. For example, a user in the accounting department may not be authorized to see any of these data except the part number and description, while a manufacturing engineer may not be allowed to see any of the data unless the part has been released. A designer may be allowed to change any data about a part he or she is working on until it is released. Once it has been released, no one would be allowed to change data. Any changes would result in creating a new version of the part, not changing the original one. All of these authorization rules are built into the database definition and are enforced automatically by the DBMS. If the user does not have the necessary authorization, the request will not be processed.
3. Assuming the user has the necessary authorization, the DBMS would then go to another part of the database definition to determine how the data are logically structured in the database. The DBMS would use this information to decide how to search the logical data structure to find the data it needs to answer the request. For example, does it need to join data from several relations? If so, what order is best?
4. The DBMS would next look at the physical database definition to determine exactly how the data are stored and how to physically process the logical structure.
5. At this point the DBMS would actually search the database and extract the appropriate records. Using data from steps 3 and 4, the DBMS can optimize the way it processes the various parts of the query. It is essential that the DBMS do

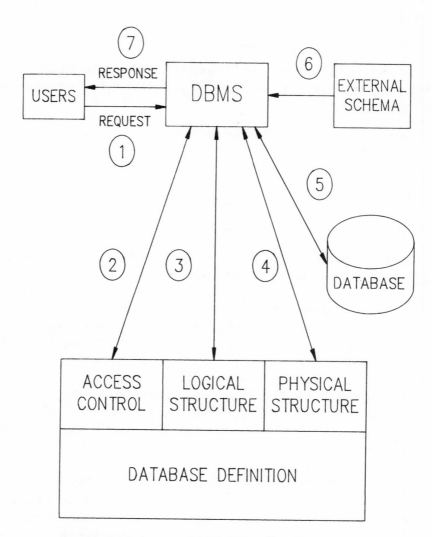

Figure 5.3   DBMS steps in query processing

this optimization step rather than assume the user has stated the request in the best way.

6. The DBMS would then go to another part of the database definition to determine exactly how this user or application program wanted to see the data. It would then do the necessary conversions so the user would see the data exactly the way he or she expected. For example, of the ten fields in the record, the user may want to see only five of them. The data the user wants may actually be stored in several different record types, but if the user wants to see them as a single record the DBMS would make the necessary conversion. The DBMS would also convert any encoded data values for the user—for example, material 23 could be returned to the user as titanium.

7. Finally, the requested data are returned to the user or the application program in the proper format. The DBMS has done much processing to satisify the request. Without a DBMS all of this work would have to be done by the application. The programmer would have to concentrate on how to process the data, not simply on what data are required. However, some of the processing is necessary because of the generalized way the data are stored and the generalized DBMS routines. The only way to avoid this generality and conversion is to store the data in exactly the form expected by the application. This forces the programmers to know how the data are stored, not simply how they need the data for further processing. Moreover, if many applications are going to use the data, there is no way the data could be structured as desired for all of them. It would have to be stored several times in different formats to meet these various needs.

Database Administration and Data Administration

Database Administration Functions

The previous section described operations used by a user or an application to query or update the database. In a database environment certain critical administrative and technical functions must be performed if the organization is to effectively use its DBMS. These functions are called *database administration*. Depending on the size of the organization, this may be done by a single individual or by a department. Database administration consists of five functions:

1. Selecting and acquiring of the DBMS
2. Designing and defining the database
3. Controlling access to the database
4. Providing tools to increase the database availability
5. Providing backup and recovery procedures

The first database administration function is to select and acquire a DBMS. To do this, the database administrator (DBA) must determine the organization's data management requirements. At the organizational level this involves strategic data planning. At the technical level it involves identifying what the organization needs in terms of database management functions, data structures, and support functions. Because of the importance of this function, Chapter 19 discusses the database selection issue and key evaluation criteria in more detail.

The second database administration function is designing and defining the database. After working with groups of users to understand their requirements, the DBA must identify the logical data structure underlying what they are trying to do and the various types of entities with which they are working. (One formal approach to this database design process is described in Chapter 6.) Based on the various types of entities, their attributes, and the relationships among them, the DBA designs the logical structure for the database. Then, based on the applications and the relative frequencies of queries and updates against the database, the DBA determines an appropriate physical structure for implementing the logical database design. The DBA then defines the database in terms of a specific DBMS by converting the results of these analyses into a conceptual and an internal schema using the data definition language of the selected DBMS. The DBA also defines the various user views or external schemas for all of the applications.

The above design and definition activities occur only once. There are, however, some design activities that occur repeatedly over the life of the database. Over time the DBA also modifies the database structure as necessary when new applications are added or when existing applications are modified. However, when making these changes—in effect modifying the database to meet new requirements—the DBA must ensure that existing applications and users can continue to get the data they need from the restructured database. These recurring activities involve either redefinition or reorganization of the database. Redefinition involves changing the logical structure of the database or the logical access paths through the data. With redefinition the DBA must ensure that current users and applications can continue to access the data they need, preferrably without any change on their part such as program modification. With reorganization the DBA is simply changing the physical organization of the database (i.e., the internal schema). Its logical structure and access paths are not affected. This means that existing users will still be able to access the data, but their response times may be affected.

The third function is access control. The reason for access control is to protect the data, a valuable corporate resource. These controls involve both the DBMS and administrative procedures. The DBA will also define administrative controls for the computerized data that must be used in conjunction with the access controls provided by the DBMS. Based on corporate policies and input from the users and originators of the data, the DBA specifies as part of the database definition who has what type of access to which data. A user may be allowed no access to some of the data, retrieval- only access to other data, and update access to still other parts of the data. Update authority is further divided into adding data to the database, modifying data, and deleting data. Different DBMSs have different levels of access control built into the software. Many of them also allow the DBA to define additional access controls as database procedures which the DBMS can then use as part of the system. The type of access controls a DBMS supports is one of the factors that must be evaluated in the selection process.

The fourth database administration function is to provide support tools to make the database easily available to both end users and application programmers. Most DBMSs provide some of these tools, such as high-level query languages (like SQL) and report writers. Most DBMSs also allow the DBA to add special database procedures and define user views and standard transactions and reports. The availability of these types of tools and the extent to which the DBA can add organizationally specific features is a significant factor in DBMS selection.

Performance is also an aspect of database availability. Therefore, the DBA must also monitor the performance of the database and, when necessary, modify its physical data structures to ensure continued adequate performance. This is important because over the life of the database, as its logical structure grows and changes, as new applications are added, and as the organization's priorities change, the system's performance changes. The DBA is responsible for tuning the performance of the system.

The final database administration function involves backup and recovery. Two types of failures can occur. First, all or part of the database can be destroyed, in which case it must be reconstructed from backup data. Second, errors may be introduced into and propogated through the database, in which case the effects of the errors must be backed out of the database and the transactions reprocessed correctly. Most DBMSs provide several mechanisms for backup and recovery, including before and after images, transaction logs, logical and/or physical database dumps, and procedures to roll back or bring forward the database when an error has occurred. The DBA must decide which of these mechanisms to use for which parts of the database. These decisions depend on application requirements, such as how long having the data unavailable can be tolerated and the costs incurred by the various mechanisms. For example, some mechanisms incur relatively low overhead for each transaction but pay a high price whenever a problem does occur. Other mechanisms allow a much faster recovery, but incur a higher penalty for each transaction. The DBA must balance these costs against the combined requirements of all of the applications using specific parts of the database.

The DBA needs certain tools to operate effectively. The main tool is a data dictionary/directory system (DD/DS). The DD/DS documents what data are in the database, how they are stored and in what their format, and which external schemas and applications use the data. The early DD/DSs were simply passive documentation tools that had to be created and updated separately. They were not an integral part of the database definition. Today many of these DD/DSs are active in the sense that they are integral parts of the database definition. When the database definition is changed, the DD/DS is automatically changed since it uses the same database definition. Most DBMSs also provide many standard reports such as documenting which applications may be affected if these data items are changed. Other DBA tools monitor the use of the database to help the DBA tune the physical design for optimal performance.

Data Administration Functions

This section describes the broader function—data administration—and explains the relationship between database administration and data administration. It also describes the two major data administration functions: strategic data planning and standard setting.

Many organizations had problems when they installed their DBMSs and defined their databases because in most companies not all important data are stored in a database or even on a computer. All shared information is a valuable corporate resource that must be managed, not just computerized data. Data administration functions involve providing the necessary administration, control, and coordination of all of these data resources. In this broader context, database administration is a subset of data administration.

Table 5.2 helps explain the distinction between these related sets of functions. Initially, organizations start with neither data nor database administration (I). In the early 1970s many companies bought a DBMS, frequently without setting up a database administration function. After a few years most of them discovered that they were not getting the benefits they had been promised. Things improved once they set up a formal database administration function (II). However, they still were not completely satisfied. This led to the broader data administration function

**Table 5.2   Data Administration and Database
Administration Migration Paths**

DATA ADMINISTRATION

		NO	YES
DATABASE	NO	I	III
ADMINISTRATION	YES	II	IV

74

(IV). This combination of functions is being called information resource management, but this path (I-II-IV) is not the only possibility. Many organizations that are now moving into database management are taking a different path. They are starting by establishing a data administration function (III). Once they have this function under control and have completed a strategic information plan, then they move to database administration (IV). This is the preferred path today.

The two key data administration (DA) functions are strategic data planning and standardization.

Strategic data planning involves finding opportunities for data sharing within the organization. These opportunities are often unanticipated because each part of the organization is focused on its own narrow area. The data administrator with a broader information modeling perspective is more likely to identify these data-sharing opportunities, which can have major corporate benefits.

Standardization involves developing policies and procedures so that the potential data-sharing opportunities can be exploited. Areas where standards are required include data naming, data definition, backup and recovery, and security. Without these standard policies and procedures and some assurance that they will be enforced, users will be reluctant to release control of their data to the DBA function. Under the best of conditions this is a difficult cultural change—moving from the perspective of "my data" to a view of data as a corporate resource to be shared.

Summary

This chapter has provided an overview of DBMS concepts. It identified the reasons for database technology, described what a DBMS system is, and explained its major components. It then discussed basic DBMS concepts, including the network and relational data models on which most current systems are based. Finally, it described the data administration and database administration functions, without which an organization cannot effectively use data management technology.

Further Reading

Date, C. J. *Introduction to Database Systems*. 3rd ed. Vol. 1. New York: Addison Wesley, 1981.

Leong-Hong, Belkis W., and Bernard K. Plagman. *Data Dictionary/Directory Systems: Administration, Implementation, and Usage*. New York: John Wiley and Sons, 1982.

Martin, James. *Principles of Data Base Management*. Englewood Cliffs, N.J.: Prentice-Hall, 1976.

_____. *Managing the Database Environment*. Englewood Cliffs, N.J.: Prentice-Hall, 1983.

_____. *Strategic Data Planning Methodologies*. Englewood Cliffs, N.J.: Prentice-Hall, 1983.

Ross, Ronald G. *Data Dictionaries and Data Administration: Concepts and Practices for Data Resource Management*. New York: AMACON, 1981.

Synnott, William R., and William H. Gruber. *Information Resource Management: Opportunities and Strategies for the 1980s*. New York: John Wiley and Sons, 1981.

6

Database Design

Importance of Logical Database Design

Overall Methodology

Information Analysis—Basic Concepts

Information Analysis—Advanced Concepts

Geometric Database Example

Summary

Information is the key to integrating CIM. Therefore, good information models and database designs are essential.

This chapter provides an introduction to NIAM (Nijssen Information Analysis Methodology). It also provides some of the basic training necessary to understand and use it. Several examples are used to explain and clarify the basic concepts. In Part Three this methodology is used to describe the information requirements for each of the design and manufacturing functions.

Importance of Logical Database Design

All application development is dependent on the information model and the logical database design. This concept of data-driven design is one of the key differences between database-oriented development and the design of independent applications, each with its own special file formats. With independent applications only the data needed by the specific application are included in the data model. The file design and format are then physically optimized for the application. On the other hand, with the database approach all of the relationships among a set of objects (i.e., a subject area) are identified and structured. The information model and the resulting database design can then easily be modified and extended for new or modified applications.

However, poor design is a major problem with large, complex databases. It usually occurs when the real data structures to be modeled are not completely understood. To avoid this, the analyst should try to identify the actual relationships in the real world rather than focusing too much on the initial applications.

There are several methodologies for logically designing databases. The information analysis approach described in this chapter and used throughout the rest of the book is called NIAM (Nijssen Information Analysis Methodology). For database design it is probably the most powerful modeling methodology available today.

A good information model and the resulting logical database design satisfies the initial applications and is easily extendable to meet future needs. It does this by capturing the underlying real-world information model, not simply the data structure needed by the initial applications.

The scope of the information analysis must include more than a single application's data. It must include the entire subject area and all of the related objects. Some of these data and their relationships may not be needed until later applications are added. In other words, the logical design should cover the entire subject area, even though the physical design and implementation will only include the data needed by the initial applications.

NIAM helps logical database design in three ways. First, it provides an effective communications tool for the users (e.g., subject matter experts) and the information modelers. This ensures that they understand each other. It does this by focusing on the information structures and relationships in the real world rather than on the physical data structures within the computer and the application. This involves the users more deeply in the design and development of the system and increases their commitment. Once the problem area and the model are understood and agreed to by the users and the information modelers, automated tools can convert the information model into a physical database definition for a specific DBMS.

Second, NIAM is a formal, easy-to-learn methodology that can be used by both information modelers and users. This methodology ensures that critical questions are raised before misunderstandings are embedded in the database design.

The third benefit of this methodology is that it allows subsets of a very large and complex database to be defined independently and then easily tied together. This avoids building a data structure appropriate to only one set of applications and then having to change it when other applications are added. Such flexibility reduces application development and maintenance costs and time. If the initial logical database design is correct, then future changes will mainly involve adding new object types, new attributes for these new object types or for existing object types, or new relationships among old and/or new object types.

Consider a specific example. A part has a certain hardness, strength, and flexibility. One database design would attach these attributes directly to the part. This model may be adequate for analyzing the stress on a part. However, later you may want to develop an application to evaluate various materials and determine which one is best for the part. Now there is a problem because the logical data structure is wrong. In reality a part does not have material properties. A part is made of a certain material, and it is the material that has these properties. With this more complex, but correct, logical data structure the database can support either type of application—analyze the stress on the part or select the best material for the part. With the first logical structure the new application would have required a major change in the logical structure, which could have forced changes in the existing applications. A good database design methodology like NIAM should ensure that these problems do not occur.

The logical data structure is determined by the types of objects, their attributes, and how these objects are related in the real world. The physical data structure (i.e., how the data are actually stored within the computer) is determined by both the logical structure and the way in which the data will be used by the various applications. Process analysis, another step in the overall methodology, determines how the data will be used and the relative frequencies of different types of use. While the physical structure is important for the performance of the applications, it is the logical structure that determines how easily the database can be modified to meet new requirements. The information analysis methodology in this chapter involves only the logical modeling.

Overall Methodology

This section describes the context within which information analysis is done. The context is important because information analysis is simply one step in an overall system development process.

This methodology consists of the six steps listed below:

1. Identify the problem.
2. Identify the requirements.
3. Define the requirements (functional analysis, information analysis, process analysis).
4. Prototype the system.
5. Design the system.
6. Implement the system.

First, the user must clearly identify the problem. He or she must identify the specific symptoms, analyze them, and relate them directly to one or more problems. Furthermore, the problem statement should not predefine a solution. That is, problems should not be stated in a way that implies the cause and the solution. For example, "Our product development cycle is too long" is not a good initial problem statement because it implies a solution—simply speed up the development cycle. It also involves an interpretation, not a visible symptom such as "Our competitor always gets a new product to market before we do." Once the symptoms have been identified, analyzed, and clustered, then the problem can be defined.

The second step is to identify the requirements that must be met by any acceptable solution. This step identifies only the general requirements; the detailed requirements analysis and definition occurs in step three.

These first two steps define the problem or application area and help limit the scope of the analysis. Scoping the problem is particularly important with this methodology since a complete information model links many types of objects. If uncontrolled, the analysis can easily get out of hand. Step three, the requirements analysis, is the critical step. It includes functional, information, and process analysis. These steps are discussed below in more detail.

In step four a prototype of the system is built to validate the requirements. With a good DBMS and a high-level query language, it is quick and easy to build a prototype so that the user can ensure that it does what is needed. In fact, the automated tools that support this methodology will generate a prototype database design and the schema for any one of several DBMSs. If the problem is small and simple enough, the prototype may be all that is needed. With large, complex problems the prototype simply validates the requirements and is followed by the fairly traditional systems design and implementation activities of steps five and six.

Database design focuses on the third step—the requirements analysis. This step consists of three activities: functional analysis, information analysis, and process analysis.

The functional analysis picks up where the requirements identification leaves off. It begins with a high-level analysis of the functions that must be performed to meet the requirements. Each of these high-level functions is decomposed into its subfunctions. In a recursive process these subfunctions are further decomposed until they are defined in a sufficient level of detail. For each function the inputs, outputs, and controls are identified. These inputs, outputs, and controls define the linkages and relationships among the various functions. Figure 6.1 shows a functional analysis diagram. (Functional analysis is described in more detail in Chapter 7.)

The modeler or analyst interviews users and experts in the area to determine the data needed for each function, the meaning of the data, and the relationships between the various data items. The flow of the data indicate how the functions are connected. The functional analysis also helps to limit the scope of the information analysis because many of the objects and their data are also related to irrele-

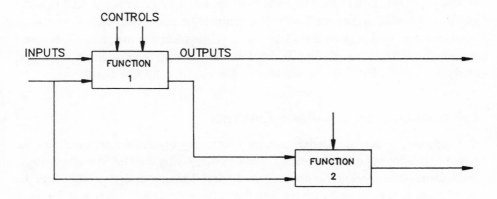

Figure 6.1   Functional model

vant objects and functions. For example, a project management system includes data about employees who may be assigned to one or more projects. Some of the personnel data, such as skills and salary, are relevant and must be included in a project management system. Other personnel data, such as dependents and benefits, are not relevant. If the data are all related to the system functions, the information analysis is tightly focused.

Information analysis is the second part of the requirements analysis. Good database design requires close communication between the user or subject matter expert and the database designer. NIAM is a database design methodology that facilitates this communication. People communicate using sentences to express facts. During an information analysis the subject matter expert uses facts to describe the real-world information relationships to the information modeler. The results of this exchange is an information model that captures the relationships among the data in the real world. It does not focus explicitly on the specific data structures needed by an application, although the scope of the information analysis is determined by the type of applications that the database must support. For example, if the information analysis is determining the various objects and relationships for a bridge, the scope or the functions to be included will determine whether the applications involve engineering design and analysis or a transportation study. Different types of data are needed by each of these application areas, but parts of the data structure would be common to both areas.

The third part of the requirements analysis is process analysis. Process analysis describes the dynamics of the information flow through the system. It identifies who needs what information when, as opposed to the information analysis that focuses on the static structure of the data. The dynamics of the data flow are used to make physical database design trade-offs. For example, if two types of data are always used together, they may be combined into a single record in the physical database design. However, these trade-offs are done later during the design step. Process analysis simply identifies and documents the required information flows.

Information Analysis—Basic Concepts

The top-down functional analysis draws a boundary around the area and sets the scope of the objects that the database must model. Using the NIAM methodology, the information model and eventually the logical database design is built from the bottom up. It is built up by identifying the various types of objects and the ways they are related.

There are two basic types of objects—real objects and lexical objects. Real objects are real things that exist in the real world, such as parts, people, machine tools, and dollars. Lexical objects are symbolic objects used for identifying and describing real objects. Examples of lexical objects include part number, name, social security number, and department number. Lexical object types are called LOTs and nonlexical or real objects are called NOLOTs. (From this point on only the term *object* will be used unless it is important to distinquish between real and lexical objects, in which case the necessary adjective will be added.)

NIAM, developed by G. M. Nijssen, is based on linguistic rather than computer science concepts. It is built on three axioms. The first is the ENALIM (Evolving NAtural Language Information Model) axiom, which states, "Each permitted communication between a user and an information system can be considered to consist of a set of elementary sentence instances." The NIAM methodology defines the grammar for these sentences. This is stated in the INSYGRAM (INformation SYstems GRAMmar) axiom, "Each permitted communication between a user and an information system can be completely prescribed by one single grammar." The information analysis identifies the types of sentences to be used in these permitted communications. Individual records or tuples within the database are instances of a sentence of a type predefined by the analysis. The third axiom, the SENE (Senko Entity Name Entity) axiom, states, "The deepest structure of each sentence can be considered to consist of a set of ideas about objects, and a set of bridges between objects and lexical objects."

Objects and lexical objects have been explained above. Ideas are relationships between real objects or NOLOTs. Bridges are naming conventions for identifying objects (i.e., linking NOLOTs to LOTs). There are three reasons for making this distinction between ideas and bridges. First, ideas are more stable, whereas naming or identifying conventions may change over time. Second, naming conventions can be confusing, especially when there are several ways to identify or name the same object. For example, an employee can be named by name, employee number, or social security number, but cannot necessarily be uniquely identified by name alone. Finally, using ideas to relate objects forces you to clarify the concepts you are describing.

Information analysis involves analyzing sentences describing ideas and bridges about objects. More complex sentences must be decomposed into elementary sentences. Elementary sentences are simply sentences that cannot be further decomposed without losing information. For example, "A part has a part number" or "A part was designed by a designer" are both elementary sentences. "A part has a design and a process plan" is an example of a compound sentence that can be decomposed into two elementary sentences. A deep-structured sentence relates two (or more) objects and their bridges. For example, "A part with part_no x was designed by a designer with employee_no y." This sentence can be decomposed into three elementary sentences—one idea and two bridges.

All of the above elementary sentences have been binary—i.e., they relate two types of objects. However, it is possible to have elementary sentences that are not binary. For example, some machineability data involve tool material, work piece material, and coolant. Eliminating any of these factors loses information. However, nonbinary elementary sentences should be checked very carefully because frequently they indicate a missing concept or idea.

As an example, assume we want to define part of a data model relating parts to their process plans. The complete deep-structured sentence describing this relationship is "The part with part_no 1234 is made using the process plan with plan_no 6789." The single sentence is decomposed into three separate elementary sentences—one idea and two bridges, each of which is documented graphically in Figure 6.2. The solid circles represent NOLOTs. The broken circles represent LOTs. The rectangles represent the roles relating the objects in the sentence. There are two roles for each pair of objects because there are two distinct roles depending on the direction of the relation. One way to interpret the idea is that a part is made using a process plan. The other way is that the process plan tells how to make a part.

Since examples help clarify the more complex relationships, population tables are used to relate specific examples to sentences. Table 6.1 shows five examples or instances of the "part is_made_using process_plan" idea. The first three are simple examples—a single part is made using a single process plan. However, with information analysis the population table forces us to ask some additional questions because there are several additional possibilities. The population table asks these questions in a clear, easily understood, unambiguous way. Consider example 4, where a second part is made using process plan A. Does this make sense? According to Figure 6.2, this situation is not possible. When process plan A appears

Table 6.1 Population Table

POPULATION TABLE

IS—MADE—USING	
PART	PROCESS PLAN
1	A
2	B
3	C
4	A
1	D

in the population table, it must be unique. The lines shown by the rectangle in Figure 6.2 is a graphical way to document this uniqueness. Since uniqueness constraints are included in the database design, the DBMS can automatically enforce them.

The population table also raises the inverse question. Can several process plans be used for making a part? The table indicates that part 1 can be made with either process plan A or D. But, the way Figure 6.2 is drawn, this cannot happen. The lines by both the part and the process plan role mean that a value in either column can appear only once in the table. In effect, this means that a process plan indicates how to make only one part and that each part has only one process plan.

These uniqueness constraints are sometimes determined by actual physical constraints in the real world. In other cases, however, they are determined by company policy decisions. For example, some companies may have several process plans for making a single part. There may be one plan for making the part in lots of 1,000 or more and a very different plan for making small batches of less than 50. In this case there would not be a uniqueness constraint on the part side of the rectangle.

As part of the NIAM methodology, every idea and bridge may be expanded with a population table, which is then analyzed to determine the uniqueness constraint. The "V" in the diagram is the total constraint. Every process plan must be related to a part. However, a part may not be related to a process plan — for

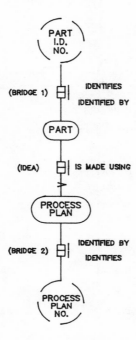

Figure 6.2   Idea and bridge example

example, the process plan may not have been done yet. (There are many other types of constraints, the more important of which are considered in the next section.)

Figure 6.3 shows an extension of Figure 6.2. A part also has a designer, a cost, an inventory level, a weight, and is composed of a certain type of material. A process plan consists of one or more operations, with each operation done on a machine tool, which has a maximum load. As with Figure 6.2, population tables can be built for each of these additional ideas and similar types of questions can be asked.

Notice the constraint on the part-designer idea. A single line goes across both roles. This means that only the combination is unique. A part can have many designers and conversely a designer can design many parts. The only thing that is unique is the combination—i.e., the population table would not have two rows with the same part-designer combination.

In Figure 6.3 the part-cost idea has a simple constraint. A part has a single cost, but several parts can have the same cost. Again, in a different company the constraint might be different. For example, if the part could be made in one of several plants, it could have a different cost for each plant. This would change the data structure because the elementary sentence to represent this idea would be a tertiary one involving part, cost, and plant.

Similarly, Figure 6.3 shows simple uniqueness constraints on inventory level. In both cases more complicated constraints would be possible in some situations.

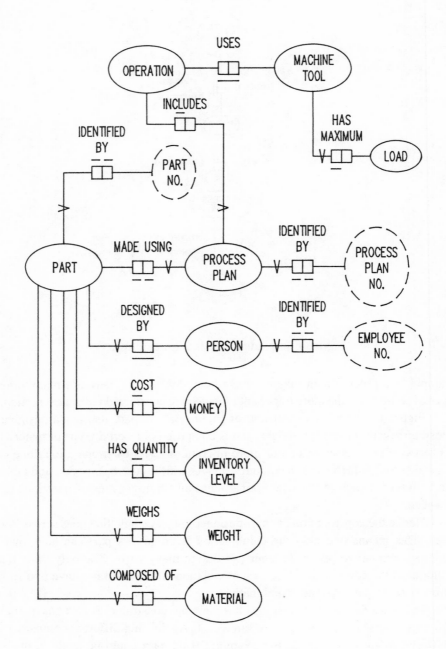

Figure 6.3   Initial part example

With the process plan the combination of process plan and step number is unique. Either one alone could appear many times in the population table. The figure also indicates that each step in the process plan involves only one machine tool and each machine tool has a maximum load. Note that while a step has only one machine tool, there is not a similar constraint on the machine tool. A machine tool can be used in any number of steps and therefore in any number of process plans. (As an exercise you might consider what would happen if the process plan involved a workcell with several machine tools.)

There are two assumptions, really subtle mistakes, in the above analysis. If undetected during the design process, they would create serious problems later. Without a formal methodology to raise and clarify issues, subject matter experts can argue among themselves and with analysts for days. In an actual project such an arguement arose about an order, until it became apparent that some people were talking about customer orders, others about purchase orders, and still others about shop floor orders.

The first problem involves the idea relating part and material type. Are parts composed of only one material or can they be composed of several different types of material? The population table and the need to put uniqueness constraints on each idea forces us to consider this question in more detail. In the interviews with users some will say that a part consists of only one type of material, while others will insist that a part can have several different types of material. The important point is not that one response is right and the other one is wrong, but that there is some confusion that must be resolved. In some cases one answer will be right and the other one wrong, and if this is the case then you must determine the correct answer. In other cases, and this is one of them, the disagreement is caused because different users are talking about different types of objects that are mistakenly being called the same thing.

At this point each person needs to identify precisely what a part really is. All parts have part numbers, but there are at least two different types of parts. There are component parts, which may be machined from a single block of metal or produced from a single mold. Component parts are made out of a single material. There are also assembly parts, which are combinations of several component parts and/or subassemblies. In an assembly the different component parts may be made from different material, although each component is made of only one material. Thus, the NIAM has helped identify a mistake in the data structure. There are really two types of objects instead of only one.

The question is how to deal with this distinction. In this case the objects are not completely different. They are only subtypes of an object called a part. This means there are three types of objects—a part and two subtypes, a component part and an assembly part. This refinement in the design requires reconsidering all of the ideas that included a part. The analysis must determine whether each of these ideas relates to a part in general (i.e., to the supertype) or to one of the two subtypes. Figure 6.4 shows the corrected representation of the ideas related to part and its subtypes. In this particular case all of the other ideas (designer, inventory level, and weight) are common to all parts, not to only one of the subtypes. Only material type must be moved from part to component part.

In an actual information analysis the subject matter experts and the information analysts would continue identifying the types of objects and the roles relating them. This would include clearly distinguishing objects and roles that are related to all parts and those which are related to only one of the subtypes of parts. This distinction is important even if initially they are only interested in one of the subtypes. For example, every part has a process plan, but there may be important differences between process plans for component parts and those for assembled parts.

The other mistake in Figure 6.3 involves the distinction between weight and load. Figure 6.3 assumes they are different types of objects. Figure 6.4 shows the correct representation. There is really only one object-weight. A part has a weight and a machine tool can accept a part with a certain maximum weight. These are simply two different roles for the same object. This is important because only objects of the same type can be compared. Thus it is reasonable to ask whether a part is too heavy for a certain machine tool. In the initial representation this was not a reasonable query. It would be like comparing a design to a machine tool.

The NIAM methodology and the use of these ENALIM diagrams to document the information model are easily learned by both subject matter experts and database designers. For subject matter experts the formal methodology helps them better understand their problem and how its various aspects are related. The diagrams provide an excellent communications tool, especially when working with experts in several different areas. In some companies once users have been trained in NIAM and participated on one or two projects, much of the further NIAM work is done primarily by these users with only occasional consulting from methodology experts.

Information Analysis—Advanced Concepts

This section discusses two of the advanced concepts used in NIAM—constraints and protoptyping.

The above analysis has described the basic information model. However, a complete information model must include numerous integrity constraints that must be enforced. In the past most of these constraints have been enforced by the application program or not at all. Now if they are identified and captured as part of the information model, the DBMS can enforce them automatically. Ideally, these constraints should be defined to the DBMS and enforced automatically. In other cases the database administrator may write complex database procedures to check for special constraints that cannot be defined to the DBMS. Some constraints are inherent in the information model, but others are simply the result of administrative policies and procedures of the organization. For example, departments must have budgets, but employees may or may not work on several projects.

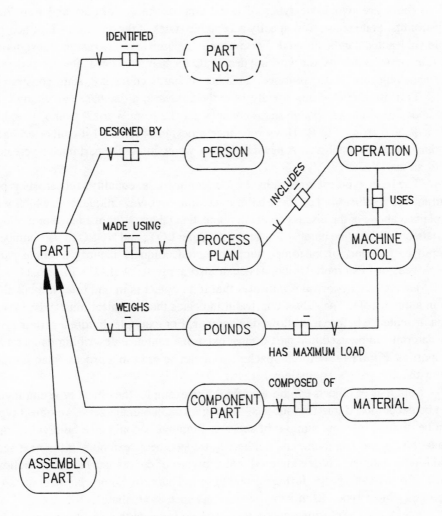

Figure 6.4   Part subtypes

Information analysis helps to identify many types of constraints and provides a graphic way to document the most common ones. This section describes those constraint types and shows how they add to the information provided in Figures 6.3 and 6.4.

There are two basic types of constraints: state constraints and transition constraints. State constraints specify acceptable states of the database—i.e., acceptable values that can be entered. For example, a company may assign a design one of four status codes: W for working design, C for being checked, P when it passes the checking, and R for released. This set of status codes is a state constraint.

Transition constraints specify how the values in a database can change. In the above example acceptable status changes may be from W to C, from C to either W or P, and from P to R. However, once a design is released it cannot go back to one of the other statuses. A new part or a new version of the part must be created with status W.

The basic types of constraints include uniqueness, equality, subset, subtype, and mutual exclusion. The most basic constraint involves uniqueness, which was explained above in the discussion about population tables. Within an idea or a bridge certain objects may be unique. For bridges linking LOTs and NOLOTs part number, employee number, or customer number should uniquely identify a single part, employee, or customer. Uniqueness can also apply to NOLOTs in ideas.

The equality constraint indicates that if an object is in one role, it must also be in another role. The subset constraint indicates that an object must exist in one idea or sentence before it is allowed in another. For example, before a certain type of material can be used in a part it must exist in a sentence describing its material properties. Similarly, before a machine tool can be used in a process plan it must be in the company's equipment list.

Subtypes of objects can be specified. For example, the object type employee can be decomposed into two subsets—managers and nonmanagers. An object type can be divided into any number of subsets. Employees could also be divided into managers, board members, and neither. In the geometry example in the next section higher geometry is decomposed into subtypes of curves, surfaces, and solids. Each of these subtypes is further decomposed. There are some characteristics of the main object type. Each subtype also has special attributes.

The mutual exclusion constraint is used to indicate that an object cannot be a member of two subtypes of objects. For example, if parts were classified into two subtypes, released and unreleased parts, then the mutual exclusion constraint would apply. In other cases an object can be a member of several subtypes of the same supertype.

Once an information model and all of the constraints have been defined, a prototype database design can be created. With some software tools this can be done automatically from the information model. The prototype is not designed for performance. In fact, the process analysis, which is required for the physical design trade-offs, may not have been completed yet. The prototype only needs to model the logical access paths in the information model. Users can then write high-level queries to exercise the prototype to ensure that it adequately reflects their requirements. Often this prototyping further refines the information model. After this prototyping, physical database design can be done with much greater confidence.

Geometric Database Example

This section outlines the way a CIM database can be designed to manage data at the record level. (This is in contrast to managing data at the file level, which was described in Chapter 4 with the database as a directory approach. This example would be for the full engineering database approach.) Geometry is used for this NIAM example because it is shared by many design and manufacturing applications. This example is a simplified subset of a more complete information model. The full model resulted in almost 500 logical record types, some of which were combined in the physical database design.

All of the geometry is built up from three basic object types—scalars, points, and vectors. These primitives have three of the same types of attributes. Each has a name or identification number, a current value, and a definition, although the form of these attributes are different for each object (e.g., the current value for a scalar is a single value, whereas the current value for a point is an xyz coordinate). The definition is important because a user can define the same geometric object type in many different ways, although there is only one way each type of object is stored in the database. For example, while a point may always be stored as an xyz coordinate, it may be defined as a coordinate or as the intersection of two curves. The definition would also determine whether the initial intersecting curves define a fixed point or whether the point should move if one of the curves moves.

Points and vectors also have display characteristics, such as whether or not the object is displayed, and if it is displayed its color and display mode (e.g., whether a vector is displayed as a solid, broken, or dotted line). Figure 6.5 is the ENALIM for a vector.

Higher geometric objects are built up from these primitives. Figure 6.6 shows the subtype structure among these geometric objects. These higher object types include curves, surfaces, and solids. There are many different types of curves, surfaces, and solids. Some examples of curves include straight lines, circles, circular arcs, parabolas, hyperbolas, and splines. Similarly, examples of surfaces include planes, cones, spheres, surfaces of revolution, and Coons patches. Examples of solids include boxes, slabs, solid cones, solid spheres, and tetrahedrons.

When there is a hierarchy of subtypes, attributes should be attached to the highest level at which they apply, not at the lowest. For example, all curves have common display characteristics such as color and solid/broken mode. Therefore,

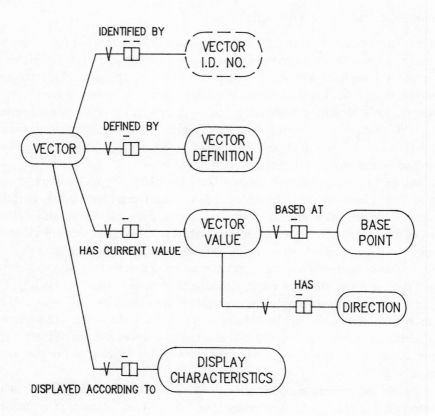

Figure 6.5   ENALIM for vector

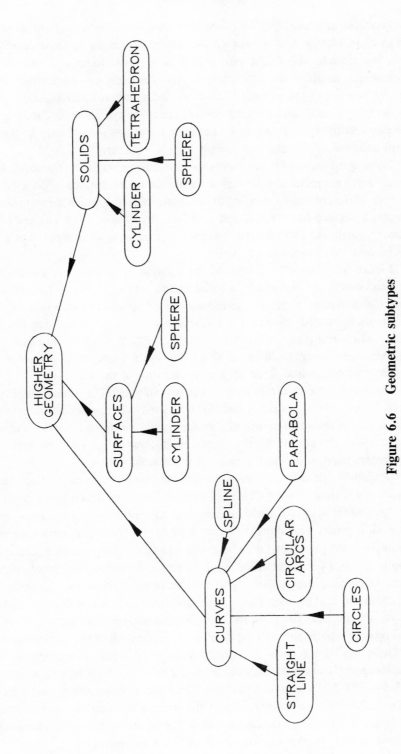

Figure 6.6   Geometric subtypes

display characteristics should be attached to curves, not to the individual subtypes, such as lines, circles, and splines. (*Note:* The experienced database designer may object that these levels of subtyping will require access to several records instead of just one, as would be the case if the display characteristics were attached directly to the subtypes. The answer is that this information modeling example only considers the logical data structure at this point. In the physical database design these two record types may well be combined, but this should only be done after we are sure we understand the correct logical structure.)

Some geometry such as spheres can be either a surface or a solid. In these cases the same geometrical information defines either the surface or the solid object. However, different nongeometric attributes are related to surfaces and solids. For example, a surface has a finish and a reflectivity. These attributes exist for any surface, regardless of its subtype. On the other hand, a solid is made of a certain material and has a moment of inertia.

Figure 6.7 shows the ENALIM for a circle, a sphere, and a solid sphere. All three objects are defined by a point in the role of center point and a scalar in the role of radius. Since the surface and solid sphere are symmetrical, only a center point is needed. However, a circle is not symmetrical in three dimensions because it lies in a plane. Therefore, in addition to the radius the circle needs a local coordinate system to define it. This local coordinate system consists of a point in the role of origin and three vectors in the role of the three axes.

Geometric objects are related by the way in which they share other types of objects. The local coordinate system for box 1 may also be used for circle 2. The origin point for the local coordinate system could be defined by the intersection of two curves. The scalars for the length, width, and height of a box could be the same scalars used to define the radii of three solid spheres.

Obviously, an extensive information analysis is required to map out all of the geometry needed by most CIM applications. However, this brief example shows how a geometric database could be designed. Once the logical database structure is defined, a prototype database can be defined and populated with sample data. Test queries and updates can then be executed against the prototype database. For example: given a point identifier, find its value; find all of the local coordinate systems with this point as the origin; find all of the curves that use this point in their definition; find the identifier, finish, and reflectivity of all the surface spheres that have this point as their origin. If the logical database design is correct, there should be access paths through the database to process all of the requests correctly.

Given the intricacies of this simple example, it is easy to see how the design of a comprehensive geometric database would be very complex.[1] An actual design included almost 500 logical record types. The only effective way to deal with large, complex CIM database designs is to partition them into smaller subsets whenever possible and to use automated design tools. The information analysis methodology described in this chapter supports both of these approaches.

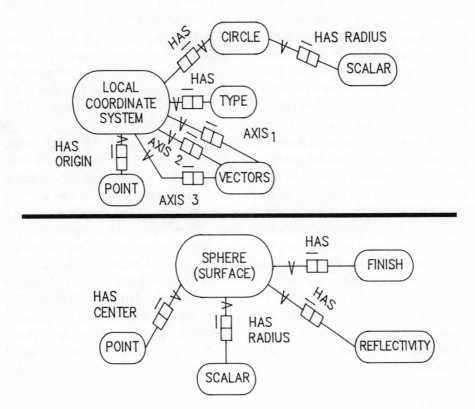

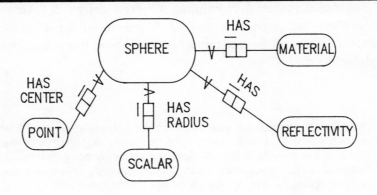

Figure 6.7   ENALIM for circle, sphere, and solid sphere

During an information modeling session these models are built and modified on the fly as users describe what they do and the data they need. These working models, such as the one shown in Figure 6.8, can become very complicated. Part of the complexity comes from the subject area itself, but part of it is from the way the working models are constructed—i.e., with all of the roles connected directly to the objects (circles). Figure 6.9 shows an easier-to-understand review model format. This more organized structure is usually much clearer and easier for reviewers (either managers or other users) to see and discuss. Furthermore, needed changes can be made in a different color so they stand out.

An additional problem in some review sessions, especially with management, is that an information model can become so detailed that reviewers lose the overall perspective—the big picture. The solution is to show this big picture in a less detailed model—but which details do you eliminate? This process, called "model abstraction," eliminates everything except "important objects" and "important facts." Important objects are objects that have unique identifiers—such as parts, machine tools, employees, and departments. The less important objects that are eliminated are those without identifiers—such as color, weight, and location. (Locations are uniquely specified not by a single identifier but by several other objects. A unique location may be identified by the combination of room, building, address, city, and state.) Important objects often correspond to the high-level entities in the entity-relationship approach, but they are derived from the analysis. Important facts are simply those facts that relate important objects. Figure 6.10 shows an abstracted model of Figure 6.9.

Summary

This chapter has explained the importance of good database design and the role of information modeling in ensuring a correct design. It reviewed an overall methodology and provided a detailed description of the information modeling methodology that will be used throughout Part Three. It concluded with an example applying the methodology to geometry.

Note

1. A more recent approach can greatly simplify the design of a geometric database. With this approach almost all of the geometry is modeled using only one type of object—a NURBS (Non-Uniform Rational B-Spline). Several systems are being built using this approach. While it simplifies the database structure, it increases the amount of processing required for some operations and for the checking of some constraints.

Further Reading

Thompson, Paul. *CIM: The Information Engineering Methodology.* Boston: Digital Press, forthcoming.

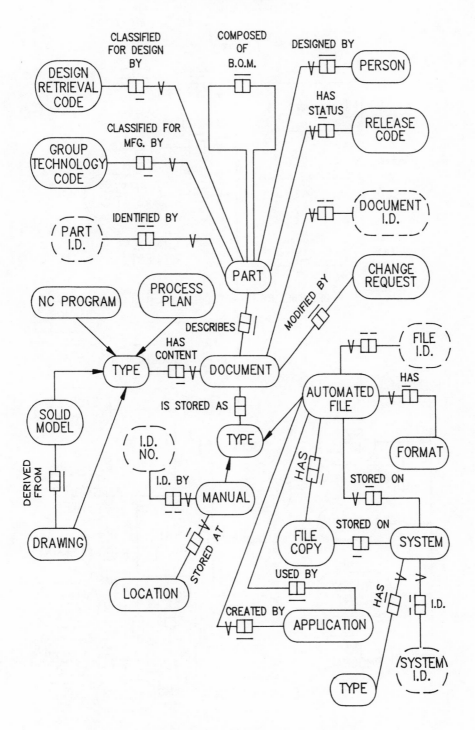

Figure 6.8   Working model example

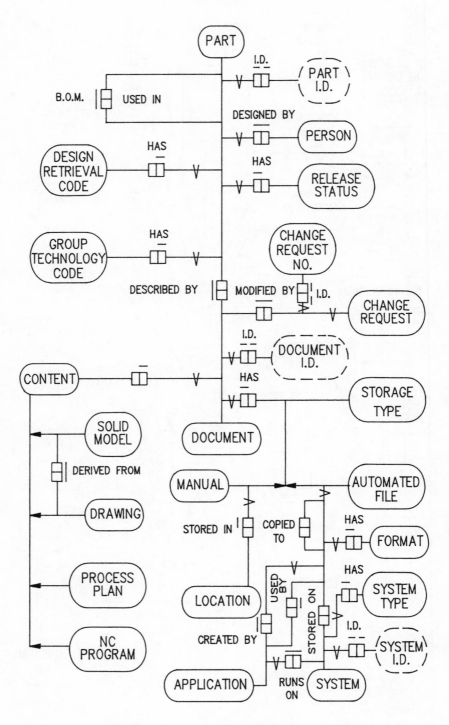

Figure 6.9   Review model example

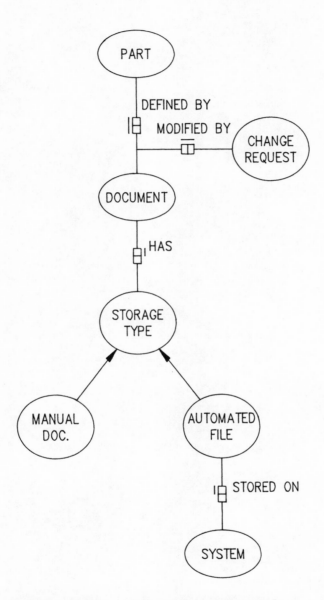

Figure 6.10 Abstracted model example

Part Three
Design and
Manufacturing Functions

This part is the core of the book. The first two parts have provided design and manufacturing engineers and information systems analysts with the basic background they need in each other's area. Against this background Part Three discusses the major manufacturing functions. For each function, it explains what the function is and how it evolved. It then describes a generic information model to support the function. Although every company performs these functions somewhat differently, the generic models provide a good starting point. Engineers and information systems analysts can use these generic models as a common starting point for their discussions. The NIAM methodology described in Chapter 6 provides an excellent communications tool for these discussions. The common objects that appear in various models are the key points of integration. Expanding these models to fit the way their company operates is an important step for a CIM task force. Specific chapters address design retrieval and group technology, product structuring and configuration management, geometric design, analysis, process planning and manufacturing engineering, production planning and scheduling, quality control, robotics, and flexible manufacturing systems.

Part Three
Design and
Manufacturing Functions

7

Overview of Design and Manufacturing

Functional Analysis

Function Overview

Function Descriptions

Function 1: Create Math Model
Function 2: Design Mechanical Model
(Engineering Design)
Function 3: Retrieve Design Using a Design Database
Function 4: Document Design
Function 5: Perform Analysis
Function 6: Design, Build, and Test Prototype
Function 7: Plan Manufacturing Processes
(Process Planning and Routing)
Function 8: Control Inventory
Function 9: Manufacture Product
(Fabrication and Assembly)

Summary

As a background for the rest of Part Three, this chapter provides an overview of the design and manufacturing process. This background is important because many readers are familiar with only one or two areas, not the entire process. Each of the remaining chapters in Part Three describes a single function in much greater detail. This overview is important because the entire design and manufacturing process must be understood and integrated as a whole. Although everything cannot be automated at once, there must be a general understanding of how the total system will fit together before the individual pieces are implemented.

This chapter first explains the functional analysis methodology. Second, it provides a short narrative describing the design and manufacturing process. The third section provides a more detailed description of each of the functions. The chapter also includes structural charts and functional diagrams to relate these functions.

Functional Analysis

Functional analysis is one step in the requirements analysis methodology described in Chapter 6, which concentrated on the information analysis step in the methodology. The basic concepts of functional analysis are included in many information systems design methodologies, although each has its own jargon.

The purpose of functional analysis is to identify what the system must do. It is not interested in how each function is performed. The how is determined later during systems design. Even the order in which the functions are performed is not important in the functional analysis.

The functions are identified using a top-down structured approach. This hierarchical decomposition of functions is shown in a structure chart (see Figures 7.1 through 7.6). A function is decomposed into two or more lower-level functions, which are then further decomposed. This decomposition continues until sufficient detail is obtained. The structure chart shows only this decomposition.

The information flow is documented in a function diagram (see Figures 7.7 through 7.10). These diagrams show the relationships among functions. Normally they relate functions at a comparable level, but they can also be used to relate functions at different levels.

Each block in the function diagram represents a single function. The inputs, both information and materials, are shown on the left. The outputs are on the right. Controls enter the block from the top. The flow through a set of functions is shown by the relationships between the inputs and outputs, with the outputs of some functions becoming the inputs to others. This flow indicates the sequence in which the functions are performed. In some cases a particular function may not be performed, while in other cases it may be performed several times as part of a feedback loop (e.g., design, analysis, and redesign). The latter case is particularly true in a process as complex as design and manufacturing, where there are many feedback loops and iterative steps.

Each of the functions in the functional diagrams is described later in this chapter. The inputs, outputs, controls, and the data structures needed to support each function are discussed more completely in later chapters, although some functions are combined in a single chapter—for example, creation of the math model and prototype simulation is in the analysis chapter.

Function Overview

The design and manufacturing process starts with a set of product requirements. These requirements may come from market research, or, in a job shop environment, they may be part of the order from a customer. Once the product requirements are defined, by whatever means, the part or product must be designed. The first step is to do a design retrieval to determine whether there is already a product that will meet the requirements or whether one can be easily modified to meet them. If a new product must be designed, this is done in a series of steps, each of which adds more detail to the design. This process frequently involves a conceptual design, a preliminary design, a detailed design, and sometimes a prototype of the product. During this step-wise design different types of analyses are performed, depending on the type of product and its requirements. Once a final design is determined, it is documented and released. The basic form of documentation today is the engineering drawing. An engineering bill of materials is also critical except for simple component parts.

At this point the released design is passed to manufacturing. The manufacturing engineers or process planners then must develop a plan for manufacturing the product. Sometimes the product cannot be manufactured as it was designed because of technological limits or because of the specific machine tools the company currently uses. Therefore, only in the simplest cases does the manufacturing engineer just determine how to build the product. In some cases he or she must recommend design changes to improve the produceability of the product. This can lead to different engineering and manufacturing bills of material. When this occurs, the manufacturing bill of materials is the one used for production. In some cases manufacturing engineering may need to design special tooling or recommend new or different types of machine tools for the company.

The plan for manufacturing or the process plan specifies how the product will be manufactured—i.e., the raw materials to use, the manufacturing operations needed, the sequence in which specific types of machine tools are to be used, the tools and fixtures, and the tasks each tool is to perform. At this point the manufacturing bill of materials is specified. Given the product's demand, a production schedule is planned for the next production period. Based on this schedule, the bill of materials, and the current inventory levels, the necessary purchase orders are generated.

Work orders control the detailed shop-floor activity to manufacture the desired product mix. These work orders or shop orders and the feedback on their status constitute the shop-floor control system. Today shop-floor control systems are relatively traditional business applications, but the automated factory shop-floor control provides a much more detailed level of control. It includes direct computer control to and accepts feedback from numerically controlled machine tools, robots, and material handling systems.

Function Descriptions

Figures 7.1 throught 7.6 are structure charts showing the decomposition of the design and manufacturing functions. Figure 7.1 divides one function—manage/perform the design/manufacturing function—into nine subfunctions. Figures 7.2 through 7.6 show further explosions of these subfunctions.

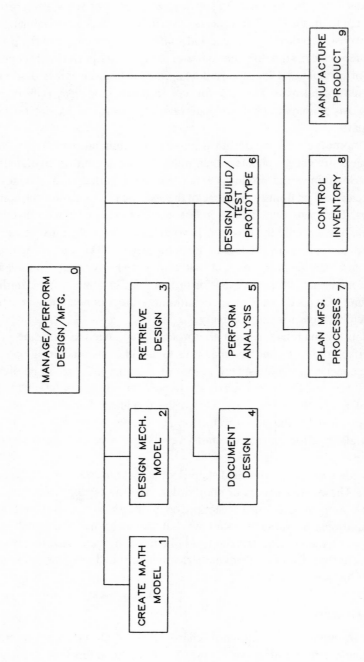

Figure 7.1   Structure chart—Manage/Perform Design/Manufacturing

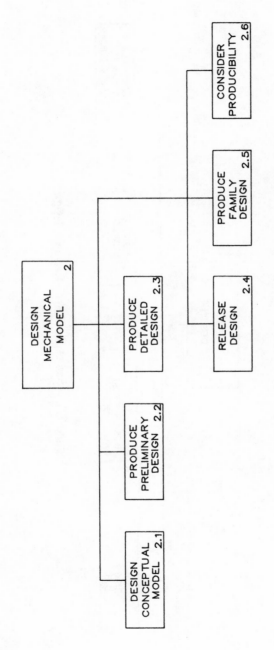

Figure 7.2 Structure chart—Design Mechanical Model

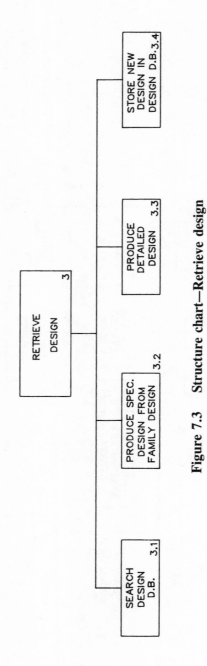

Figure 7.3   Structure chart—Retrieve design

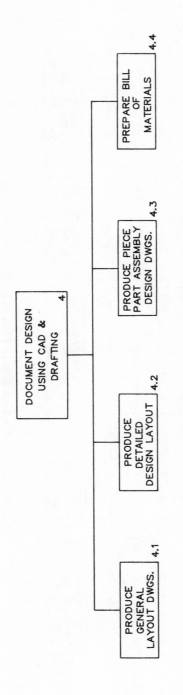

Figure 7.4   Structure chart—Document design

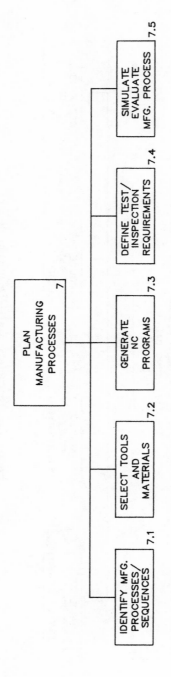

Figure 7.5   Structure chart—Plan manufacturing process

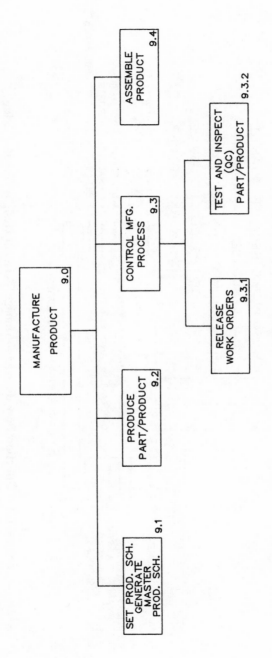

Figure 7.6   Structure chart—Manufacture product

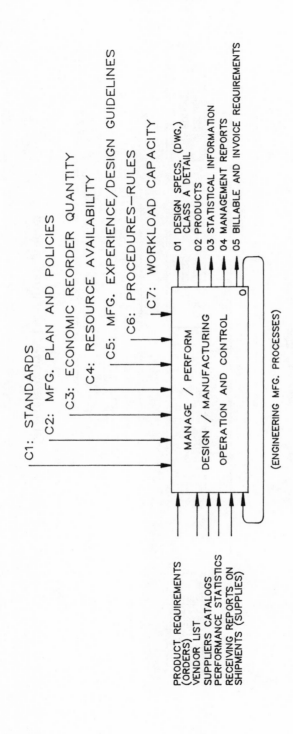

Figure 7.7 Function flow diagram—Manage/Perform Design/Manufacturing

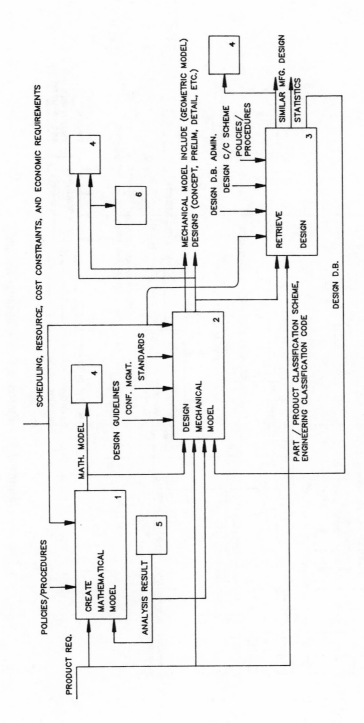

Figure 7.8 Function flow diagram—Design 1

113

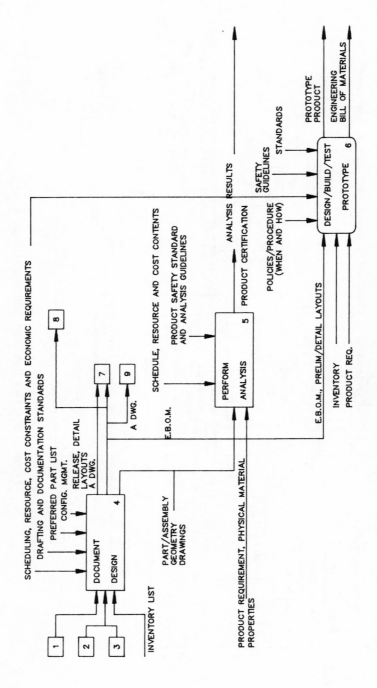

Figure 7.9 Function flow diagram—Design 2

114

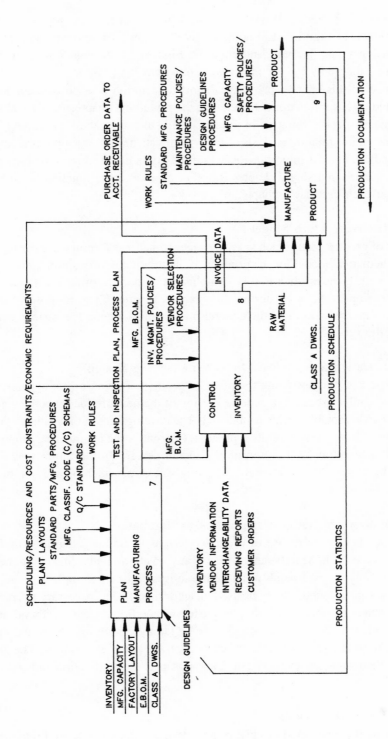

Figure 7.10 Function flow diagram—Manufacturing

Figures 7.7 through 7.10 are function diagrams for the nine top-level nine functions shown in Figure 7.1. Figure 7.7 is the high-level summary that identifies the major inputs, outputs, and controls. Figures 7.8 through 7.10 show the more detailed diagrams for the nine major functions.

The rest of this chapter provides a short description of each of these nine functions and their subfunctions. In general, the remaining chapters in Part Three each describe a specific function in greater detail, including the inputs, outputs, controls, and an information analysis of the type of data needed to support the function. Depending on their importance and complexity, some of these functions are discussed together in a single chapter. In other cases a single function is further divided, and each part has a chapter of its own.

Function 1: Create Math Model

Given a set of product requirements, the designer sometimes formulates a relatively simple mathematical model for the product. If the product is very simple, this step may be omitted. If the product is very complicated, a more rigorous mathematical model is developed and used during the analysis function. The purpose of this function is to define and model the general relationships among the various components of the product.

Function 2: Design Mechanical Model (Engineering Design)

This is the first step in designing the physical product. Based on past experience in designing similar products, a generic version of the new product is defined and refined until an acceptable design is obtained. The development of the mathematical and mechanical models is an iterative process. Currently, the engineering drawing is used to document and communicate the model design. In the future much of this modeling will be done with solid modeling software, which provides a more complete definition of part geometry.

Function 3: Retrieve Design Using a Design Database

This function checks a database of previous designs to find any that are similar to the new product. The search can be done at any level — an individual component part, an assembly, a subassembly, an entire subsystem, or a complete product. If a similar design is found, it may be used intact or modified as necessary to create the new product. In some cases the design for a specific part can be found and reused or modified. In other cases a generic or family design may be found and a specific design created by specifying the necessary parameter values. The key to an effective design retrieval system is an appropriate classification and coding system.

Function 4: Document Design

In this function the completed product or part design is documented and released.

If the design is modified after this function, a formal change control procedure must be used. Once the proposed changes are approved, this function is repeated and the changes are incorporated into the documentation.

Function 5: Perform Analysis

Depending on the specific product, the design is analyzed in various ways. Usually these analyses are done in sequence, with the results of each one being further analysis, modification, or acceptance of the design.

Function 6: Design, Build, and Test Prototype

This function involves building and testing a prototype of the product or some part of it. The purpose of the prototype is to learn more about how the product will work and the operations required by its various subsystems and components. Depending on the industry and the company, the prototype may or may not be very close to the final product. Improved CAE systems and more detailed analysis are reducing the amount of prototyping needed. Companies are also beginning to shift from physical prototypes to numerical prototypes and computer simulations.

Function 7: Plan Manufacturing Processes (Process Planning and Routing)

This function takes the design of the product as specified by engineering and determines how to build it, either as designed or with changes to improve its produceability. This function determines the manufacturing processes that should be used, the desired sequence of the operations, and the specific machine tool types and materials to be used. Although in some cases the designers have specified what materials to use, these materials may be changed to improve the produceability of the design. This function also generates the programs for any numerically controlled tools that will be used. Finally, test and inspection procedures, using manually and/or numerically controlled devices, are defined to ensure adequate quality control.

Process planning assumes a given set of machine tools and considers only minor changes in the set of equipment in the plant. There are, however, two additional functions that are done occasionally, usually only once for a major product line. One is plant layout. Given a set of machine tools, plant layout determines how much space to allocate to them, where to place them, what type of material handling system to provide, what paths are needed for the material flow, and what machine tools to cluster into workcells. The other function is determining which machine tools to acquire. This is done initially when the plant is designed. Subsequently, new machine tools are added when new products require new manufacturing capabilities or when current machine tools become obsolete. For the automated factory this type of information—such as plant layout, the material handling system, and the material flow—must be included within the design and manufacturing database. Some of these decisions are made when the plant is designed, but others can be tailored to a certain extent during process planning.

117

Function 8: Control Inventory

This function controls the inventory and integrates the effects of all of the company's manufacturing operations. This function should also include controlling both material (raw materials, work in process, and finished goods) and tools. At one level this function involves determining what items to carry and the inventory level for each item. At the other level it tracks the inventory level and monitors the flow of material through the plant. Production scheduling, material requirements planning, and purchasing all effect inventory control. (Function 8 and parts of function 9 are sometimes grouped together and called production scheduling and control.)

Function 9: Manufacture Product (Fabrication and Assembly)

This function involves generating the master production schedule, issuing and tracking work orders, and in the automated factory actually controlling the operations on the shop floor. This involves controlling the material handling system and the individual machine tools and robots. The actual production operations (such as fabrication, assembly, and testing) must be done regardless of the extent of factory automation. Increased automation simply means that this function is done in different ways.

Summary

This chapter has explained the functional analysis methodology. It has also provided an overview of the design and manufacturing process. The remaining chapters in Part Three provide a more detailed functional and information analysis for each function.

Further Reading

Bo, K., and F. M. Lillehagen (eds.). *CAD Systems Framework*. New York: North-Holland, 1983.

Encarnacao, J., and E. G. Schlechtendahl. *Computer-Aided Design: Fundamentals and System Architectures*. New York: Springer-Verlag, 1983.

Stover, Richard. *An Analysis of CAD/CAM Applications with an Introduction to CIM*. Englewood Cliffs, N.J.: Prentice-Hall, 1984.

Yeomans, R. W., A. Choudry, and P. J. W. ten Hagen. *Design Rules for a CIM System*. New York: North-Holland, 1986.

8

Design Retrieval and Group Technology

The basic purpose of data management is improved data sharing throughout an organization. This chapter describes design retrieval and group technology, two important functions that emphasize data sharing.

Design retrieval enables engineers throughout a company to share design information more effectively. With design retrieval, engineers can frequently find and reuse existing designs rather than redesigning the same part. Even when the existing designs are not exactly right, design retrieval locates similar designs that can be used as a starting point. This can dramatically reduce the design effort.

119

Group technology involves two functions, one of which is the manufacturing equivalent of design retrieval. Group technology identifies parts that are manufactured in similar ways, so their process plans can be reused. Although group technology helps locate process plans that can be reused with or without modification, it was developed primarily to facilitate production scheduling. The setup time to change a machine tool from one part to another similar part is much less than the setup time for a completely different part in another group.

This chapter explains design retrieval and shows how it can be used. It describes its major benefits and identifies the type of company that will benefit the most from such a system. However, virtually all manufacturers will get some benefits from design retrieval. The chapter also provides the same background for group technology—what is it and what its benefits are.

The discussion includes a basic information model that a company can use to support design retrieval and group technology. Some of the implementation issues are also described. Finally, since the key to both effective design retrieval and group technology systems is a good classification and coding scheme, the chapter identifies the essential characteristics of good classification and coding schemes for each function. The similarities and differences between design retrieval and group technology are also explained.

What Is Design Retrieval?

Design retrieval allows engineers to find design and engineering data about existing designs. They may find either a design to satisfy current requirements or a similar design that needs to be only slightly modified. In other cases they may want to review certain types of designs to get some ideas for a current design. A design retrieval system is simply another CIM application, although it is one that impacts many other applications.

The four components of a design retrieval system include a classification and coding system, a base of existing designs, a database linking these existing designs to the classification and coding system, and a user interface that allows the engineer to ask questions to find similar designs.

A database management system is the main information system tool for implementing design retrieval. The classification and coding scheme identifies the key design attributes that the engineer uses to search the design database. The database relates these attributes with the actual design data (e.g., solid models, analyses, and drawings in either automated or paper form). The details of a design retrieval database are shown in a later section.

In the long term the design retrieval database may contain the actual design data. However, today most design retrieval databases include only the attributes of the design and the pointers to the design data. The actual design data (in paper form or as a computer file) are stored elsewhere. If the design is on a CAD system, the pointer indicates the file name and the system on which it is stored. If the design is not on the computer, the pointer will indicate the document number and storage location.

For example, suppose a designer needs a hollow aluminum rod about 18 inches long, 3 inches in diameter, and with threads on the outside at both ends. A design retrieval system today could give the designer the file names or the drawing numbers for similar parts. The designer then requests the drawings or attaches the files on the appropriate CAD system. Additional software in the user interface could invoke the appropriate CAD program and attach the file automatically. For the design retrieval system to invoke the appropriate CAD system and attach the correct design files, these CAD systems would have to be networked together.

Today there are two benefits for isolating the design retrieval data from the actual design data. First, it greatly simplifies the data management problem so that almost any existing DBMS can be used for this application. Second, it provides greater flexibility in the type of design data that can be included in the design retrieval system. With this approach the design data can be stored under many different CIM systems. In addition, the system could include noncomputerized design data, such as paper drawings.

The basic architecture for such a system is shown in Figure 8.1. A centralized design retrieval system resides on one system with the design retrieval database. This system may or may not also have a CAD application and data files. It is networked to other CAD systems, each with its own workstations and data files. All design retrieval requests enter through the user interface, which invokes the design retrieval application. The design retrieval application searches the design retrieval database and finds the similar designs and the types of documents that are requested (e.g., models, drawings, etc.). In the simplest design retrieval systems only the file names and their locations are returned to the user, who must then request them. More sophisticated systems would then let the user pick specific designs to see and actually transfer them. If there are different types of CAD systems, then some translation would also be necessary.

Since users may want to modify the designs obtained through the design retrieval system, it should include a check-out/check-in mechanism to prevent several engineers from modifying the same design simultaneously. In most cases, however, a design would not be changed. First, only released designs or those stable enough to be under configuration control would be in the design retrieval system. It would not include working designs that are still being developed. Second, if the design can be reused as is, there is no need for a change. Finally, if the design is close but needs some modification, then the original design is copied into a new design or a new version of the old design. The original design is normally not modified because it is still being used by many other products.

This same basic architecture also applies for a group technology system (described in a later section), except that it has a different database and retrieves different types of data (e.g., process plans instead of drawings).

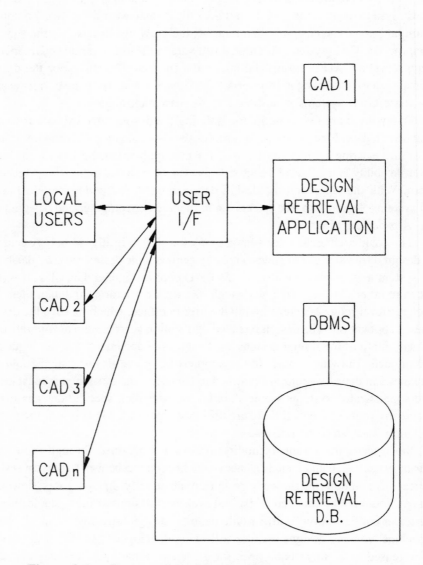

Figure 8.1   Basic architecture for design retrieval system

Benefits of Design Retrieval

Even before CIM, part proliferation plagued manufacturers. As the number of products and product families increased, the number of parts also increased. Ideally, this increase should level off. The twentieth new product should not require as many new parts as the second. Unfortunately, this leveling did not occur because many parts were being redesigned instead of reused.

In most companies it is easier to design a new part than to find a similar existing one because the only way a drawing or other design data can be retrieved is by part number.

Almost all companies have this problem—many designs for essentially the same part. In large companies ten to twenty duplicate designs for some parts are not uncommon. Since this duplication occurs for many parts, it is expensive and wasteful. The part proliferation problem can occur even in small companies where the engineers know each other. It is inevitable in large companies with different divisions scattered across the country. Therefore, for larger companies design retrieval is critical.

Design retrieval is one of the most obvious and dramatic examples of the benefits of data sharing. If engineers can find parts that have already been designed, they avoid the wasted effort of redesigning the same part. More importantly, these cost savings occur throughout the entire design and manufacturing process. If a new part is designed, then someone has to analyze it. Someone has to determine how to manufacture it. Finally, the new part must be stocked both in the factory and in the field for maintenance. Depending on the part, new raw material may also be needed.

If a design is reused many times, then it is worthwhile to optimize both the design itself and the process plan for manufacturing it. Constantly redesigning the same parts keeps the design and manufacturing engineers so busy that they cannot evaluate many alternatives and select the best one. For example, in extreme cases the manufacturing costs for the duplicate designs can differ by an order of magnitude.

How significant are the savings from design retrieval? A 1981 study in *American Machinist* addressed precisely this question.[1] For the average new product, 40 percent of the parts already existed, exactly as needed. Another 40 percent required only slight modification of an existing design. Only 20 percent of the parts in the typical new product needed to be designed from scratch.

Therefore, in the extreme case a company with an efffective design retrieval system can build the same product with 40 to 80 percent less design effort compared to one not using design retrieval. Similar savings occur in manufacturing engineering.

These cost savings directly impact the company's bottom line because they are reduced expenditures. A dollar saved is essentially an additional dollar of profit. It is not like an additional dollar of revenue, which may generate only a few additional cents of profit. Thus design retrieval can have a major impact on a company's bottom line.

More importantly, design retrieval provides corporate management with greater strategic flexibility. A product can be designed with less effort and at a lower cost. This lower cost can be used in either of two ways. First, the product can be sold at a lower price, thus increasing market share and making it harder for other companies to compete. Second, the company can maintain its original price but realize a much larger profit margin.

Alternately, a company can use design retrieval to dramatically shorten the product development cycle. With a design retrieval system the same number of designers can complete the product design much faster, drastically shortening the product development cycle. This faster time to market can provide important competitive advantages. Still another alternative is for the company to provide a more tailored product with far more options for the customer. Today there is a clear trend in many industries toward more customized products. Design retrieval provides a company with the type of flexibility it needs to offer this type of customization without major cost increases.

In summary, design retrieval offers one or more of the following benefits. First, it can reduce the price of a product, thus making it more competitive. Second, it can improve a company's profit margin, making it better able to compete. Third, it can shorten the product development cycle, allowing a company to get its new product to market before its competitors. Fourth, it allows a company to provide a broader range of product options.

Although design retrieval offers benefits to any company that adopts it, there are some situations in which it is much more important. In some of these situations the payoff in each individual instance may be relatively small, but these instances occur so frequently that the cumulative effect is significant. In other cases the payoffs may not occur very often, but when they do they are so large that they justify the system. Design retrieval is important for companies that have these characteristics:

- many designs or design variations
- complex designs
- short product development cycle
- low-cost products

First, a company with a large design group creating many new designs will benefit from design retrieval much more than one with a fairly stable set of products. It has more opportunity to reuse or modify existing designs. It also has a larger design database from which to find possible designs. The savings occur whenever a design is reused, regardless of how simple or complex it is.

Second, the more complex the company's designs, the greater will be the savings whenever they can be reused. This is important because companies with very complex designs frequently have little opportunity to reuse their designs.

However, because of the complexity of their designs and the effort they involve, each opportunity to reuse one provides significant savings. In fact, one of the reasons some complex products are so expensive and have such frequent and high cost overruns may be because of the lack of design retrieval and the failure to learn from modifying and enhancing an existing design. For example, nuclear power plants are essentially designed from scratch, whereas aircraft are primarily variations from a common design. Boeing does not design every 747 from scratch. It starts with a common design and customizes it as required by each airline.

Third, a short product life cycle or development cycle also suggests design retrieval. Finding and reusing or modifying existing designs can significantly cut the development time and costs for a new product. Therefore, any company that needs a rapid product development cycle should consider design retrieval. There are always time and cost trade-offs between optimizing a new design and adapting a relatively standard existing one. In fact, there are frequently marketing niches at each extreme.

Fourth, when a company's strategy is to be the lowest-cost producer, design retrieval is essential because it saves both costs and time. This, of course, assumes one of the above conditions also applies. Design retrieval would not help the low-cost producer with a stable set of standard products. Design activity would be such a small part of the total costs that cutting the design phase in half or even reducing it to zero would not dramatically effect the company's overall cost.

To be effective, design retrieval must be accompanied by a classification and coding scheme, the use of standard or preferred parts, and a design database supported by a DBMS. A family design methodology, while not essential, increases the usefulness of design retrieval. Classification and coding are discussed in more detail in a later section

What Is Group Technology?

Group technology traditionally concentrates on identifying parts that are manufactured in similar ways so they can be scheduled and produced together as a group. It also helps a company design workcells and more effectively schedule its production. However, the same classsification and coding scheme also allows the manufacturing engineer to reuse or modify existing process plans and tooling rather than creating them from scratch.

Group technology was originally developed in the early 1900s to effectively schedule the production of small batches of related parts. It groups similar parts together using a classification and coding scheme. However, a group technology classification and coding scheme can support additional functions beyond the original scheduling one. In this chapter all of these functions are called group technology.

Focusing on the original function, Hyde defines group technology as "a technique for manufacturing small to medium lot size batches of parts of similar process, of somewhat dissimilar materials, geometry, and size, which are produced in a committed small cell of machines which have been grouped together physically, specifically tooled, and scheduled as a unit."[2]

Most manufacturing involves small or medium-sized lots (i.e., fewer than 50 units). This raises production cost because of the short runs and the frequent setups required to change to a new part. Furthermore, the way most factories are laid out, a part may be routed all over the shop floor to get to the four or five machine tools it needs.

Group technology addresses both of these problems by identifying parts that are produced with the same set of machine tools (i.e., the same manufacturing processes) and similar tooling and fixtures. This allows a company to improve its production in two ways. First, the production runs will be longer and the setup between batches will be minimized because all of the parts in a group are scheduled and run together. Second, a set of machine tools can be clustered in a workcell so that all of the parts in a group can be manufactured in one workcell. This eliminates much unnecessary part movement throughout the factory. These benefits are especially important to job shops, which usually have very small lot sizes.

A group technology classification and coding scheme can also be the basis for a retrieval system. A group technology retrieval system can provide manufacturing with many benefits similar to design retrieval. If designs can be reused as is, then manufacturing documents (such as process plans, shop and assembly drawings, NC programs, and machining instructions) can also be reused rather than created from scratch. Similarly whenever an existing design is modified, the corresponding manufacturing documents can also be modified. This saving also applies to any special tooling or fixtures needed for a design.

Benefits of Group Technology

Competition requires that companies get new products to market quicker, produce them cheaper, and do more tailoring and customization. Group technology, like design retrieval, helps in all of these areas by offering two types of benefits — one-time initial benefits and repeated benefits that occur whenever the parts are produced.

First, there are initial, one-time benefits that occur in getting the product to market. These benefits are almost identical to those for design retrieval, except that a different part of the company benefits. By reusing existing manufacturing documentation and tooling either as is or with slight modification, the manufacturing engineering for new products is greatly reduced. This results in a combination of lower development costs and a short time to market. It also allows greater product variety with the same resources. Although these benefits would help any company, they are especially important to companies with these characteristics:

- many designs and design variations
- complex manufacturing plans and specialized tooling

126

- short product development cycles
- low-cost production

As with design retrieval, some companies will benefit from group technology retrieval through modest savings that occur many times, while other companies will be able to reuse manufacturing data and tooling only occasionally but with substantial savings in those cases.

The second type of benefit occurs repeatedly whenever the parts are produced. This savings comes from more efficiently scheduling longer production runs by group instead of by individual part. Additional benefits occur if the company goes further and reorganizes its production facilities into work cells based on the group technology classification, but this is a more complex, long term step.

Hyde[3] provides six case studies of group technology, some of which occurred before CIM became a factor. The cases described are Perkin Engines Ltd. (1956), Cincinnati Milacron, Inc. (1976), Hoover Worldwide Company (1970), Coles Crane Ltd. (1976), Serck Audco Valves (1960), and Boeing Commercial Airplane Company (1969).

In summary, the objectives of both design retrieval and group technology are the same—to find related parts. The difference is in the types of data used. Design retrieval focuses on the initial design data whereas group technology concentrates on manufacturing-oriented data. Group technology also has a critical role in effectively scheduling production, the initial objective for which it was developed.

Information Analysis for Design Retrieval

Since a design retrieval database and a group technology database are similar, Figure 8.2 summarizes an information model to support both functions. The central type of object is a document. Documents describe parts. Documents are subtyped in two ways—what they contain and how they are stored.

The first is based on content. A document could be a solid model, a drawing, a process plan, an NC program, or any one of many other types. Some facts are common to all types of documents. For example, all documents have a document I.D. and may have change requests. Other facts relate only to specific subtypes of documents. For example, a drawing may be derived from a solid model. However, all solid models are not necessarily related to drawings, and a drawing may not have been derived from a solid model. This fact may relate some solid models and drawings; therefore it needs to be included in the information model.

Another way to classify documents is by how they are stored—i.e., manual or automated. All documents have an identification number, but only manual documents are stored at a location. An automated document is stored in a file identified by a file identifier. There may be multiple copies of the file, each with its own identifier. Each copy is stored on a computer system, which has both a type and an identifier. The file, and therefore all of its copies, were created by an applica-

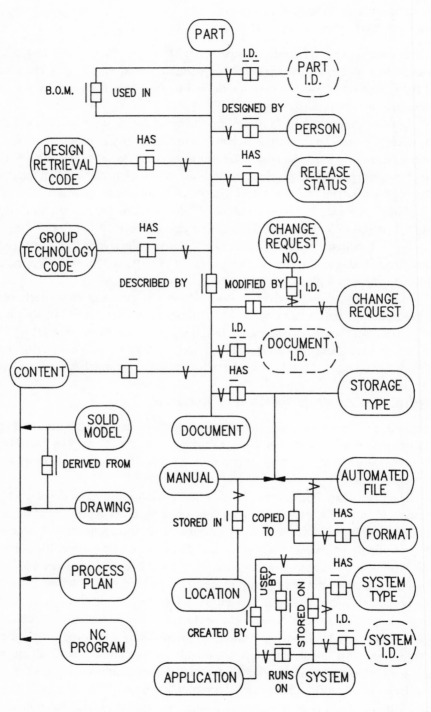

Figure 8.2   Information model for design retrieval and group technology

tion and may be used by other applications, which define its format. When a file is translated from one format to another, it becomes a new file, not simply another copy of the original file. The CAD applications are stored on a file.

To relate this information model to those in other chapters, we must remember that a document describes a part, which has a part identifier, a designer, and a release status. Parts are composed of other parts, which provides the product structure. Parts can be classified using any number of classification codes. This figure simply shows a design retrieval and a group technology code.

The design retrieval code includes information about the part geometry, its function, and design features (e.g., holes, threads, keyways, etc.). The group technology code includes part material, shape, features, and the processes for producing those features.

For an actual implementation this model would be expanded in much greater detail. However, this simple model supports queries such as:

1. Find all drawings for parts of a certain type.
2. List all solid models for parts in a certain subassembly.
3. Do we have any automated drawings for certain types of parts, and, if so, what system are they on?
4. Find the process plans for all parts of a certain type.
5. Order the following list of parts by group technology code so all of the parts in a group can be scheduled together.

In Chapter 9 Figure 9.1 shows extensions to this model to support change control and configuration management functions. Chapter 12 describes process planning and provides an information model for that function. The link between this information model and that one should be apparent. A process plan is a type of document that may be stored on paper or in an automated form.

To reemphasize a point made earlier, the information models in each chapter describe one aspect of the design and manufacturing process. They can be linked together easily because many types of objects are common across several models. From the information modeling perspective, CAD/CAM integration involves building and implementing these models in manageable pieces and then linking them together.

Implementation Issues

When a company decides to install a design retrieval and/or a group technology system, there are several implementation issues to resolve.

First, there is the scope of the system. Should it cover just design retrieval, just group technology, or should it include both areas? A related issue is whether it be only a directory system with pointers to the actual drawing and process planning documents, which are stored elsewhere in computer files or on paper. Alternately, the system could be part of a more complete engineering database. This chapter describes only a directory type of system containing only design and manufacturing attributes and pointers to the actual data files or documents. Very few, if any, vendors are today able to capture both the design and manufacturing attributes and all of the detailed design data in a common database. Part of this issue also involves whether the system should retrieve only electronically stored data or all data.

Second, a classification and coding system must be selected or developed. Developing a classification and coding scheme is a specialized activity, and a company must decide whether it wants a customized scheme or can use a generic off-the-shelf one. If a company opts for a combined design retrieval and group technology system, then two classification and coding schemes are needed.

Third, a small or new company could load attributes for all of its parts into the retrieval system, but most companies need a priority scheme for deciding which parts to load now and which ones later as well as when to load these later ones.

The scope issue addresses how broad the retrieval system should be. Unfortunately, many people, both vendors and manufacturers, define design retrieval in a relatively narrow sense. For some it is drawing retrieval, although they may include paper drawings as well as those on a CAD system. Other people include all types of design information but limit it to information stored on a CAD system. Although this could include drawings, solid models, finite element models, and NC programs, it is still too narrow a focus. These system are also frequently limited to data stored on a specific vendor's CAD system, not even all of the data stored in a heterogeneous CIM network. However, these limited perspectives are gradually broadening.

As was shown in the information model in the previous section, the scope of the ideal retrieval system should encompass a wide range of design and manufacturing data. It should include this information regardless of whether it is stored on paper or in an automated form. Furthermore, it should also be integrated with a configuration management system, which is described in Chapter 9. All these components will probably not be implemented at once, but the initial planning should assume that eventually they will all be part of a common database. In other words, the initial information analysis should include the related objects for all of these areas, although only part of this information model and the related applications may be implemented in the first phase. Subsequent phases will complete the coverage. The order in which areas are added should be based on the company's priorities and resources.

For example, in one company the sequence might be retrieval for drawings (both manual and automated), retrieval for other types of automated data, configuration management, and then retrieval for other types of the manual documents. Another company might emphasize configuration management first, then retrieval of automated documents, and finally retrieval of manual documents. Still another company with a group technology orientation could emphasize process plans, then drawings, and finally configuration management.

Many companies hesitate to get into design retrieval partly because of the complexity of developing the necessary classification coding scheme. Ideally, a customized scheme is developed for each company by a firm specializing in this service—Brisch-Birn is one of the best known. A sample of the company's parts are selected and a scheme is developed from them. The development of such a customized scheme is expensive and time-consuming. Additional time and costs are required to actually classify the company's parts and load the database.

Some people are now proposing to speed up this process by using a more generic scheme applicable for a number of companies or industries. While this approach is a compromise, it can be effective for many companies. A company can easily take a sample of its parts, classify them using a generic scheme, and evaluate its effectiveness. The question then becomes whether the marginal gain from a customized scheme is worth the increased costs and time.

Once the company accepts the scheme, it then classifies its parts and loads the design database. This raises the third issue—which parts should be loaded when. This is similar to the question a company faces when it acquires a CIM system—which parts should be put on the system and which ones should be left as manual designs. A first reaction is that ideally the company should load all of its parts. However, this may be impractical for a company with 20,000 or more designs, especially if many of them are inactive. Therefore, the company could start with only active parts and enter them by priority: those most likely to be reused and those that would eliminate the most design effort because of their complexity.

Over time all of the company's parts (at least the active ones) should be classified, although the detailed design and manufacturing data files for many of them may not be loaded into the design database. The retrieval system must include all part data whether they are in the computer or on paper. As more and more parts are classified, some categories will begin to accumulate many parts. But upon closer examination only a few of them may be significantly different, the others being simply variations. Only the basic designs need to be entered in the CIM system. Furthermore, one or two of them may be defined as standard or preferred parts. If possible, one of them should be used whenever a part in this category is needed. Gradually, one of the standard parts will replace the other variations in the company's products.

In effect, the process of implementing a retrieval system helps a company identify and eventually eliminate most of its duplicate designs. In some cases the inventory savings alone are enough to justify the system.

Classification and Coding

This section discusses an essential component of both an effective design retrieval and a group technology system—a classification and coding scheme. Classification and coding schemes for design retrieval and group technology have similar, but not identical, characteristics.

Design Retrieval Classification and Coding

A good classification and coding scheme for design retrieval has the following four characteristics, the first two of which are essential:

- all-inclusive
- mutually exclusive
- logical, sequential decision tree
- permanent design characteristics

First, every design must fit somewhere in the classification scheme. If a design does not fit in the scheme, it cannot be retrieved and thus must be redesigned each time.

Second, the categories must be mutually exclusive. There should be only one logical place in the scheme for any given design. An ambigious scheme that allows a design to fit into several places creates problems in both loading and using the data. When the designs are initially being classified and then loaded into the design database, there is no reliability if the same design can be put in different categories. An engineer who needs a part in category A would miss any similar designs that had been placed in category B. Some reusable designs would be missed because the classification scheme allowed ambiguities.

A logical, sequential decision tree is a tool to avoid this ambiguity. It helps the people who initially classify a company's designs and load the database as well as the engineers who try to find a design. The decision tree is determined by the actual classification scheme, but it must also be related to the way the designers think about the parts they are trying to design (e.g., which characteristics they think of first).

The classification scheme for design retrieval should be based on permanent part characteristics. Otherwise, minor changes in the design could result in having to reclassify it. For example, the classification scheme for piping should not include what the pipes are made of, which could change in later revisions. The scheme could, however, include characteristics that could be a function of the material. For example, one might want to classify piping by whether or not it was potentially toxic, such as lead pipe. Such a scheme would not distinguish between copper and plastic pipe unless there were other factors that were important.

Group Technology Classification and Coding

A classification and coding scheme for group technology has the following characteristics:

- all-inclusive
- mutually exclusive
- based on permanent manufacturing characteristics

The first two characteristics are the same as those for a design retrieval scheme.

A group technology classification and coding scheme must include all parts and classify them unambiguously. The third characteristic is what tailors the scheme for manufacturing rather than design. For example, material is more important than the exact shape because parts of different materials, such as metal and plastic, are produced by different manufacturing processes. Similarly, a group technology code includes information about both features and how the features are created, whereas a design retrieval scheme needs to know only the features. For example, different manufacturing processes must be used to make holes of different tolerances.

A related issue is how to classify the special tools and fixtures used to make a part. One approach is to consider them as just other parts and classify them independently. However, they are interesting only in terms of the parts they are used to produce. Therefore, an effective approach some companies are using is to give them the same classification code as the part they are used to make.

With a classification and coding system the key characteristics are included in the clasification code. The part number is simply a way of identifying a specific part or design. It provides no information about the part characteristics.

Types of Coding Schemes

There are two types of coding schemes—monocodes and polycodes. A monocode is a single integrated classification code. The digits in the code are not independent. Each digit or set of digits further qualifies the previous one. For example, one digit may specify that a part is axial, and the next digit would specify whether it had one or several radius dimensions. A monocode coding scheme is essentially a hierarchical decision tree. Therefore, once a classification scheme is designed, it usually cannot be changed short of a major revision, except for adding details to an unused branch. One normally retrieves designs using the entire code. A request can stop at any point going down the decision tree, but there is no way to query an attribute at a lower level without having worked down all of the decision tree above it. Monocode schemes are used primarily for design retrieval systems.

The hierarchical nature of the monocode approach provides the design discipline by which an engineer specifies the requirements for a part. In most cases these coding schemes are developed specifically for a company and its unique set of parts. The procedure for developing a classification and coding scheme was described above.

There are several other classification schemes, such as MI-Class or D-Class, but many of them are either general hierarchies or polycodes tailored to group technology rather than design retrieval.

With a polycode each digit or group of digits is independent of others and describes a single part characteristic. A polycode can be of any length and is frequently very long, some over 40 digits long. Polycodes are easily extensible because adding a new characteristic simply requires adding another digit or set of digits to the code. Parts can be retrieved using any one or more of the characteristics included in the polycode. Furthermore, the characteristics can be specified in any order. In summary, polycodes are very flexible and easy to use. Their primary use is for group technology classification schemes. Only occasionally are they used for design retrieval.

Summary

This chapter has discussed design retrieval and group technology. It described each function and its benefits. It reviewed an information model to support these functions. Finally, it discussed some implementation issues and explained the different classification and coding schemes.

Notes

1. George H. Schaffer, "Implementing CIM," *American Machinist* 125 (August 1981): 151–174.
2. William F. Hyde, *Improving Productivity by Classification, Coding, and Data Base Standardization: The Key to Maximizing CAD/CAM and Group Technology* (New York: Marcel Dekker, 1981).
3. Ibid.

Further Reading

Hyde, William F. *Improving Productivity by Classification, Coding, and Data Base Standardization: The Key to Maximizing CAD/CAM and Group Technology.* New York: Marcel Dekker, 1981.

Hyer, Nancy Lea (ed.). *Group Technology at Work.* Dearborn, Mich.: SME, 1984.

Knox, Charles S. *CAD/CAM Systems: Planning and Implementation.* New York: Marcel Dekker, 1983.

9

Design: Product Structure/ Configuration Management

Product Specifications

Top-Down Design

Product Structure

Configuration Management/Change Control

Summary

This chapter, the first of two on design, concentrates on the top-down approach needed to design complex products and assemblies. Overall product requirements, product structure, and configuration management are key issues for this aspect of design. The other aspect of design, which is discussed in Chapter 10, involves creating and modifying the detailed part geometry. Geometry is also involved with assemblies, but the geometry of an assembly is usually derived from the geometry of the parts in the assembly rather than being directly or explicitly defined.

Product Specifications

The designer starts with a set of product specifications. These specifications may have come from marketing ("Our customers want these features" or "This is what our competitors are providing"), or they can be driven by technology ("We have this new capability in either component or production technology; how can we use

135

it to improve our current product or to develop a new product?"). These specifications may be global and relate to the overall product, or they may relate to only one or more of the components or subsystems in the product. Finally, specifications may be in absolute or relative terms—for example, we need a car to provide 40 miles per gallon or we need a 20 percent improvement in fuel efficiency.

Most products have many different specifications. Some are independent, but others are closely related, such as the payload and range of an aircraft. There are several approaches for related specifications. One approach is to treat some of them as independent or given and then derive the others. Another approach is to combine them, possibly with a weighting factor, into a composite specification for the product.

The specifications for the product and its subsystems and components determine the types of analyses that must be done on the design. For example, analyses can involve structural or thermal characteristics. Components may be rigid or deformable. Analyses may also involve static or dynamic and linear or nonlinear assumptions. Analysis is described in more detail in Chapter 11.

Top-Down Design

The initial design process is a top-down process. Given the major product specifications, the designer must identify the major subsystems and assemblies in the product and then the individual components within these subsystems and assemblies. At any level the designer may identify an existing element (e.g., subsystem, assembly, or component) that can be used in the new product. Whenever this is done, the design process is simplified because the entire design tree below the reused element already exists and does not have to be redesigned and reanalyzed.

For complex products the top down design may be generic down to a certain point, and then specific elements are identified or designed. For example, an aircraft generically consists of an airframe, propulsion, and avionics systems. The airframe consists of a fuselage, wings, and a tail assembly. The propulsion subsystem consists of the engines and the fuel system. The design work is simplified if an existing engine can be used for a new aircraft. Similarly, stretching an existing airframe is much easier than designing a new airframe from scratch. A similar design decomposition can be done for most other products—cars, lawn mowers, televisions, washing machines, or machine tools.

Complex products can have several subsystems, tens of major assemblies, and thousands of individual components. Even relatively simple products can have ten to twenty components. Product structure, configuration management, and change control are important mechanisms to help manage this complexity.

Product Structure

A product structure (sometimes called a bill of materials) specifies what goes into a product. It identifies the subsystems, assemblies, and individual components. It also specifies how many are used in each higher-level assembly. In a product structure each part (which may be an individual component, an assembly, a subsystem, or the entire product) is identified by a part number and is related to other parts in the product. This product structure is used in many ways. It is essential for MRP (material requirements planning), and it tells the shop floor how the product is assembled.

Several situations occur that complicate the product structure. There may be many variants of the product. For example, most models of a car are available with any one of several different engines and transmissions. Every car must have an engine and a transmission, but the buyer can select which one of several engines or transmissions. Therefore, the product structure must allow for alternate parts or assemblies at various points. However, these choices can only be made at certain locations, not anywhere in the product structure. For example, the product structure will go down so far and then call for an engine. It may call for a generic engine, with its own part number, to be replaced by one of the following acceptable engines for that model car. However, having selected an engine, the customer cannot select which valves to use. Only the engine is a variant, not its subassemblies and components.

A related problem occurs with options. An option is a part that may or may not be included in the product. For example, a car may or may not have an air conditioner or a radio. The fact that the part may not be included in the product is what distinguishes an option from a variant in the product structure. (In common use the term *option* usually refers to either a real option or a variant; however, the difference is important in the product structure context.)

For a given product structure the way it is used can be more or less complicated depending on how the company or the industry does business. The product structure and its use is relatively simple if the company makes standard products. It becomes more complicated if the products can be customized with variants and options. Given a product structure with variants and options, the way it is used to run the factory becomes much more complex if the company manufactures to order rather than to inventory in a relatively fixed ratio of models.

Finally, the product structure is still more complex if serial or lot traceability is required. Normally each product has a single structure, regardless of how many are produced—one or a thousand of them. However, for some critical products serial traceability is required. This means that if ten units of the product are produced, there are ten separate product structures (or bills of material). In addition to the basic product structure, they also identify which specific units were used to make each unit of the product. With lot traceability the individual units do not have to be identified, only the lots of materials and parts from which they were made. The reason for serial or lot traceability is that if a lot or a specific item is bad, it is possible to find out exactly where it was used. For example, if you discover that a certain lot of raw material was bad, you can determine that it was used to machine the turbine blades for two specific jet engines, which are installed in two specific aircraft. Clearly, for some critical products this traceability is important.

The most serious and most common complication to the product structure arises because of the poor communications between design and manufacturing. In many companies a product does not have a single product structure or bill of materials. The designer engineers develop a bill of materials during the design process. This engineering bill is sent to the manufacturing engineers as part of the design documentation. However, manufacturing engineering often makes changes to improve the producability of the product. Some of these changes cause modification of the product structure. Now the company has both an engineering and a manufacturing bill of materials. (In extreme cases further changes may be made during the actual manufacturing operations, so there may also be an "as built" bill of materials.) These conflicting bills must be reconciled. The manufacturing product structure must become the standard one since it normally is the "as built" bill. The engineering bill of materials is simply a first approximation of what will be the final (i.e., the manufacturing) bill of materials.

Configuration Management/Change Control

Configuration management and change control are the mechanisms for resolving these differences. Configuration management is a discipline for identifying, tracking, and controlling changes to approved or released design and manufacturing documents. It tracks the changes and the resulting product structure as it evolves over time. Some changes may be the result of natural product evolution, but others may be the result of errors in the initial product design.

Configuration management deals only with released documents or documents in the process of being released. As long as a designer or a design team is working on and revising a design before it has been approved, these documents and their changes do not come under configuration management.

Once they are satisfied with the design and are ready to send it to manufacturing engineering, then it must go through a formal release and approval cycle. At this point the design is frozen, and any changes must be formally approved under a change control procedure. This mechanism ensures that only consistent sets of changes are done and that the necessary people are notified of any changes.

Figure 9.1 shows the basic information model required to support change control. Someone generates a change request to modify a set of documents, which describe one or more parts. This part (or parts) may be used in one or many products. The change request is generated on a date and has an effective date. There is also a reason for the proposed change—such as to improve the produceability, reliability, or cost of the part or because there was an error in the initial design.

Several assumptions have been made to show the integrity constraints on the information model. First, only one person is responsible for generating any single

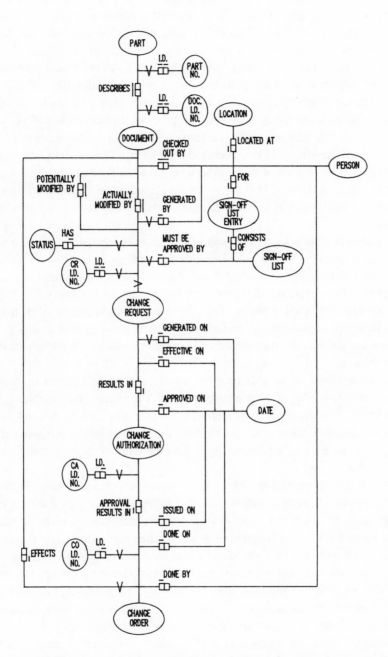

Figure 9.1   Information model for configuration management and change control

change request; however, a person can generate many different change requests. Second, the change request has only one date of generation and one effective date. Third, a single change request can effect many different documents and any single document can be affected by many different change requests.

After evaluating the request, the Change Control Board may determine that the request affects more documents than were originally identified. For example, suppose the designers of product A want to change part x. If part x is also used in product B, then there may be additional product B documents that are affected that the product A designers did not know about. As part of the change control process, all of the effects of the change should be considered. Part of this process may involve notifying all of the people who have checked out or used any of the documents to be modified. The change control system cannot automatically decide whether these people will be affected, but it should at least ensure that they are notified.

Assume that the designers of product A want to change part x so that it becomes part y. This may result in a better design for product A but not for product B. In this case the designers of product B will decide to ignore the change and continue to use part x. However, in other cases the change may be because of a design flaw in part x that is corrected in part y. Then the change should also be made in product B. Configuration management and change control ensures that at any point the company knows the structure for all of its products and can track any changes to those products.

There are three types of change documents, although in some companies they may be combined. They are the change request, the change authorization, and the change order. The change request identifies the documents to be changed, specifies the changes for each document, and explains the reasons for the proposed changes. Following a review and evaluation by a Change Control Board, certain changes are approved.

A change authorization identifies the approved changes. In some cases all of the requested changes are approved, but in other cases only a subset of them are approved. In a few cases the review and evaluation may identify additional documents that must be changed but that were missed in the original request. In these cases the authorization would include more changes than the original request. Some companies will keep a one-to-one relationship between change requests and authorizations. Other companies may consolidate several change requests affecting the same documents into a single authorization. Either approach can work, but the information model shows the one-to-one relationship.

Change orders specify the changes for a single document. A change authorization may approve a related set of changes to several documents. This authorization would result in several change orders, one for each document. Different types of documents are controlled by different organizations and people, all of whom must be notified to make the approved changes. The change order provides this notification. To ensure that the changes are made, there should be feedback to the change order specifying who made the change and the date the change was made.

When a document changes, one of three things can happen to the part it describes. The first possibility is that both the part number and version number can stay unchanged. Second, the part number may remain the same, but the version number changes. Third, the part number changes. There are precise configuration management rules to determine which of these alternatives occurs. These rules relate to the interchangeability of the old and new part for fit, function, and traceability.

The simplest case is when neither the part number nor the version number changes. This happens if the document changes do not directly affect the part – for example, if information in the label block, such as the designer, changes.

If for any reason it is necessary distinguish between the new and old part, then either the version number or the part number must change. Some people contend that if the changes were such that the parts are completely interchangeable for fit, function, and traceability (e.g., the new and old parts could be dumped into the same bin, and it would make no difference which is used), then neither the part number nor the version number have to change. However, without a new version number any future traceability is lost.

If the modified part is completely interchangeable with the old part, then only the version number needs to change. The part number can remain the same. If the modified part is no longer interchangeable, then the part number must change. A new part number must also be used if the material used in the part changes.

This decision about the version number and part number for the modified part is only the beginning. The same decision process must be repeated up the entire product structure. To decide what to do at the next level, such as a subassembly, realize that it is just another part so the same decision rules apply. If the modified part is a component in a subassembly, then a decision must be made about the subassembly. Is a new part number or version number needed for the subassembly? There has clearly been a change in one of its components and therefore in its bill of materials. For traceability the version number at least must change. If the modified subassembly is not interchangeable with the previous one, then it would need a new part number.

Summary

This chapter has addressed the top-down, high-level design process. It has described the transition from a generic product structure to a detailed one using existing parts or newly designed ones. It has also explained the importance of configuration management and change control in ensuring the integrity of the product structure.

10

Design: Geometric Design

Historical Perspective and Future Directions

Types of Geometry

Two-Dimensional
Three-Dimensional Wireframe
Three-Dimensional Solids

Information Analysis

Geometry
Features

Summary

This chapter focuses on the geometric aspect of design. Geometric information, which is used throughout the design and manufacturing process, describes parts and assemblies. In process planning and NC program generation part geometry is used in conjunction with the geometry of the machine tools, fixtures, and cutting surfaces of specific tools. Geometry is also important in tool design, since a tool is simply another part that is being designed. Robotics programming and the animation to verify these programs also use geometry. Finally, geometry is important for describing plant layout and evaluating material handling systems and the flow of material through the plant.

From the data management perpective geometry is one of the least understood and discussed areas. Therefore, this chapter provides an introduction to geometric concepts, construction, and data structures. This background is useful for the other chapters because geometric data are needed to support many of the functions they describe.

The first section explains the origins of the geometric design function in CAD/CAM and its evolution toward feature-based design in which the designer implicitly rather than explicitly defines the geometry. The second section describes the three basic alternatives for representing geometry: two-dimensional, three-dimensional wireframe, and three-dimensional solids. It also relates the geometry to the way in which it is created (i.e., explicitly or implicitly). The third section is an information model to support geometry and features.

Historical Perspective and Future Directions

CAD/CAM has supported the design function for a long time. The computerization of geometric design was originally called computer-aided drafting (CAD). This terminology accurately described what the system did. Drafting is the creation of the engineering drawing for a part or a product. This engineering drawing was, and in many cases still is, the primary form of engineering documentation. Most other forms of documentation are used in conjunction with it and expand on it.

The engineering drawing, even for a relatively simple part, is very complex. Creating the drawing was a difficult, time-consuming, and error-prone task. Interpreting and using such a drawing, especially for a complex part, was not much easier. The engineering drawing is a precise two-dimensional representation of a three-dimensional object. It required three separate two-dimensional views (usually orthogonal) of the object. The person creating the drawing had to be able to visualize a part, which usually did not yet exist, and figure out how it would look from the three selected views. The person using the drawing had to look at the three views and integrate them to understand how they were related before he or she could visualize the part.

Changing a finished engineering drawing was also difficult. Therefore, a finished engineering drawing was usually made only when a design was completed or fairly stable. Until this point in the design process engineers used sketches and working drawings. In spite of this, designs did change (e.g., to correct errors or to create new versions of a part). In extreme cases the entire drawing would have to be redone, but often smaller drawings were attached showing only the modified part of the drawing. The user then had to integrate not only the three views but also any changes.

Computer-aided drafting addressed the creation and modification of engineering drawings. A great deal of skill was still needed to create, modify, and interpret the drawing. CAD did, however, greatly improve the productivity of the people creating and maintaining drawings. For example, the system could automatically create the necessary mirror image so only one part of a symmetrical part had to be drawn. And if a small part of the drawing was changed, the system could easily redo the entire drawing, so the person working with the drawing did not have to consider both a master drawing and a separate set of modifications. However, these benefits were limited. The draftsman still had to determine and create the three separate views of the part. If the part was changed, then each of these views had to be modified independently. In effect, CAD simply assisted in the documentation of a design, not in its creation (i.e., the actual design process). The next step required these systems to give up their two-dimensional orientation.

The first step toward true computer-aided design occurred with the three-dimensional wireframe systems. With these systems the designer could create a three- dimensional representation of the part by defining points and curves in space. Although this wireframe approach did not provide a complete geometric representation of a part because it did not define the surfaces, it was a significant improvement. The designer could define the part geometry, move the part around in space, and look at it from different perspectives. Using hidden-line removal, the designer could create the views of the geometry needed for the engineering drawing. This allowed the designer to create the part geometry once and then relatively easily generate the necessary geometry for the three views required by the engineering drawing.

This approach had several benefits. First, the designer or draftsman no longer created each view in the drawing independently. All of the views could be generated from a common wireframe model of the part. The draftsman did, however, have to add some drafting detail, such as annotation and dimensioning, to each view. Second, changes could be made once to the wireframe model and then propagated to each of the drawing views since they were no longer independent views. However, these changes to the drawing views cannot be made automatically. Finally, in some cases the wireframe model was easier for most people to understand and interpret than the engineering drawing, particularly if the hidden lines are removed. However, automatic hidden-line removal is beyond simple wireframe modeling systems primarily because it requires so much processing power as well as surface information, which was not present in the early wireframe systems. Some of the early wireframe systems forced the designer to manually remove all of the hidden lines. This approach was very tedious because the hidden lines that need to be removed are dependent on the view, not simply the geometry. However, the increasing processing power of engineering workstations has reduced this problem. Many of the wireframe CAD systems now do automatic hidden-line removal, but to do this they assume that planar surfaces connect the wireframe.

In the early 1980s the wireframe approach seemed to promise significant improvements in designer productivity. However, two more recent thrusts have made the wireframe approach obsolete: solid modeling and feature-based design.

With these two new approaches CAD is changing even more to represent design rather than drafting.

The solid modeling approach capitalizes on the benefits of the wireframe approach but avoids its weaknesses. With a solid model there is still a single common geometric model of a part or an assembly. But unlike the wireframe model, the solid model provides a complete geometric definition of the part. This complete geometric definition allows fully automatic hidden-line removal. This means that the designer can define the part geometry as a solid model and move it around in space to examine it from different perspectives, but always seeing an easily understandable image of the part with the hidden lines removed. This approach takes more processing power and more sophisticated software, but it increases the productivity of the people using the system. Much of this productivity improvement also comes from the ease of passing model data between CIM functions, not simply because the designer work has become easier.

Originally solid modeling systems were very hard to use because the designers had to use a command language, often in a batch mode, so they could not see the intermediate results they were creating. Now with more powerful workstations and real-time graphics displays these systems are becoming easier to use because the designer can select model components on the screen and watch them move in real time. Since these solid models are now easier to create and modify than a wireframe model or an engineering drawing, people doing this work can be more productive. Furthermore, although they do require a different way of thinking about design, the solid modeling system can be used effectively by people with less experience and training. And because these solid modeling systems (or wireframe systems that include surfaces) can produce images that are clearly understood, a common part definition can be used for many additional functions, such as marketing literature and assembly and maintenance instructions.

Although solid modeling systems are becoming easier to use, there is still a problem because everything is defined in terms of geometry. Clearly, one can define much of a part design in terms of geometry. However, it is much simpler to design the part directly in terms of basic features, such as holes, fillets, and slots. To the system a feature such as a hole is simply geometry, but the designer thinks in terms of holes to be drilled in the part. Therefore, in addition to defining the solid model as geometry, the designer should be able to define and attach features, as parameterized pieces of geometry, to the part. For example, a hole is simply a cylinder with a certain radius, depth, and angle between its axis and the normal to the surface. Features may also be added to a part design by a process planner.

Feature-based design systems allow this additional capability on top of a solid modeling system. The feature-based approach has two benefits. First, it makes an easy-to-use solid modeling system even easier to use by allowing the designer and manufacturing engineer to work in terms of familiar features rather than pure geometry. Second, subsequent applications, such as process planning and numerical control programming, can usually identify the features they need to work with, eliminating the need to reconstruct them from the raw geometry.

Many CIM systems today provide a solid modeling capability, which is frequently added as another application, relatively independent of their existing system. However, most of these vendors do provide a migration path to convert from the solid modeling data structures to the ones normally used by their system, which are frequently based on a wireframe model. Some vendors are now building their applications directly on a solid modeling capability although several additional vendors have added a solid modeler to their offering. Those that do are beginning to include a feature-based design capability and this is clearly the trend. In the future few if any new CIM systems will be developed without this capability.

The next section discusses the three geometric approaches underlying CAD/CAM systems. Because of the trend described above, most of the emphasis is on three-dimensional solid modeling. The information analysis for geometry in a later section also emphasizes solid modeling.

Types of Geometry

Geometry is a fundamental type of data needed by CIM applications, although additional attributes may be attached to the geometry. Sophisticated graphics systems are used to display the geometry and manipulate the display. However, for the users and most of the designers of CIM systems, geometry (as it is represented and stored in the database) is the important factor. Graphics display is not the key. Therefore, this chapter focuses only on the geometry.

Two-Dimensional

Two-dimensional CAD systems are essentially drafting systems. Today they are either relatively old systems or primarily for small microcomputers and workstations with limited power. A few years ago these systems were the most common CAD systems, and they are still bought by the smaller manufacturing companies. Their use by larger companies is slowly being replaced by 3-D systems. Declining hardware costs and increasing power have made the more sophisticated three-dimensional systems accessible to many medium-sized or even smaller companies. Solid modeling applications are available on almost all engineering workstations and many microcomputers, so their use is slowly expanding.

Although two-dimensional systems are used primarily for drafting, they do allow designers or draftsmen to work with basic geometry. The two-dimensional geometry they support is a subset of the geometry supported by the more sophisticated three-dimensional systems. They define points and curves in two dimensions rather than three, but they include most of the same types of curves. They lack the more complex surfaces and solid primitives (i.e., those requiring the third dimension).

With all geometry—two- or three-dimensional—there are two key issues: how the geometry is stored and how it is created and manipulated. Most systems store each type of geometric object (e.g., a point, a line, or a circle) in one common or canonical form, although the common form for some types of objects is different for different systems. This common storage form makes it easier for the system to manipulate the objects in most cases.

On the other hand, there are many ways in which a geometric object can be created and manipulated. In addition to storing geometric objects in a common form, many systems also keep information on how the object was constructed.

Let's consider two simple examples—a point and a line. A point is stored as simply xy coordinates. However, it may be constructed in many different ways. It may be specified in terms of actual xy coordinates by either entering the numbers or by pointing to a position on the screen. It may be defined in absolute terms or terms relative to a specified base point. It may be constructed as the intersection of two lines or more generally as the intersection of any two curves. The intersection of some curves, however, may define several points (e.g., as with the intersection of two overlapping circles), in which case the user must then specify which of the points is the desired one. In most cases geometric manipulation is relatively easy given a point's coordinates. In some cases, however, one also needs to know how the point was defined. If it was defined as the intersection of two lines, it still has a coordinate. However, if one of the lines is moved, the point may also need to move. In fact, if the lines no longer intersect, the point may actually disappear. To facilitate these types of operations (i.e., those in terms of the objects used to define a geometric entity), many systems also store information about how the object was constructed.

Similarly, any line segment may be stored as its two end points, although it can also be defined in many other ways. For example, a line could be specified as a base point, a distance, and a direction. However, many of these construction methods simply involve other ways of specifying the points defining the line.

Other types of geometric entities supported by most two-dimensional systems include circles, circular arcs, and conic curves (e.g., parabolas, ellipses, and hyperbolas). Some systems also allow more arbitrary curves such as splines. In addition to the geometric nature of these entities they also have certain display characteristics such as font (e.g., solid, broken, or dotted) and color.

Once the geometry is created, the user needs to edit or modify it. The user may add geometric entities to a drawing or select entities that already exist and then modify, delete, or move them. If a drawing is symmetrical, the user may only create one part of it and then have the system create the necessary mirror image. Another operation involves changing the scale of part of the geometry (e.g., double the length of a line). All of these edit operations actually change the geometry— i.e., the values that are stored.

Other operations change only the image the user sees on the display, not the actual geometry as it is stored in the system. Conceptually, the drawing is being created on a very large sheet with the display simply showing one area of the sheet. A small drawing may comfortably fit entirely within the display area, but a large drawing maybe too big for one display. With a large drawing the display window can pan over the drawing to show different parts of it. The user can also zoom in on a part of the drawing and display it much greater detail. Similarly, the user can zoom out to show the broader context for a part of the drawing. In all of these cases the actual stored geometry remains unchanged. Only the display data changes.

These two-dimensional geometric designs can be created directly by the designer or derived from more complete three-dimensional designs. Given a three-dimensional wireframe or solid model, the designer can look at it from a particular viewpoint and project it onto a plane to create a two-dimensional view of the geometry. As mentioned earlier, without hidden-line removal the projection from a wireframe model is hard to interpret. The pure wireframe geometry does not include enough data to do this hidden-line removal automatically, but a solid model does. To avoid this problem many wireframe systems assume planar surfaces.

Some companies are now beginning their design process with a solid model, although they still use the engineering drawing as the basic documentation. They initially create the design as a three-dimensional solid. They then determine the desired viewpoints, such as three orthogonal views, and let the system project the design geometry (i.e., the solid model) onto the appropriate two-dimensional planes. A draftsman then needs to add only the drafting entities to the drawing. The entire geometry does not have to be recreated. Today solid modeling systems do not allow drafting information, such as tolerances, to be directly attached to the solid model.

The traditional, nongeometric drafting information is the essential data that must be added by a two-dimensional system or by a three-dimensional system that allows a two-dimensional projection. The reason for this is that most drafting entities are dependent on both the geometry and the specific view of that geometry.

There are five types of drafting data—labels, dimensions, tolerances, annotation, and exploded detail, all of which are shown in the sample drawing in Figure 10.1. The drawing label is essentially text and is not directly related to the geometry. Because the label is independent of geometry, it is the easiest to support. Each company has its own standard for its label format and what data are included. These data generally include part number, version or revision level, date created or modified, and designer.

Dimensioning information provides additional information about the part geometry in a form easily readable by the people who must work with the drawing. Even when the drawing is drawn to scale, having the dimensions explicitly included makes the drawing easier to use. There are several different types of dimension entities—linear, radius or diameter, and angular. A dimension relates several distinct objects in the geometry. First, there is the geometry itself, which may be a line, an angle, a circle, or some other type of curve. Second, there are witness

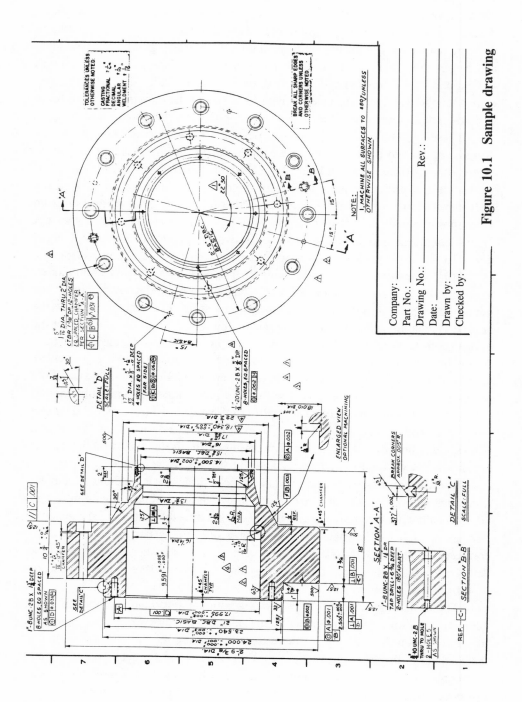

Figure 10.1 Sample drawing

150

lines to specify precisely what is being dimensioned. Third, there is the actual value of the dimension. (In the case of a family drawing the dimension value is a variable, not an actual number. This can be a problem for some systems.) A drafting system needs flexibility so it can be tailored to various national and company drafting standards.

In the earliest drafting system the dimensioning was manual in that the user had to specify all of these entities. The system did not know about or maintain any relationship among them. Most systems today are semiautomatic in that the system keeps track of some of the data and the relationships. For example, if a line in the geometry is lengthened, the witness lines and the dimension value are automatically changed. However, no current system has fully automatic dimensioning in the sense that given a set of design geometry, it will automatically do all of the dimensioning.

Tolerances specify how precisely a part must be made. Tolerances are not simply additional data attached to part geometry; they are the key to how the part is defined. Specifying that two holes must be 10 inches apart is not the same as specifying that the first hole must be 5 inches from the edge and the second 15 inches. In the first case the tolerance of the first hole position is added to the tolerance of the second hole position, whereas in the second case it is not. Therefore, the second approach more precisely defines the position. In the drawing tolerancing is shown as part of the dimension (e.g., 10 inches $\pm$ 0.001 inches). CAD systems today do not represent effectively the concept of tolerances.

Annotations provide additional nongeometric information about the part. For example, an annotation may specify the type of material or certain processing to be done to the material. In other cases an annotation may refer to a design standard or other document to be used in conjunction with the drawing.

The last additional type of data is exploded detail. This information is less important in CAD drawings than in manual ones. It consists of representing a certain part of the drawing with much greater detail. With a CAD system this can be accomplished automatically be zooming in on that part of the drawing. However, since hard copies are often produced from CAD systems, exploded details are still needed.

Three-Dimensional Wireframe

The second type of geometry is three-dimensional wireframe modeling. The geometry in a wireframe model consists of points and the curves connecting them. Topology relates the various parts of the model geometry. For example, a box can be defined geometrically by six planar faces. Topology identifies which faces are connected together along which edges (i.e., which faces are adjacent). The curves define edges. Two edges meet at a vertix. A set of one or more loops define a face (i.e., a surface or part of a surface). A closed set of faces defines a topological solid. Most of the geometry and topology in a three-dimensional wireframe model

151

are the same as for the two-dimensional geometry, except that they exist in three-dimensional space rather than on a two-dimensional plane.

Since a wireframe model is created in space, it can be moved around and viewed from any perspective. Furthermore, the wireframe model can be projected onto a plane from any of these views to create the basic geometry for an engineering drawing. This operation projects all of the edges onto the plane, so the hidden lines have to be removed to make the resulting figure meaningful.

Wireframe models (without added surfaces) have several basic representation and construction problems that prevent them from being the best form of geometry for CAD/CAM. First, a three-dimensional wireframe model is not topologically complete. This has several implications. The system cannot ensure the topological integrity of a model—i.e., its completeness and consistency. Thus the system will allow the user to create impossible Escher-type designs that cannot be made. This means that parametric design methods, such as part families with variable dimensions, are not very effective because there is no guarantee of the integrity of the resulting design. Similarly, high-level geometry construction and modification methods are not feasible.

Second, a wireframe model lacks surface and solid information. For example, a wireframe model for a box could represent either a solid box or a hollow one. And a wireframe model cannot distinguish whether the material is inside or outside of the model. With many wireframe systems the surfaces of the part are not explicitly defined. They must be inferred, and such inferences are frequently ambiguous. Most of the wireframe systems that allow surfaces assume planar surfaces, so they cannot represent curved surfaces. This drastically reduces the number of parts that can be modeled.

Without surfaces all of the edges in the model are visible. This means that pure wireframe models of even relatively simple parts are difficult to understand and interpret. Face or solid information is needed for the system to identify and completely and accurately remove the lines that are hidden from a given view. Unless this information is explicitly in the system, the system must infer where the surfaces are and which lines are to be removed. Wireframe systems can avoid this problem by assuming planar surfaces. However, since hidden lines are view-dependent, this removal must be done for each view.

Third, since the wireframe model does not specify the bounding surfaces, certain types of analyses cannot be done with this type of model. Interference analysis cannot be done if you do not know the boundaries of the parts. And if you do not know the boundaries of an object, you cannot calculate its mass properties.

Finally, without surfaces NC programs cannot be generated. Although NC generation is only one small step in the CIM process, it is a commonly available function. Any geometry that cannot support NC would have serious problems as the basis for a CIM system.

Despite these problems, three-dimensional wireframe models are an improvement over the earlier two-dimensional drafting systems. They allow the designer to create a three-dimensional model of the part and move it around. This capability helps significantly in the design process, even if the model is not complete.

Once wireframe systems became acceptable, people began to develop solutions to some of their most serious problems. This led to the development of hybrid systems, which were essentially wireframe systems to which surfaces were added. This single addition allowed these enhanced wireframe system to support a broader range of manufacturing applications, such as NC program generation. These hybrid systems were easier to use and could support more types of applications. However, even with the addition of surfaces, these systems were still not topologically complete so they could not ensure consistent designs.

Wireframe modeling seemed to be a development whose time had come. While not perfect, it was being improved and becoming more widely applicable. Most people assumed this trend would continue for a number of years before developers could solve the solid modeling problems and develop production-quality solid modelers. However, this was not to be the case. Our understanding of solid modeling and the software and hardware to support it became available much sooner than anticipated. Thus, before it could really take off, wireframe modeling was made obsolete by solid modeling systems.

Three-Dimensional Solids

In the future three-dimensional solid geometry will become the dominant way of defining and storing the geometric component of CAD/CAM data. Although it will be many years before there is widespread industry acceptance and use of these systems, many CIM vendors already have such products on the market, and many of the leading, more sophisticated companies are beginning to use them. The rest of this section identifies the main components of a solid modeling system, describes the two main approaches for representing solid geometry, and provides an example of how each approach would be used to define a simple assembly.

A solid modeling system consists of three distinct components—a solid modeler, viewing programs, and application programs. The solid modeler is the software that allows the user to create, modify, and manipulate the geometry. Most of today's modelers also actually store and retrieve the geometric data. In the future, however, the actual storage and retrieval of the data will be done by a database manager that is independent of the modeler itself. The solid modeler will then be simply another application using data stored in a common CIM database.

The viewing programs are those routines that create the desired display given the geometry and a viewpoint. They may create a color solid model, a shaded image, a wireframe with or without the hidden lines removed, a sectional or cutaway view, or an exploded view of an assembly. The programs to create these types of views are simply other application programs, but they are sometimes considered a part of the modeler because they enhance its usefulness.

The application programs perform various functions on the solid model. Common examples include interference checking, calculation of mass properties, finite element modeling and analysis, and NC program generation and verification. The number of applications using solid models is rapidly increasing as more vendors are converting their old applications or developing new ones based on the data structures supported by solid modeling systems. Many CIM applications were developed before solid modeling, but they are being converted to use this more powerful approach.

Solid modelers and applications are being developed and marketed in either of two ways. Some vendors are providing integrated or bundled systems. In these systems the modeler, its data structure, and the applications using it are all tightly integrated. The benefit is that all parts of the system are linked to the same data structures, so there is much more flexibility in moving among the various parts of the system. For example, if a problem arises in generating an NC program, the user can directly change the geometry at that point. (Administratively this flexibility may not be desirable. For data integrity and security reasons only the designer may be authorized to change part geometry. Using a database management system to manage the geometric data allows both the flexibility and the necessary access controls.) The trade-off is that it may be hard for a company to add its own applications or to acquire other applications that run against the modeler's data structures.

As an alternative, some vendors are providing stand-alone or independent solid modelers. These system include only the modeler, its viewing programs, and the data structures to support them. Using this open-system approach, the modeling vendors specify their data structures and encourage other people to write application programs on top of their modeler. In the long term there will probably be more applications written for these systems so a company will have more flexibility in choosing or building applications for its specific needs. If these models are built on top of database managers that allow other applications to directly operate on the database, then this approach can also lead to well-integrated applications.

In many cases today, to preserve the data integrity for the modeler, other applications cannot work directly against the database. The model data must be translated or put into another form for the other applications. This reduces the degree of integration. For example, if the solid model data must be converted into another form before the NC application can be used, then there is little or no integration. The geometry for the NC program may be changed, but the change is not automatically reflected in the solid model. Alternately, the user may have to exit the NC program and enter the solid modeler, change the geometry there, and then reconvert the changed model.

This approach occurs frequently today as a transition phase because most applications need only part of the data in a solid model. This is an example of the file interface approach described in Chapter 4. As CIM shifts from this file-processing approach to a database management approach, this method of passing data to applications will be replaced. The rest of this chapter assumes an integrated database approach.

A solid model provides a complete and consistent definition of a part geometry. (However, recall that more than geometry is needed to completely define a part for manufacturing—for example, tolerances and material type.) It ensures that the part geometry being designed is real and can be manufactured. To provide such integrity, the solid model must maintain and check many complex relationships among the basic geometric and topological entities. This requires a far more complex data model than that required to support three-dimensional wireframe models. The information analysis in the next section shows part of this complex data structure.

As with the other types of geometry, with solid models there is a distinction between how a geometric entity is defined and how it is stored. Each type of geometric entity is usually stored in only one form, although it may be defined in many different ways.

The two main ways of representing three-dimensional solids are constructive solid geometry (CSG) and boundary representation. (A third approach, spacial occupancy, is also possible, but it is ignored in this section because very few systems use it.) These two fundamentally different approaches define the geometry in terms of different types of entities. They are not simply different ways of defining the same types of entities, such as a point. For example, the CSG approach defines a solid model as a combination of primitive solids, with the surfaces defined implicitly as part of the primitives. On the other hand, the boundary representation explicitly defines the surfaces of an object. The enclosed geometry (i.e., what the CSG approach would call primitives) is defined only implicitly.

Initially, solid modelers used one of these two approaches exclusively because these early systems were developed primarily by researchers concentrating on either constructive solid geometry or boundary representation to show the capability of their favored approach. However, as users started evaluating the two approaches, they discovered that some of their applications were best supported by CSG and some by boundary representation.

As a result of this application-oriented evaluation, the two approaches are beginning to merge and to include some of the entities and data structures used by the other. This introduces redundancies in the data models because some implicit data that could be derived is also being stored explicitly. However, as long as the solid modeler knows that this redundancy exists, it can do the necessary integrity checks to ensure that the completeness and consistency of the geometry is maintained.

These redundant data structures are added to the modeler data for one of two reasons. First, some of the redundant data can dramatically improve the performance of some applications. This is especially true for geometric retrieval and manipulation, although there are fewer benefits if the geometry is being modified. Second, nongeometric attributes often need to be attached to specific types of geometric entities, such as surface tolerance or color. This creates a problem if

155

these entities are stored implicitly rather than explicitly. In some cases certain types of entities are thus added explicitly to facilitate defining and maintaining these relationships.

The rest of this section describes constructive solid geometry and boundary representation. This includes the concepts underlying each approach as well as its benefits and problems. It also describes how a simple assembly would be defined using each approach.

The CSG approach uses solid primitives to build up complex solid geometric objects. Typical primitives include box, sphere, cylinder, tetrahedron, torus, ellipsoid, and paraboloid. An instance of a primitive is created by specifying the appropriate parameter values and a position in space.

More complex geometry is built by combining the primitives using three basic operations—subtraction, union, and intersection. Subtraction of the cylinder from the box defines a box with a hole in it. In general, subtraction represents material removal. Union of the box and cylinder results in a box with a cylinderical projection. Union represents an extrusion or connection operation such as welding. The intersection operation requires that the resulting geometry be in both primitives. The physical analogy to this operation is not as clear as with the subtraction and union operations. The order in which the primitives are combined is important only with the subtraction operation.

A complex part geometry is built up using a CSG tree. Figure 10.2 shows a solid model for a simple part, a box with four holes. Figure 10.3 shows a CSG tree that represents this model. This CSG tree is just one of many that could also

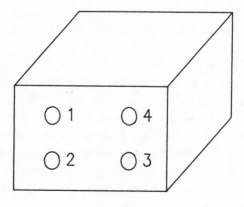

Figure 10.2 Box with holes

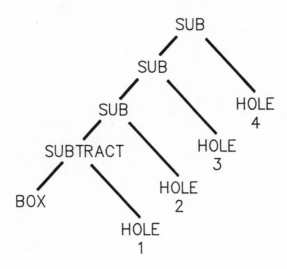

Figure 10.3 CSG tree for box with holes

represent the same model. A CSG tree not only defines the geometry but also specifies how the geometry is created. Each leaf node in the CSG tree is a geometric primitive. Nonleaf nodes are combinations of other geometry and usually represent two pieces of geometry (i.e., two subtrees, each of which is also a CSG tree) as well as the Boolean operation combining them. In some cases the operation at a node is simply a transformation of a set of geometry, in which case the node has only one subtree.

The benefit of the CSG approach is that it is relatively easy to learn and use, especially when compared to wireframe systems. However, there are several problems with the pure CSG approach. First, the CSG tree for an object is not unique. Since the same object can have several representations, it is hard to test for equality. Second, it cannot represent arbitrarily complex geometry because it uses only a basic set of primitives.

To better understand the CSG approach, consider the simple assembly shown in Figure 10.4. It consists of a block and a plate, both with four bolt holes, and the four bolts. Consider the following four operations:

1. Create the assembly.
2. Change the thickness of the bottom block.
3. Change the diameter of the bolt holes.
4. Remove one of the bolt holes.

157

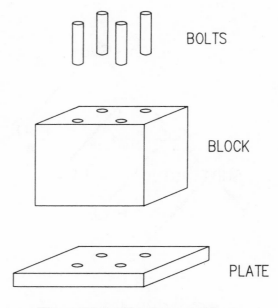

Figure 10.4 Simple assembly

Creating the assembly requires only four solid primitives with four instances of two of the primitives. The model can be constructed using only the union and subtraction operations. One approach is to union the block and the plate. Then the cylinder that represents the bolt holes is subtracted from each of the corners. Finally, the cylinder that represents the bolt is unioned into each of the bolt holes. Figure 10.5 shows the CSG tree from this model.

This approach raises two questions. The first is how to represent multiple use of the same geometry (e.g., the bolt holes and the bolts). Depending on the specific system, this can be done in either of two ways. In any system the designer would create two cylinders, one for the hole and another for the bolt. In some systems the designer would then place four instances of each in the proper locations. The system would automatically maintain the relationship between each instance and the original geometry that defined it. The implication of this approach is that, to change the diameter of the bolt holes, the designer would only have to change the original geometry. Each instance of that geometry is used would be automatically updated to reflect the change. If a system did not have this instancing capability, then the designer would create distinct copies of the geometry and move a copy to each corner. This approach may be slightly faster for the system because it does not have to maintain as many relationships. However, it is harder to use. To change the four bolt holes, the designer would have to explicitly change each one because the system does not realize they are related. Ideally, a system should have the flexibility to allow either the instancing or the copying approach.

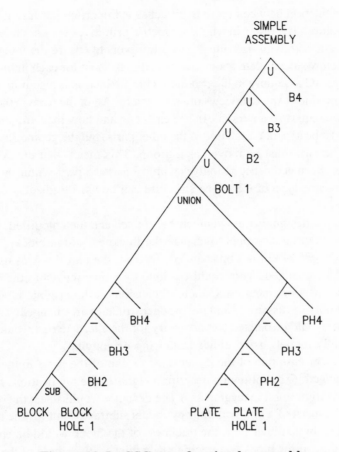

Figure 10.5 CSG tree for simple assembly

The second issue involves the validity of this approach to constructing an assembly. That is, is it necessary to know how the assembly will be built to define the proper CSG model? To understand the problem, consider two cases. First, assume that the base and the plate are really only one piece of material. The model says, in effect, to take the one piece of material, defined by the two geometric primitives, and drill four holes in it. To this single part, then add the four bolts. In this case the construction method is valid. For the second case assume there are two distinct parts in the assembly—a base and a plate, both with the four holes. In the construction method described above these two parts do not exist because the holes are not created until the base and the plate are combined. Therefore, the way in which the model is constructed should be related to how the product is actually assembled. In general, the geometric primitives should be combined to define individual parts. Assemblies should be created using instances or copies of these parts rather than individual geometric primitives.

The distinction between these approaches is important because it affects the product structure. The order in which geometric primitives are combined is essentially irrelevant within an individual part. However, to ensure the integrity of the product structure, a complete geometric model must exist for each individual part, subassembly, and assembly in the product. This distinction is also important if the system is to produce exploded views of an assembly. All of the parts in the assembly must be moved apart so a person can see each one and how they are put together. Each part must be separated relative to the other parts, but the geometric primitives making up the part must be moved as a group. This means that the system must distinguish between geometric primitives within a part and parts within an assembly, although the same type of CSG tree structure can be used to display either parts or assemblies.

During the design process geometry is created and then modified. For example, assume the designer wants to change the thickness of the block. To do this, the assembly itself would not be changed. Instead, the part that was used for the block would be changed. This could be done by either replacing the block part with a thinner part or changing a single dimension on the original block part. In the first case only the assembly and the product structure are changed. The original part geometry would be deleted and geometry for the alternate part would be added to the assembly model, using either instancing or copying.

In the latter case one of the dimensions of one of the parts in the assembly would be changed. (The following description ignores the implications for change control and configuration management.) The designer would select the block part, which would consist of a box with four cylinders subtracted out for the bolt holes. By changing a single dimension, the thickness of the block would be changed. In some cases (e.g., if the block were being made thicker) the length of the cylinders for the holes would also have to be changed. The designer would then have to go back to the assembly model and replace the original block part with the new version of the block. Propagating a change in a part to all of the affected assemblies cannot be done automatically, but there is research in this area.

As a final example of a change, assume you wanted to remove one of the bolt holes. The operation would be the same regardless of whether instancing or copying were used. The designer would indicate the appropriate bolt hole, and it would be removed. With instancing the pointer to the pattern would be removed; with copying the entire copy would be removed.

All of these changes affect the mass properties of the assembly. The mass properties, such as center of gravity and moments of inertia, are calculated from the solid model. However, because of the processing involved, they are not automatically updated whenever the model is changed. They are calculated only when the designer requests it. All the system needs to ensure is that, once the model has been modified, its mass properties are flagged as invalid so that they will not be used until they have been recalculated for the new model.

Now consider how the sample assembly would be defined using a boundary representation geometry. This approach explicitly defines the faces and edges that form the boundaries of the solid while the actual solid is implicit.

How the parts and the assembly are defined is dependent on the capabilities of the system. The most straightforward approach could be used with a very limited system. In this case the base and the plate are each defined as six faces, with each face being defined as a separate operation. The bolt holes would be defined as cylindrical surfaces. The bolts would be defined by cylindrical surfaces with planar surfaces at each end. As with the approach using solid primitives, the base and plate would be similar parts but with different thicknesses. The holes would exist independently in each part rather than as a single cylindrical surface passing through both parts.

With more powerful modeling capabilities the same surfaces and edges would define the part, but the construction method would be easier. For example, with some systems the designer could create a two-dimensional square with four circles in it. Assume this were done in the xy plane. This entire figure could be swept or moved perpendicular in the z plane for the thickness of the base. This sweep operation on a surface creates a solid. (Some solid primitive systems also allow this sweep operation on certain types of surfaces.) However, in a pure boundary representation approach the sweep operation is actually performed on the curves or edges defining the surfaces. The four edges of the square are swept in the z plane to form four of the sides of the base while the circles form the holes.

As mentioned earlier, these surfaces implicitly define the solid part, whereas with the CSG approach the solid primitives implicitly define the surfaces. However, both of these representations provide a complete geometric definition.

Conversion between these representations, subject to certain limitations, is possible but not necessarily easy. The main problem is that the CSG representation of a part is not unique, whereas the boundary representation does provide a unique representation. A second problem involves the set of curves and surfaces that can be modeled in the two systems. Regular solid primitives have regular, well-defined surfaces so there is no problem converting between them. On the other hand, the boundary representation approach frequently provides more flexibility by allowing the designer to create irregular curves and surfaces. These irregular geometries do not translate easily back into regular primitives.

One of two approaches is used to solve this problem. First, some systems do not allow the designer to create geometric objects that cannot be converted. In the past this has not been a problem because the usual conversion path has been from the more limited solid primitives to the more general boundary representation as a step along the path to a wireframe or two-dimensional drawing. However, the actual model was always defined in terms of the solid primitives. The conversion in either direction will become more important in the future when a single model may be defined in terms of both solid primitive and boundary representation entities and the system must maintain the consistency of the model.

The second approach is to provide an exact and an approximate model. This approach is adequate for some applications but not for others. Approximations are usually not accurate enough for NC program generation. Depending on specific cases they may or may not be accurate enough for mass properties or interference analysis. Approximations are usually adequate for display and animation applications, except where the animation is done for interference analysis. In fact, improving the display performance is one of the main uses of this type of approximation.

Most modeling systems allow the designer to create an exact model. However, some of the algorithms for these models can be very time-consuming for display and some analysis. Therefore, for better performance some systems will create for the user a polygonal approximation of this exact model. In a polygonal model all of the surfaces are approximated by regular polygons. In principle, any degree of accuracy is possible by using small enough polygons. The designer can then display, move, and analyze this approximate model very quickly. The approximate model can be used for experimentation and refinement. To get the final results, the exact model can then be used. With some systems all the manipulation is done directly against the exact model, with the approximate model used only for display. However, approximate models are a valuable tool, especially for complicated models. In the future, however, they will become less important as processing power (especially in the form of special high-speed chips for geometric processing) and memory increase.

Systems that support these approximate models require a slightly more complicated data model. The complication is not with the approximation model itself because all of these systems can support a model of that complexity. The complication is that there are now two models of the same part and the relationship between them must be maintained. An analysis is not done on a part; it is done on a specific model of that part. Furthermore, the system must keep track of the congruency of the two models (e.g., which approximate model was derived from which exact model) and have changes in one reflected in the other.

Information Analysis

Geometry

This section describes an information analysis for a subset of the geometry needed for CIM. The subset is large enough to show the complexity of a logical data model for geometry and to support most of the operations described earlier in the chapter. It is not a complete data model for geometry, which is beyond the scope of this book.

Companies can use this information analysis model as a starting point for designing their own geometric database for CAD/CAM or preferably for understanding the design of a vendor's database so they can extend it to better meet their own needs. Extensions would usually take one of two forms. In some cases they would add new types of geometric entities (e.g., a torus solid or surface), while in other cases new facts or attributes would be added to existing geometric entities (e.g., reflectivity or tolerance for a surface). Nongeometric entities and attributes could also be added to the database. The database design methodolgy described in Chapter 6 can be used to identify the needed enhancements and determine how they should be added to the database.

Figure 10.6 shows some of the many types of data that are associated with a part. Some of those data involve geometry. Within geometry there is a hierarchy of subtypes. At one level geometric entities can be subdivided into basic, curve, surface, and solid entity subtypes. Each of these subtypes can be further divided into subtypes.

Figure 10.7 shows the diagram for these basic subtypes. All of the basic subtypes have certain facts in common, while other facts relate only to specific types of basic objects. The common facts for all basic object types include name/identifier, type (i.e., constant or variable), and definition. For this example, the definition can be considered simply a text string of the command creating the object. (In a more complete analysis the definition would have a more detailed structure, some of which would be dependent on specific subtypes of objects.) Basic objects, shown in Figure 10.8, have three subtypes—scalar, point, and vector. A scalar has an identifier and a current value.

Points and vectors have both geometric and display attributes. The geometric facts about a point involve an identifier and a current value. The current value for a point is a coordinate triple (xyz) or some other coordinate system. The display characteristics indicate whether the point is blanked or unblanked (i.e., whether or not it should be displayed) and its point display mode. The display mode indicates how the point should be displayed, (e.g., as a dot, a small circle, an X, or with some other symbol and perhaps the color in which it should be displayed). A point (or any other displayable geometry) has a display mode, regardless of whether it is actually displayed.

A vector also has an identifier and a current value. However, a vector current value is not the same as a point current value. A vector current value includes a base point, a direction, and a length. A point and a vector can be related through the role of base point. Length is a role relating a vector and a scalar. Blank and unblank serve the same function with a vector and a point. The display mode for a vector includes a line and an arrow. A vector could be displayed as a solid, broken, or dotted line in a color.

Curves are a subtype of object at the same level as basic objects. Common facts for all curves include identifier, type, blank/unblank, display mode, and definition. Display characteristics can be related to curves at this level because all curves have the same display characteristics whereas with basic objects each subtype has a different display mode. There are many different subtypes of curves, including line, circle, ellipse, parabola, hyperbola, splines, and composite curves. (Note that

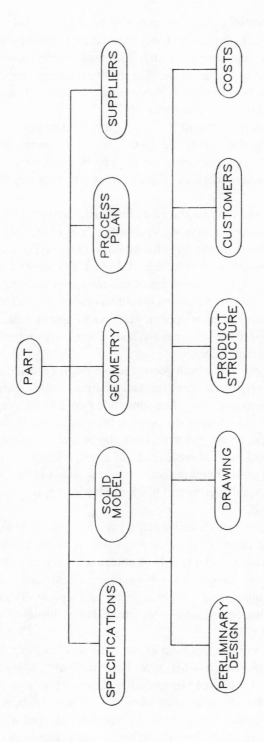

Figure 10.6   Data associated with a part

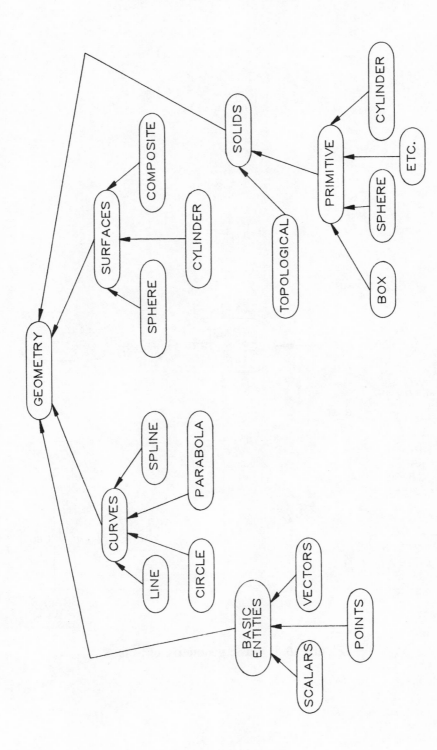

Figure 10.7 Geometric subtypes

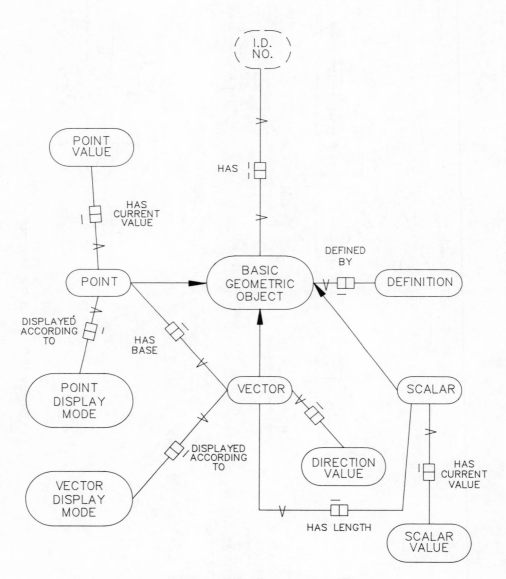

Figure 10.8 Basic geometric objects

all of these curves could be defined as either two- or three-dimensional objects. In this example assume they are three-dimensional because they can be used to construct solids.)

A line has an identifier. This is the same as the curve identifier and relates the two sets of information. A line is also related to two points, one in the role of starting point and one in the role of ending point.

Figure 10.9 shows the models for circles, a spherical surface, and a solid sphere. A circle has an identifier. It is also related to a scalar, which has the role of radius. This scalar has a current value and can be either constant or variable. A circle must have a position and orientation in space. This is provided by an object called a local coordinate system.

A local coordinate system (LCS) has an identifier and relates a point and three vectors. The point has the role of the origin of the LCS. The three vectors define the axes of the LCS. Obviously, various geometric objects can be related by having the same LCS, the same origin, or by using any of the three vectors in some way.

An ellipse has an identifier. It is related to two scalars, which have the role of major and minor axis length. The position and orientation of the ellipse are defined by a local coordinate system.

Most of the other curves can be defined in similar ways. However, splines and composite curves are different. A spline is a special type of curve that has been fitted to pass through a number of points. There are many different subtypes of splines, which are defined differently although they all involve an ordered set of points.

A composite curve is the final subtype that will be described here. A composite curve is simply an ordered set of curves with each curve forming a segment of the composite curve. A composite curve has simply an identifier and a scalar, which is the number of segments it contains.

A segment is identified by the identifier of the composite curve of which it is a part and a sequence number reflecting its order in the composite curve. A segment is also related to one of the other curve subtypes. Finally, a segment is related to two points, in the roles of starting and ending point. There is a constraint on segment data so that the end point of segment i must be the same as the start point of segment $i + 1$. Because of the way segments are identified, they can occur only once and therefore can be related to only one composite curve. However, a composite curve can have a number of segments, and a curve can be used to define any number of segments. (More precise geometric and topological terminology distinguishes between unbounded curves and edges delimited by starting and ending spots. These edges are then used to bound surfaces. This example simplifies some of these distinctions and reserves edges only to bound surfaces.)

There are three subtypes of surfaces—primitive, topological, and composite. A primitive surface is the surface for a solid primitive. The same set of parameters can define either a solid or a surface. In some cases the solid is defined explicitly

CURVES

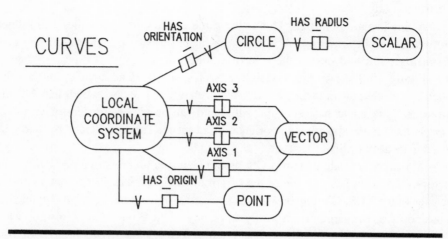

SURFACES

SOLID

**Figure 10.9 Information model for circle, surface sphere, and solid
sphere**

and the surface is implicit. The primitive surface subtype provides a way to make this surface definition explicit if necessary—for example, so that attributes can be attached to it. A topological surface is one defined in terms of edges and faces. A composite surface is analogous to a composite curve and is defined by an ordered set of surfaces. Each of these subtypes has a specific data structure. However, there are certain common attributes of all surfaces.

All surfaces have an identifier. They also have a type (primitive, topological, or composite), a blank/unblank indicator, a surface display mode, and a definition. A surface may also be related explicitly to a solid. The relationship can be in either direction. The surface can be part of the definition of a solid or the solid may define one or more surfaces. Finally, if a solid is involved, the surface has a vector to define its normal, which indicates which side of the surface the material is on.

Primitives also involve several subtypes. Examples include sphere, box, cone, tetrahedron, cylinder, and paraboloid. The data structure for several of these object types is included under primitive solids because these primitives are usually defined as solids rather than as surfaces.

Topological surfaces (sometimes called faces) are defined by an ordered collection of edges that form a closed loop. A face has an identifier and the number of edges.

An edge has an identifier, a starting point, and an ending point (also called a vertex). The ending point of one edge must be the starting point of the next edge. The start and end points imply a direction for edge. All of the edges in the closed loop defining a face must go in the same direction. In the relationship between edge and face, only the combination is unique. A face is related to more than one edge. Similarly, an edge can be used to define two or more faces. However, when this happens, the edge must have the same direction in all of the loops.

As an example of the use of these relationships, consider the base of the assembly described earlier. Using the CSG construction, the parameters defined the solid box. The same parameters also defined a box surface. Similarly, there were cylindrical surfaces corresponding to the cylindrical solids that were subtracted to create the holes.

The relationships are more complex using the boundary representation. The designer can specify the edges and the faces they create and relate them all to form the box. Given that all the faces combine to form a solid, the system knows the types of geometric constraints that must be enforced and can check them. The other construction method involved defining a square in the xy plane and sweeping it through the z plane. Sweeping each side of the square (an edge) through space defines a surface. One side of the original square forms one edge. The movement of the starting and ending points form two other edges. The fourth edge is formed by the ending position of the original edge after the sweeping operation.

This example shows why the sweeping operation is so powerful. The designer has to specify only a small part of the geometry. The sweeping operation allows the system to automatically generate much of the geometry.

Features

This section shows the difference with feature-based design by describing a specific feature, a hole. A feature-based design system would support many features — such as holes (threaded and unthreaded), slots, and chamfers.

A feature type, such as a hole, includes certain parameters which define it and other parameters which position it on the part. For example, a simple hole has a diameter and a depth, with tolerances on each dimension. A simple hole is assumed to be normal to the surface, but an additional parameter could be specified for the angle the hole makes with the parts surface. For a threaded hole there would be additional parameters to define the threads.

Additional parameters would specify the position of the hole on the part. As with defining any point, the CAD system would provide many ways to specify where to place the hole.

Obviously, the hole and its position could be defined directly in terms of geometry, although it would be more difficult. The benefit of feature-based design is twofold. First, features are easier to define and place. Second, features are treated and stored as an explicit set of geometry, to which additional attributes can be attached. This eases subsequent processing, such as process planning. For example, given a set of standard-sized holes, the drill bit needed to drill the hole could be attached to each standard-sized hole. This would make process planning much easier since it no longer has to analyze the detailed geometry to identify the features to be machined.

Feature-based design is relatively new, but in the future it will be added to many existing CAD systems, and most new CAD systems will include it.

Summary

Geometry is the most widely shared type of data in CIM. This chapter has provided an overview of the development of the CAD applications that capture and manage this type of data. It has also explained the underlying concepts, benefits, and problems of each of the major geometric representations — two-dimensional, three-dimensional wireframe, and three-dimensional solids. It described an information model for storing geometric data in a database. Finally, it briefly explained why feature-based design is a significant improvement over simple geometric design.

11

Analysis

Parameterized Design

Simple Calculations on the Actual Design

Complex Calculations on an Idealized Design

Simulation

Information Model for Analysis

Summary

This chapter describes how analysis fits into the design and manufacturing process and how it is integrated with the rest of the process. The chapter also shows the basic information model to support various types of analysis.

Analysis is a complex area because there are many different types of analysis — static and dynamic, linear and nonlinear, rigid and deformable bodies, and others. The specific types of analysis needed depend on the part and its requirements. Therefore, this chapter cannot explain how to do specific types of analysis — entire books are devoted to specific techniques such as finite element analysis or simulation. Instead, it identifies four levels of analysis and the information modeling implications of each level. The four levels are as follows:

- parameterized design
- simple calculations on the actual design
- complex calculations on an idealized design
- simulation

Parameterized Design

Parameterized design is an effective approach for relatively simple parts and assemblies. This approach integrates the design and analysis steps. The design rules are provided for a specific type of part or part family, and the designer simply specifies the parameters needed by the design rules.

For example, to design a bracket to support a shelf, the parameters include the length and width of the shelf and the weight to be supported. Given these data, a parameterized design routine can design the bracket by specifying its geometry and the material. No further analysis would be needed.

Parameterized design is similar to design retrieval. In both cases the designer provides a set of parameters (or part characteristics), and the system provides a design. The difference is that with parameterized design a new design is created each time. The system does not recognize that a similar or even identical design already exists and can be reused. As long as the parameters are within the scope of the design rules, the system always generates a new design. On the other hand, with design retrieval the system searches through the set of existing designs to find one that can be reused. While this minimizes design proliferation, sometimes it will not be able to find an appropriate design. The ideal approach would be a combination: given a set of parameters, find an appropriate existing design if one exists; otherwise create a new parameterized design.

Parameterized design creates no special problems for the information models normally used for design. All it needs is part geometry, material type, and some basic material properties. Some of these data are entered as parameters, and others are calculated during the design process.

Today this approach is used primarily for relatively simple parts. In the future, however, with more sophisticated rule-based expert systems, parameterized design will be able to deal with more complex designs.

Simple Calculations on the Actual Design

The difference between simple and complex calculations as levels of analysis relates to the interaction between the complexity of the part geometry and the complexity of the analysis.

Simple calculations are those done directly against the actual design geometry. At one extreme there are simple geometries and simple analyses that permit analytical solutions. In one sense parameterized design fits this criterion, except that it involves integrating the design and analysis functions into a single step. The other three types of analysis require two distinct steps: a design is first created, and then it is analyzed.

Simple calculations can become more complicated in one of two ways. First, the geometry can become more complex. Calculations that are simple and quick on simple geometry can become intractable as the geometry becomes more complex. For example, analysis algorithms that take a few seconds if the design is limited to planar surfaces may become prohibitive with sculptured surfaces such as airfoils.

Similarly, the analysis routines themselves can become more complex. Some analyses can be solved analytically, while others require extensive numerical approximations. Furthermore, some analyses that can be done analytically with simple geometries require numerical approximations as the geometry becomes more complex.

At some point a threshold is crossed. The combination of geometric and analysis complexity becomes intractable. This is the borderline between simple and complex calculations.

As with parametric design, simple calculations do not seriously affect the information model. The model includes design geometry, material type, material properties, and analysis results, where the last three types of data can be attached directly to the design geometry. Because these calculations are simple and cheap, several design versions may be proposed and analyzed before the final design is accepted and released. To support this, the information model only needs to include the concept of design versions.

Complex Calculations on an Idealized Design

The dividing line between simple and complex calculations is subjective and depends in part on the available computational resources. A problem that would require complex calculation methods on a workstation might be done on a supercomputer as a simple calculation (i.e., using the actual part geometry).

The difference is that with complex calculations the analyst no longer directly analyzes the actual design geometry. The analysis is done on a simplified or "idealized" geometry. For example, for the analysis a complex curve may be approximated by line segments or a complex surface may be approximated by planar surfaces. (Some solid modeling systems already use both an actual model for analysis and an idealized or faceted model for rapid display and animation.) The reason for this idealization of the geometry is so the analysis can be done in a reasonable time and for an acceptable cost.

This transition to an idealized geometry requires a fundamental change in the information model. Instead of a single design geometry, there are now at least two distinct geometries that must be related. This creates two types of problems.

First, given an actual design geometry, the designer or analyst must abstract or transform it into an idealized geometry for the analysis. However, the idealized geometry is not unique. Depending on the type of analysis (e.g., static or dynamic, structural or thermal, linear or nonlinear), the idealized models can be different. Furthermore, for the same type of analysis different analysts can transform the same actual geometry into different idealized geometry. Therefore, the first problem involves providing the necessary links between the actual geometry and the idealized geometry to be analyzed.

The second problem occurs after the analysis. The analysis results are in terms of the idealized, not the actual, geometry. Therefore, a similar problem exists in inferring what the analysis results mean in terms of actual geometry.

Finite element analysis is the most common example of analyzing an idealized model rather than the actual design geometry. There are three basic ways in which a complex geometry can be simplified for analysis. First, non critical aspects of the design can be eliminated. For example, in an analysis to model an automobile crash, the side trim is irrelevant and can be eliminated. The decorative or ornamental features of the design geometry can usually be eliminated. They often have very complex geometry that would make the analysis more difficult and time-consuming, and they contribute nothing to the part's structural integrity. Second, complex curves and surfaces can be approximated with simpler ones, such as line segments and planar surfaces. This can speed up the analysis without affecting the accuracy of results if the approximations are small enough. Third, if the part is symmetric, then only one part of it needs to be analyzed since the results will be the same for the other parts.

Today these simplifications are made by experienced analysts who understand the assumption underlying each simplification and its effects on the analysis results. The trade-off is between more simplification to make the analysis faster and cheaper versus less simplification to provide more accurate results. In the future more of this idealization will be done by expert systems using the rules obtained from these analysts.

An example of this trend is with adaptive mesh generation for finite element models. Automatic mesh generation has been possible for many years, but this was a static approach. It simply provided an initial mesh that the analyst could then modify as necessary to obtain a better analysis. The newer adaptive mesh generation is a more complex, iterative approach. It automatically generates an initial mesh and then runs the analysis. Based on the results, it then generates a finer mesh in areas of high stress and reruns the analysis. This process is repeated until the results with the finer mesh converge with the previous results. Today adaptive mesh generation is adequate for some problems and can almost replace the analyst, but for complex problems involving geometric nonlinearity, large deflections, and plasticity an experienced analyst is still essential. However, the capability of adaptive mesh generation is rapidly improving.

For the information model the critical aspect of idealizing the geometry is that for any analysis two distinct geometries must be related, and the analysis results must be related to the actual design geometry. This linkage can be done at either a macro or a micro level. At the macro level the link is between the overall design geometry and its idealized model (i.e., the design file is linked to the idealized model file, and they are both linked to the analysis output file). This is the approach described in the design retrieval chapter for relating various types of design documentation. This approach is relatively simple and can be done today. However, it does not automatically relate the analysis results to the design geometry. This step must be done manually by an analyst.

With the micro approach the connections are made at the geometric object level rather than at the overall design level. For example, if a complex curve has been approximated by a set of line segments, when a problem occurs along one of those line segments the system could directly relate the problem to the more complex curve in the actual design. Although this approach is beyond the capability of today's systems, it is a direction for the future.

Simulation

Simulation adds still another level of complexity to analysis. All of the previous types of analysis are deterministic: solve one of these problems once, and you have the answer, regardless of whether the algorithm is analytical or numeric.

Simulation, however, usually involves some random processes. Its results are like a single run of an experiment. You need to do a statistical analysis of a set of experimental results, and the larger the number of runs, the more confidence you have in the results. Therefore, with simulation you need to store, relate, and analyze the several sets of analysis results. This level of complexity is not incurred with the other analysis levels.

This definition of simulation is the more traditional one. It is not the same as a numerical simulation of a test, such as a crash test of a car. If a car hits a barrier with the same speed, angle, and orientation, then the results will be essentially the same. This not the same type of simulation considered here because there are no random processes. However, the distinction can become fuzzy.

You can run multiple crashes under different conditions. Each crash analysis or "simulation" would provide a deterministic result, but the set of results could be treated as multiple runs of a crash experiment. The results could then be summarized statistically. This approach would be similar to the simulation level of analysis described in this section, as long as the variations between "experiments" involved external factors and not design variations. If they were design variations, then there would multiple design versions, but each with only one set of analysis results—i.e., it would not involve this level of analysis.

Information Model for Analysis

Figure 11.1 shows a high-level information model to support various levels of analysis. A part has an actual design that consists of geometric features. The geometric features have parameters, which may be specified in the design or calculated as part of an analysis. Geometric features are also made of material with material properties. The analysis may be done on either the actual design or on an idealized design derived from the actual design. The analysis is done using an analysis code and produces analysis results. In most cases an analysis produces only one set of results, but with simulation it can produce multiple sets of results.

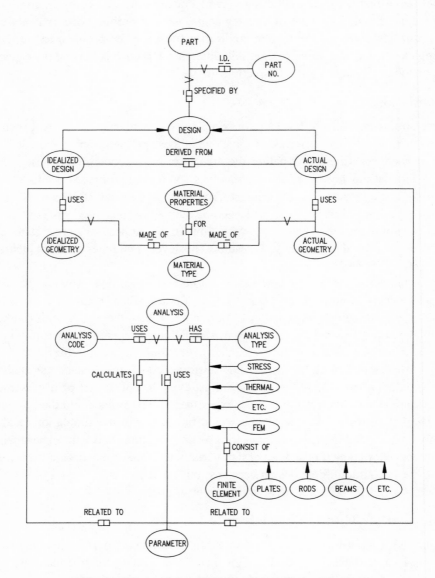

Figure 11.1 Information model for analysis

For the micro level linkage individual actual geometric features are related to the idealized geometry used to represent them. At the macro level the only connection is between the actual design and an idealized design. There can be many idealized designs for a single actual design. For finite element analysis the idealized geometry is related to specific finite elements or various types, such as plates, rods, or beams.

Summary

This chapter has described at a high level an information model for analysis. It discussed how the model becomes more complex for four different levels of analysis—parameterized design, simple calculations on the actual design, complex calculations on an idealized design, and simulation.

12

Process Planning/ Manufacturing Engineering

What Is Process Planning?

Computer-Aided Process Planning

Process Plans

Numerical Control

Generative Computer-Aided Process Planning

Summary

Once a part or product has been designed, the critical question becomes how to manufacture it. This chapter describes process planning, the bridge between design and manufacturing. The process planner (or manufacturing engineer) determines how to manufacture a specific product.

This chapter uses several terms that are essentially interchangeable, although some people make a subtle distinction between them. Process planning and manufacturing engineering in their broadest context are the same function. The main output of the process planning function is a detailed set of instructions for manufacturing the product. This output is called either a process plan or a routing. Manufacturing is used as a generic term to include both fabrication (e.g., machining) and assembly, although some people use manufacturing to mean only fabrication. In this chapter the generic term *manufacturing* will be used unless it is important to distinguish between fabrication and assembly.

This chapter first explains what process planning is and identifies two basic types of computer-aided process planning—variant and generative process planning. Then, it provides a more detailed description of what a process plan contains and shows a basic information model to relate the various objects in a process plan. It also describes the development of numerical control and its relationship to process planning. Finally, it offers a description of an algorithm for generative process planning and a simplified information model to support it.

What Is Process Planning?

Process planning is done once a part or product has been designed. A manufacturing engineer determines exactly how the part or product will be manufactured. The process plan specifies how the individual piece parts will be fabricated and how they will be put together into subassemblies and assemblies. Process planning identifies the manufacturing processes, the order in which they will be done, the types of machine tools to be used, the raw material, the design of any special tools and fixtures, and any necessary detailed instructions for the machine operators at each step.

In reality process planning is not this simple and the bridge between design and manufacturing is not always smooth. Many companies have separate engineering and manufacturing bills of material and have trouble resolving the difference. This difference occurs because most designers are not well trained in manufacturing processes and cost trade-offs. Therefore, to improve produceability, the design they send to manufacturing is often changed during process planning. However, these changes must be approved by the design engineers to ensure that the "as-built" design still meets all the original design requirements.

For example, some shapes are much easier to machine than others. If the exact shape is not critical, the process planner may change it to an equivalent one that is easier to machine. In some cases a designer may specify tighter tolerances than are necessary. Machining to finer tolerances increases the machining costs and the reject rate, so the process planner may suggest looser tolerances where they are feasible. Finally, a process planner may suggest using different raw material, perhaps one that is already in the inventory. In summary, process planning does not simply take a design and decide how to manufacture it. Process planning involves analysis and refinement of the original design for improved produceability and lower cost.

Today some of the distinctions between design and process planning are artifical. They occur because design engineers are not well trained in manufacturing processes and do not have the tools they need to evaluate the produceability of their designs. In the future with the appropriate tools the designs released to manufacturing engineering will already be refined for produceability. Then the process planners can concentrate on how to manufacture the product rather than second-guess the designers' intentions.

Manufacturing Cost/Design Guidelines (MC/DG), an ICAM program, provides a preview of this closer linkage.[1] Today designers consider material properties and design requirements to decide whether a part should be made of metal or plastic. They may use their experience or a more formal analysis program to determine which material to use. However, when they identify several alternate materials, they probably do not know the detailed cost and manufacturing implications. With MC/DG designers can evaluate the alternatives using the MC/DG database. Assume the design calls for a hole to be drilled with a certain tolerance in the part. The system will indicate the cost for drilling that hole in each type of material – specifically the costs based on the machine tools the company has. It will also show how the costs are affected by changing the tolerance on the hole. A design guidelines database allows this same type of analysis for all of the features to be machined on the part.

This type of system can be used by either the original designer or by the process planner who is trying to refine the design for produceability. An MC/DG system provides designers with the data they need to make the most of these trade-offs. They can release a more produceable design to process planning. This approach requires less manual, time-consuming, and iterative communications between the process planner and the designer than if the planner modifies the design for produceability. For the process planner this system simply makes it easier to evaluate the various trade-offs and consider more alternatives. Furthermore, the data needed by this system are the same type needed by generative process planning systems to identify and evaluate manufacturing alternatives.

Computer-Aided Process Planning

Today few CIM systems address process planning in its broader context. Although there are some computer-aided process planning (CAPP) products by vendors of specialized systems, most CAPP activity involves cooperative research and development projects with manufacturing companies, universities, and government. For example, some of the ICAM projects involve process planning, and there is a CAPP project within CAM-I.[2] Several companies such as Metcut and OIR have products that aid in process planning and optimization, and some expert-systems work involves process planning because these applications require evaluating a complex set of rules.

There are two basic types of computer-aided process planning systems – variant (or adaptive) and generative systems. Pure variant systems provide more administrative than technical support. They allow a process planner to find and retrieve existing process plans for specific parts or generic plans for a part family. A new process plan is then created by making the necessary modification to the existing one. In effect, this is the design retrieval applied to process planning.

A variant process planning system only helps the process planner identify similar parts (i.e., similar with respect to how they are manufactured) and retrieves and edits existing process plans to create plans for new parts. It does not help decide how to change the plan or how to optimize it. It is more like a word processing application than an engineering one. These limited variant systems were developed because even this limited support is better than nothing. Just as design retrieval and standard parts help a company lower its costs by reducing redundant design effort, variant process planning helps a company standardize its manufacturing operations.

The generative process planning approach does the analysis to generate a process plan from scratch. It starts with data about the part geometry, the material type, the company's machine tools, and machineability data. It then identifies and evaluates various manufacturing alternatives for manufacturing the part. This involves determining which operations to do on which machine tools, with which tools and fixtures, and under what conditions (e.g., feeds and speeds). An example of the types of analysis used by these algorithms is found in the section on generative computer-aided process planning later in this chapter.

Most of the current work on CAPP focuses on the generative approach because of its greater potential payoffs. Today's generative CAPP systems are limited in the type of parts they cover. For example, several years ago United Technologies described a generative process planning application that the company had developed internally.[3] However, it was limited to turned titanium parts. These systems are also limited by the fact that the decision rules and analyses for current systems are hard-wired into the application code. Rule-based expert systems technology will provide much greater flexibility.

Another problem with most of the generative systems today is that they take the part design as a given and concentrate on how to manufacture that design most effectively. They lack the sophistication to vary the design within certain constraints to improve its produceability and reduce costs. However, this is only a current limitation. Additional decision rules can be added in the future to allow them to make this type of trade-off.

Process Plans

A process plan explains how to make a single type of part, which may be an individual piece part, an assembly, or a complete product. Therefore, a process plan can involve fabrication and/or assembly. Normally the same process plan cannot be followed to produce different parts. Although a family process plan describes generically how to produce a part family, it is not yet detailed enough to specify an individual part.

The process plan for a part is not unique. There are usually many different ways to make any part. A process plan simply specifies one consistent set of operations that will produce the part. However, a part may have several process plans for several reasons. If a part may be made at several plants with differents sets of machine tools, then there may be a different process plan for each plant. Different process plans may also be needed for different lot sizes. With a small lot size flexibility is important, so that plan would call for machine tools with very fast stepups, even if the cutting time may be slower. For large lot sizes the machining time would dominate the setup time, so that plan would emphasize rapid cutting rather than setup. In both of these cases there are certain criteria (e.g., plant or lot size) for picking a specific process plan. Once the plan is picked it is followed precisely.

A process plan consists of several parts. First, there is basic information that identifies the part, its version, and any special conditions for selecting the plan — e.g., the plant or lot size for which the plan was developed.

Second, the body of the plan consists of a series of steps. The size of step can vary, but essentially a step defines the operations on a specific machine tool or work center (a set of related machine tools). An operation consists of processes to be done on a specific machine tool. For example, a step may involve attaching fixture ABC to machine tool X, loading and aligning a workpiece in the fixture, and drilling four one-inch-diameter holes at certain points on the workpiece using drill bit 123. The step could involve another process, such as changing the drill bit and drilling several additional holes or changing the orientation of the part in the fixture and drilling additional holes.

If the part is unloaded from this machine and loaded onto another one for additional processing (e.g., grinding), then there is another step in the process plan. Some steps in the process plan may involve assembly rather than machining. In some cases, such as in a work cell, the next step is done on a nearby machine tool, but proximity is not a requirement. For complex products subsequent steps in the process plan may be done at different plants.

To manufacture the part, each step in the process plan is performed in sequence. At some points a plan specifies alternate steps. For example, a set of holes could be drilled on one machine tool using a certain fixture and drill, or it could be drilled on an alternate machine tool using a different fixture and drill. Alternate steps identify changes that can be made when the part is scheduled on the shop floor. If one type of machine tool is down or is busy with priority work, the alternate step can be done. However, the machine tool operator normally sees only the step to be done, not the alternatives.

Each step in the process plan specifies the machine tool (by type, not by specific unit on the shop floor). There are no clear guidelines for how much to include in a single step. Therefore, a step may consist of one or more operations. For example, a step that involves milling a part of a specific machine tool may consist of several operations — one operation for each surface to be machined. The operation specifies any fixtures that are needed, the specific tools (such as drills or grinders), and the workpiece. It also provides detailed instructions for setting up the machine for the workpiece and machining a single part. If the step involves an NC machine, the process plan (at either the step or the operation) identifies the NC program. Inspection criteria are also included in the process plan either as an integral part of a step or as separate steps. The entire process is summarized in the information model shown in Figure 12.1.

Two changes are occurring in process planning. Traditionally, some operations are done on a part, and then it is inspected. Additional operations are done on the part, and then there is another inspection. The problem with this approach is that there is too much delay before the part is inspected. This can mean expensive rework or scrap because an entire batch may be completed before the inspection is done. And often only a sample of the parts in the batch are actually inspected. Ideally, quality control should be an integral part of the processing. This involves adaptive control.

Adaptive control monitors and adjusts the process while it is still occurring. For example, sensing tool wear during the machining process allows the operator to either replace the worn tool or adjust for the tool wear so the part is still within tolerance. In the future, new process plans will reflect this improved form of quality control.

The other change is occurring because companies are reorganizing the shop floor into work centers. In the past the same types of machine tools were clustered together. Workpieces had to move all through the factory to use different types of machine tools. Now, especially with group technology, companies are rearranging the factory to establish work centers or workcells. This involves clustering all of the machine tools needed to manufacture a specific group of parts. This minimizes the movement of the workpiece around the shop floor. Traditionally, NC programs were written for individual machine tools. Loading and unloading a machine tool and the interface between machine tools were manual processes not considered by the NC program. In the future, the operations for entire workcells, not simply individual machine tools, should be planned and programmed. Both integrated inspection and integrated NC programs involve major extensions to numerical control systems and a move toward flexible manufacturing systems. Therefore, the next section explains the basics of numerical control and the trends leading in this direction. Flexible manufacturing systems are described in Chapter 16.

Numerical Control

The most common manufacturing function provided by today's CIM systems is numerical control program generation. These systems use the part geometry already in the CAD system to define the tool path part of the NC program. NC program generation is part of process planning since it involves creating some of the detailed instructions for manufacturing a part. However, it is only one small part of process planning. Before the NC program can be generated, the process planner has already decided which manufacturing processes are needed, which machine tools are to be used, and even which part of the machining is to be done on which type of machine tool.

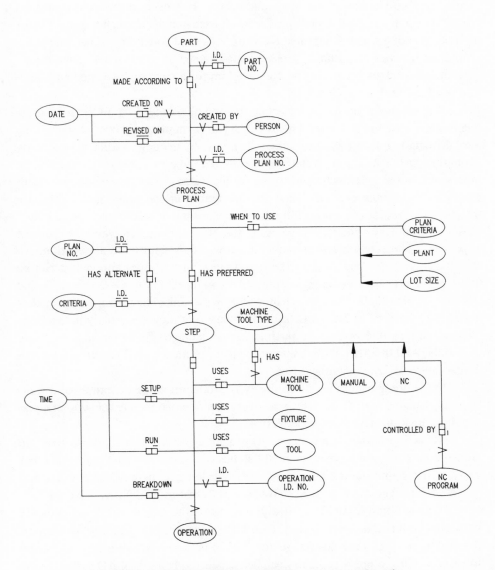

Figure 12.1   Information model for process planning

Originally, NC involved only a few types of machine tools such as drills, milling machines, and lathes. Now it applies to a much broader range of machine tools, including coordinate measuring machines for inspection and work centers made up of collections of machines and robots. However, in most work centers the NC programming is done independently for each individual machine tool. Today's systems do not generate integrated NC programs for a collection of machine tools. Although robotics is discussed in a separate chapter, in many ways robotics programming involves generating an NC program for a very sophisticated and flexible machine tool.

The process plan, the engineering drawing, and other part information show the machine tool operator how to machine the part. A numerically controlled machine gets its detailed operating instructions from an NC program rather than directly from the machinist. The machine tool operator can override the NC program when necessary, but as systems become more sophisticated, this will happen less often.

NC machining provides much greater precision and repeatability than if a machinist were directly controlling the machine tool. It also makes producing a different part easy — simply by changing the NC program. However, NC is not a panacea. The actual machining may be slower than with fixed automation. An NC machine tool is also more expensive than a manual one, although it can be more productive because its higher precision and repeatability mean less scrap and rework. Of the installed base of machine tools in the United States has only a modest percentage consists of NC tools (estimates vary, but they are usually in the 10 to 20 percent range). However, a much larger percentage of new machine tools are NC tools. And in terms of the value of the parts produced, NC represents a much larger share of U.S. manufacturing.

NC is not appropriate if a company is producing large quantities of a standard, unchanging part. Even if the part is very complex and requires close tolerances, fixed automation will be more effective.

NC is appropriate if a company is producing small or medium lot sizes. In some cases it may be producing small batches of custom-designed parts. In other cases it may be producing a standard part, but doing so in small batches to hold down inventory costs, as with KANBAN or JIT (Just-in-Time) inventory control.

If, in addition to small or medium lot sizes, the part geometry is complex or if close tolerances are required, then NC is appropriate. The repeatability of the NC is a significant advantage for both complex part geometry and close tolerances. The complex geometry can be transferred from the CAD system to the NC program generation application, eliminating human errors that can occur if the design must be manually transferred and interpreted.

NC is also favored if the part design changes frequently. This can occur during design if physical prototypes are made and refined. However, CIM systems are reducing the need for these physical prototypes, which are being replaced by more sophisticated analysis and by numerical prototypes. Design changes also occur as

186

a product evolves. Finally, customized products also involve many frequent design changes, which also result in small lot sizes, in some cases with lots of one. The ease of going from a new part geometry to the new NC program also favors NC.

As was mentioned earlier, NC programming is only one small part of process planning. Recall that a process plan consists of many steps, each performed on a different machine tool. Some of these tools are numerically controlled. An NC program is a set of instructions for one of these machine tools.

Generating an NC program involves three steps: part programming, tape preparation, and tape verification. The basic step in the process is part programming. The part program defines the part geometry to be machined and specifies the necessary machine commands, such as feed and speed rates and coolant function. The program generated at this point is in a neutral form called the CL (cutter centerline) file. While it describes the precise part geometry, the machine commands are in a generic form. For example, it includes generic commands for "coolant on" and "coolant off." However, specific machine tools have specific commands for each of these machine operations. A postprocessor program for the specific machine tool to be used converts the CL file program into the exact program for the specific machine tool. This is tape preparation. This tape is verified ultimately by actually running it on the machine and checking the part that is produced to make sure that it is the part as it was designed. However, since this requires use of a machine tool either in the NC program development group or on the shop floor, it is an expensive process. There is a growing trend to use computer simulation of the process to verify the process plan because this approach is cheaper and faster. Once the tape is verified, either directly or by simulation, it is then stored and can be used whenever the part is to be made on that machine tool.

Two changes should be noted about the tape preparation and verification process. Historically, the NC program was stored on punched tape (rather than magnetic), but these tapes are becoming a thing of the past. These programs are now created, stored, and transmitted in electronic form, so it is more accurate to describe this process as program preparation and verification. In companies with large NC operations abandoning the physical tapes represents a significant cost savings. Standard communications protocols such as Manufacturing Automation Protocol (MAP) allow the programs to be transferred quickly and easily to where they are needed from a common source. This makes it easier for the company to control changes to the NC programs and to ensure that proper versions of the program are used.

The second change involves the verification process. In the past a test part was built and checked to verify the NC program. Now with more sophisticated CIM systems computer verification is becoming possible. A solid model of the workpiece is constructed, and the computer simulates the tool path used to machine the part. This simulation verifies that the path provides the correct geometry. However, complete computer verification requires solid models for not only the workpiece but also for the machine tool, the cutting tool, and the fixture. This additional information is necessary to ensure not only that the tool path produces the correct geometry, but also that the tool does not interfere with the machine tool or the fixture.

These complete requirements for computer verification of the NC program indicate some of the extensions needed in conventional NC program generation. Today NC program generation focuses primarily on the geometry for the tool path. In addition to the part geometry, many systems also know the original shape of the workpiece and machineability data, so they can specify rough-cut and finish-cut paths. However, they still cannot calculate optimal feeds and speeds. Additional types of analyses require a much greater degree of data integration than is available today.

Some of this work is being done to develop more sophisticated computer-aided process planning. Some machine tool builders are also developing machines with sophisticated feedback systems. For example, these machine tools can sense when the stress on the cutting tool increases dramatically and reduces the feed rate to avoid breaking the tool. However, before these types of machine tools can be used effectively, the NC programming languages, such as APT, will have to be enhanced. Currently they have no way to read this feedback or adjust the NC program based on these results. These types of enhancements are being considered by the standards committees working with these languages. Machines with this type of feedback can be much more expensive.

NC programming capabilities have gone through four distinct phases. First, there was no numerical control capability, so the machinist directly controlled all of the operations of the machine tool. Without NC, the process plan and the engineering drawing told the machinist how to machine the part at that workstation. This gave the machinist much discretion in machining the part.

In the second phase much of this discretion shifted to a part programmer. At this stage the NC program was created manually by a part programmer who was knowledgeable about machine tool characteristics and performance. The process plan told the part programmer which machining process would be done on which specific NC machine tool, on which workpiece, held with which fixture, to produce which part or which workpiece for the next step in the process plan. The part programmer wrote the NC program by entering the part geometry to define the tool path and specifying the necessary machine commands at the appropriate places within the program. At this stage in the development of NC, CAD systems either did not exist or were limited to computer-aided drafting systems that did nothing more than create a hardcopy drawing.

The third phase occurred as CAD systems developed many of the capabilities they have today. The critical capability was the ability to create a model of the part, not simply a computerized engineering drawing. This model could be a 3-D wireframe with surfaces or a solid model. The essential point was that the model explicitly included the surfaces to be machined. At this point NC tape or program generation was conceived. The CAD system had enough information to generate the basic tool path from the part geometry. However, this was only the draft of the real NC program because it could not provide the exact tool path or the necessary machine commands.

The fact that this was only a draft tool path does not minimize the amount of work the computer was doing for the part programmer. It translated the part geometry from the CAD system into the tool path, and it provided extensive computational support for generating the tool path. For example, a point-to-point machine tool moves in a straight line from point to point. Given a required tolerance, the NC program generator can calculate all of the intermediate points that must be specified to ensure that the machining remains in tolerance. The system also calculates the cutter offset, since the CL file must specify the cutter centerline, not the actual part geometry, which is what is originally provided by the CAD system. Finally, a postprocessor program converts the exact NC program (once the part programmer has created it by editing the draft version) from a neutral CL file format to the specific commands for the specific machine tool.

The exact tool path required additional information—i.e., the geometry for the machine tool, the fixture, and the actual cutting tool. The machine commands required additional information about the original workpiece geometry and machineability data related to the workpiece and tool material.

The fourth stage of NC involves linking the CIM-oriented NC generation to computer-aided process planning so that a relatively complete NC program can be generated. With the additional information for CAPP the system could optimize the process plan, which could include both NC and non-NC machine tools and the various NC programs that it needs. In effect, NC programming is simply a subset of a more complete CAPP system. The next section describes generically the type of analysis a CAPP system must go through.

Generative Computer-Aided Process Planning

Generative computer-aided process planning (CAPP) systems use information about part and workpiece geometry; machine tool, tool, and fixture geometry; workpiece and tool material type; and machineability data to optimize the process plan and the machining to be done at each step in the plan. These systems use equations relating machining time and cost to the appropriate feed and speed rates for workpiece and tool material types. It also determines the power required for each machining operation. Some systems also relate surface finish to tool geometry (specifically to the tool nose radius). They may also determine the appropriate chucking (fixturing) type and location. The detailed mathematics of this analysis is explained in Halevi.[4]

The information model in Figure 12.2 shows only the parameters and their relationships, although the applications using this information model would need

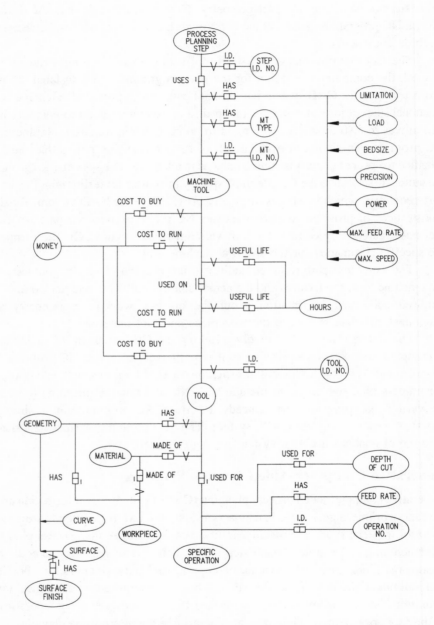

Figure 12.2 Information model for generative process planning

the actual equations. For clarity this information model has been simplified in several areas. For example, it shows only one object called machineability data. In reality, there are many types of machineability data related to the combination of part and tool material, and in some cases to their geometry. In addition, this simplified model relates part, tool, and fixture to geometry, but a more complete model would make these connections through specific geometric objects (i.e., the ones described in Chapter 10). A more complete model would describe these connections in much greater detail.

A sample generative process planning algorithm like the one described by Halevi[5] consists of the following eleven steps:

1. Compute the chucking locations.
2. Assign depth-of-cut limits.
3. Define type of cut required for each segment.
4. Ensure tool access for each operation.
5. Establish feed rate limits.
6. Compute allowable forces.
7. Compute feed rates.
8. Try to reach maximum feed rates.
9. Check the effect of step eight on the previous operations.
10. Compute economical cutting speeds.
11. Compute forces, power, and time for each operation.

The first step is to compute an initial set of chucking locations, which will be refined later. This process assumes free chucking types and minimal part overhangs.

The second step is to assign depth-of-cut limits. These depth-of-cut limits are based on the surface finish required. This begins to distinguish rough-cut and finish-cut depths.

The third step breaks the machining into a series of segments and defines the type of cut (rough or finished) for each segment. Depth-of-cut limits for each segment are used to try to combine segments.

The fourth step checks to ensure that the tool can access the part for each operation. This may result in changing the order of the operations or some of the chucking.

The fifth step calculates feed rate limits for each operation. This involves a relationship between the desired surface finish and the tool geometry. It is also related to the depth of cut.

The sixth step computes the allowable forces for each operation. The minimum limiting force may be the bending, torsion, or chucking force. These forces are based on the type and location of chucking, the surface finish, and the tolerances for the part.

Step seven recalculates the feed rates based on the allowable forces that have been calculated in step six.

Step eight is an iterative attempt to reach the maximum feed rate. If the chucking forces were the limiting ones, the system will try changing the chucking locations and/or types. It will also split the depth of cut into a rough and finished cut. It will also try varying the depth of cut to try to combine segments.

In step nine the system will check the effects of changes made in step eight on previous operations. For example, if the chucking location or type is changed, then the allowable forces will change, affecting the feed rate. Similarly, changing the depth of cut will change the feed rate limits.

Step ten calculates the economical cutting speed. This affects the power required by the machine and tool wear.

Finally, step eleven calculates the force, power, and time required for each operation, which directly affects the costs of the operation. The power requirements place constraints on which machine tools can perform the operation. With adaptive control the calculated force provides a standard against which to compare the feedback.

Summary

This chapter has explained what a process plan is and described two types of computer-aided process planning—variant and generative. It discussed the role of the NC program as part of process planning. It also provided an overview of generative process planning. Finally, it provided basic information models for process planning in general and for some of the more detailed information needed for generative process planning.

Notes

1. Much of the Manufacturing Cost/Design Guidelines work was done by Battelle Institute in Columbus, Ohio, for the U.S. Air Force ICAM project.
2. CAM-I (Computer-Aided Manufacturing—International) is a research consortium based in Dallas, Texas.
3. Charles F. Sack, Jr., "Computer-Managed Process Planning: A Bridge between CAD and CAM," in *Proceedings of Autofact IV* (Dearborn, Mich.: SME, 1982).
4. Gideon Halevi, *The Role of Computers in Manufacturing Processes* (New York: John Wiley and Sons, 1980).
5. Ibid.

Further Reading

Boothroyd, G., and P. Dewhurst. *Design for Assembly: A Designer's Handbook.* Amherst, Mass.: University of Massachusetts, 1983.
Stoll, Henry W. "Design for Manufacture." *Manufacturing Engineering* 100 (Jan. 1988): 67–73.
Tulkoff, Joseph. "Process Planning in the New Information Age." *CIM Technology,* Aug. 1987, 19–22.

13

Production Planning and Control

Production Planning and Control Functions

Production Scheduling
Shop-Floor Control
Materials Management
Maintenance
Costing and Administration

Information Model

Customers
Parts/Products
Manufacturing Orders
Machine Tools

Information Model Validation

Summary

This chapter describes the production planning and control functions that are part of operations management. It includes functions such as material requirements planning, production scheduling, inventory control, and shop-floor control. Many software vendors now have standard application packages (e.g., AMAPS) that integrate the set of function described in this chapter.

Today this area is the most integrated phase of design and manufacturing. It is also the only area in which database management is the rule rather than the exception. Although often considered a part of business data processing rather than

CIM, for effective CIM these manufacturing and operations management functions must be linked to the earlier engineering and manufacturing applications that create and modify the data they use.

Production Planning and Control Functions

The functions considered in this chapter are shown in the function chart in Figure 13.1. The discussion concentrates on three critical functions—production scheduling, shop-floor control, and materials management. The other two functions, maintenance and costing/administration, are also discussed but in less detail.

Production Scheduling

At the highest level production scheduling involves determining the level of production for each product (i.e., product mix) and scheduling operations to produce that mix. This function includes much of what is traditionally called MRP (Material Requirements Planning), but MRP usually includes parts of the materials management function.

The first major subfunction is to project the demand for each product and part. In some cases it is only for the next production cycle. However, in many cases the demand is projected for several months, quarters, or even years. The time horizon for these projections depends on the nature of the specific products and industries.

These projections use data from sales forecasts and current back orders. If new products are being introduced, their sales must be projected and estimates must be made of how their sales will affect existing products. If a product line has been in existence for many years, a significant portion of the production could involve spare parts rather than complete finished products.

The complexity of this projection depends on many factors. Is there a single standard product, or are there many variations or models of the product? Is the company producing to inventory, or is it scheduling production based on firm orders from customers and/or retailers or distributors? Does the company produce many different products or only a few? Is demand for one or more products seasonal? How flexible are the company's production facilities in terms of both different products and different production levels?

These projections involve two types of demand—external or independent and internal or dependent. The external demand arises from customers and distributors. This demand is for different products and spare parts. The internal or dependent demand is derived from this external demand using the product structure. It specifies the requirements for each part in the product (i.e., how many of each part are needed and when are they needed).

The second subfunction takes these estimates of the demand and actually schedules the production. This involves two steps: specifying the production targets for each period and determining the production schedule (i.e., the load on each

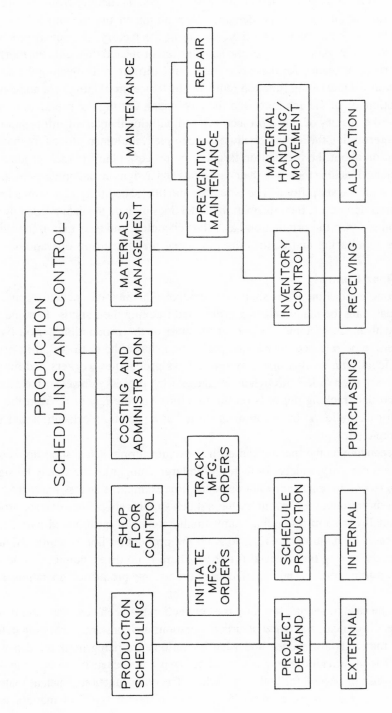

Figure 13.1 Manufacturing management functions

195

machine tool). Setting the actual production targets is distinct from the previous subfunction of projecting the demand. Depending on the inventory levels, the seasonality of the demand, and the capacity of the factory, the actual production targets may be higher, lower, or the same as the projected demand. Furthermore, the information needed for these two functions is different. Projecting the demand is essentially a marketing function requiring historical marketing data and external information about the economy and the customers. Setting the production targets requires the results of these projections and additional internal information.

Determining the actual schedule is a complex, multistep procedure that takes information about the production targets, the process plan for each product, and the available machine tools and their capacities and assigns actual products to specific machines on the shop floor. The actual production scheduling algorithms are not considered. However, the information model does include the data needed by these algorithms. Once the production has been scheduled, the next major subfunction involves monitoring and controlling the actual manufacturing operations.

Shop-Floor Control

The second major function is shop-floor control. This involves actually generating and dispatching the manufacturing orders and tracking their status. In some companies with batch systems a report at the start of the production period lists all the orders to be released during that period and shows the status of all in-process orders. Ideally an on-line query system allows production workers and management to track shop orders through the manufacturing process. However, the accuracy of such order tracking depends on the timeliness of the feedback from the shop floor—for example, when an order is started at a specific workstation and when it is completed.

Depending on the specific approach to manufacturing, actual shop-floor control procedures can vary widely. In fact, within large companies there may be significant differences among factories or divisions. For example, a factory mass-producing a commodity product for inventory has a much simpler shop-floor control problem than a small job shop producing many small batches of customized parts. In the former case the main objective is to keep the production line running efficiently and keep delivering the material it needs. There is no direct connection between specific customer orders and manufacturing orders, and production operations rarely change.

In the case of a small job shop the connection between customer and production orders is critical, and manufacturing operations are constantly changing in terms of what materials are needed and what operations are being done at each workstation. The information model described below is comprehensive in that it includes the relationships needed for both approaches. The other functions, such as materials management, have more commonality across different types of manufacturing operations.

Materials Management

The third major function is materials management, which can be subdivided into inventory control and materials handling. Inventory control involves purchasing, receiving, and allocation of inventory. Materials handling involves the actual movement of materials through the factory.

The purchasing function gets material requisitions from MRP and orders the material from the appropriate vendors with enough lead time so it will be on hand when needed. To do this, MRP requires information about production targets, product structure, current inventory levels, outstanding purchase orders, and vendor performance. In some job shops where there is enough lead time, parts and materials may not be ordered until there is a customer order that requires them. On the other hand, longer lead time items may be to be ordered and stocked in anticipation of customer orders. This is particularly true when the competitive environment requires that customer orders be processed quickly.

The receiving function accepts the parts and material when they arrive and places them in the inventory where they can then be allocated when needed. Receiving also includes reconciling what was received with what was ordered, performing any quality control to ensure that the material meets any specifications, and recording vendor performance (e.g., whether it was received on time and whether it met the desired quality standards). An additional function must reconcile the invoices with the original purchase orders and pay the vendors, but this is an accounting function that does not directly affect manufacturing.

Finally, there is the allocation of inventory to actual production. For example, there may be 100 units physically in the inventory, but 90 may have already been allocated for scheduled production. This means that there are only 10 units that are available for allocation to new production or for shipment to customers.

Misallocation of inventory can lead to major scheduling problems. For example, if 20 units are used for a special high-priority manufacturing order, then there will be a shortage of 10 units for later scheduled production. The importance of expediting in many factories shows that this problem has not been eliminated. Ideally the system should reschedule the high-priority order, reallocate the needed material to it, and then reschedule one or more of the orders for which the 90 units were originally committed. However, without faster, more sophisticated information systems many companies simply are not able to respond this quickly. The allocation function can be more complex in a job shop than in a mass production facility. However, the impact of a shortage can be much more severe with mass production because a shortage could shut down the production line.

The inventory control function and its three components are becoming much more important in all types of manufacturing operations. As the labor component of a product's cost decreases, the inventory cost component can become much more significant unless it is effectively controlled. Inventory turns is a major criterion in evaluating company performance.

JIT (Just-in-Time) inventory control is one way to reduce inventory carrying costs by keeping a minimal inventory on hand. However, success of this approach requires close coordination between production scheduling and materials management as well as a close relationship between the manufacturer and its suppliers. A delay in a shipment from a supplier can quickly shut down a factory using JIT inventory control.

The importance of improving inventory turns is evident in studies showing that, material is simply sitting in inventory 95 percent of the time it is in the factory. Only 5 percent of the time is it at a machine tool ready to be worked on. Furthermore, it is being processed for only half of this time (i.e., value is being added to the material). Clearly in most factories materials management can be dramatically improved.

The other major materials management function is material handling. In many factories today the automated part of material handling simply produces the appropriate orders for moving material from one point to another in the factory. The actual movement itself is still done manually. However, in more automated facilities the movement itself is also being automated. Automated warehouses, wire-guided vehicles, and robotics all contribute to more automated material handling.

With an automated warehouse the system knows exactly where the material is stored and how is placed. Therefore, when a request arrives for certain material in the inventory, the system can automatically send a vehicle (using either a wire-guided system or a less flexible one) to collect all of the requested parts. (A similar approach is used to store material from receiving.) This type of automated material handling system can be used in either a distribution center or a factory. In a distribution center it would primarily handle finished goods and move them from inventory to shipping, where they would be sent to the customer.

An automated warehouse linked to a factory could be much more complex, depending on how they were linked. If, for example, material came from many different parts of the factory rather than a single receiving point, the system requirements would be more complex. However, this complexity could be avoided if the material were moved from the end of the various production lines to a central receiving point either manually or by a factory material handling system rather than by the automated warehouse system. This would be a cleaner interface and a simpler warehouse system.

A more complicated system would be needed if the automated warehouse were at the front of the factory and supported its manufacturing operations. Although this approach would be more complicated, it would provide much greater benefits if it were integrated with other automated systems within the factory. The greater complexity is caused by several factors. First, the system would probably have to deal with more different types of parts and materials, which implies different sizes, shapes, and weights. These differences would require a more flexible or more complicated picking mechanism and vehicle. Alternately, different types of vehicles could be used for different types of parts, but this would complicate the traffic flow through the factory and would create timing dependencies for when different types of vehicles arrived at the same workstation or workcell. Second, since materials must be delivered to many different points within the factory, the routing and guidence system would be more complicated. Again an alternative is to have the automated warehouse system bring the material to a central distribution point where it is then reloaded on wire-guided vehicles for movement through the factory floor. Although ideally this intermediate step is undesirable, it may be worth the trade-off if it simplifies the interface between the different systems — for example, if the automated warehouse and the material handling system within the factory were from different vendors.

Maintenance

The maintenance function is becoming more critical in automated operations because failure of a single machine tool can affect the entire production line. When a single operator has to run several machine tools or an entire workcell, it may take longer to spot a problem with one of the machines. Furthermore, when the operator is repairing one machine, he or she cannot be working another one. Finally, more complex workcells may require specially trained maintenance personnel. All of these reasons emphasize the importance of preventive maintenance, rather than simply waiting for a failure to occur and repairing it.

An effective operations management system should include extensive support for maintenance. Maintenance schedules should be included in the database to indicate what actions should be taken when. When production is scheduled, it is assigned to specific machines, and there is an estimate for how long it will take. This allows these systems to track the number of hours on each machine tool. By keeping track of when every repair or maintenance action was done on each machine, the system can also schedule preventive maintenance. This would ensure that preventive maintenance is not required halfway through a production run.

In addition, when a machine tool breaks, the system can check and see whether any other maintenance work is needed in the near future. If so, it may be done while the machine is already down for repairs. This would minimize the down time for the equipment. However, most maintenance operations are not yet this sophisticated.

Costing and Administration

Costing and administration is a business support function, but it requires data from the manufacturing operations. All manufacturers need costing data to determine the effectiveness of their operations and improve them. However, access to accurate and current cost data is even more important for job-shop-oriented companies because they must frequently bid on work.

Capturing cost data directly from the shop floor on a routine basis (rather than as a special study) allows them to identify and track cost changes quickly. In some cases the changes are acceptable, but they must be factored into future bids. However, other changes may indicate that certain costs are beginning to slip out of control. The quicker and more precisely these changes can be identified, the easier they are to correct and the less damage they do.

Most of the standard manufacturing management products provided by vendors today already include extensive cost tracking and reporting. However, much of this reporting is done on a clerical basis from the shop floor. In the future more of this data will be directly monitored and captured from the CIM system.

Information Model

This section describes the information models needed to support the functions described above. The information models in this chapter focus on four types of objects—customers, parts, manufacturing orders, and machine tools.

Some of these objects and roles have already been described in other chapters. For example, parts, geometry, and machine tools have been described in more detail elsewhere. They are included here for two reasons. First, they are essential for production planning and control and must be included for the information model to make sense in the context of these functions. Second, additional object types and roles essential for the manufacturing management functions are added to and integrated with the information model that is being developed. However, where possible, simplifications are made both to avoid redundancy and to clarify the model. For example, in some figures in this chapter there is an object called "part geometry" to link this model to the complex information model for geometry.

Customers

A company always has customers. These customers may or may not directly affect the manufacturing operation. If a company or a plant manufactures standardized products only for inventory, then individual customers and their orders do not impact the manufacturing operations directly. They are only important as statistics for projecting demand. Even if a customer buys in very large quantities and receives a substantial discount, manufacturing is not affected—only accounting. As long as the customer orders are filled from inventory, there is no direct linkage to manufacturing.

In other cases customer orders directly drive the manufacturing operations. The most common case is a company building to order rather than to inventory. In this case the manufacturing order is not generated until a customer order is received. Sometimes combined production occurs when part of the output is built to inventory while part is built to specific customer orders.

Figure 13.2 shows the part of the information model related to customers and customer orders. Since this model applies for all customers, it also supports

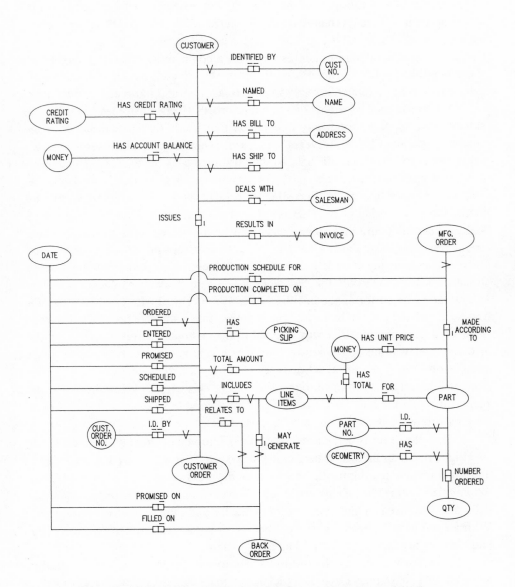

Figure 13.2   Information model for customers and orders

the linkage between specific customers and manufacturing operations. The basic customer information includes an identification number, a name, one or more addresses (usually a bill-to and one or more ship-to addresses), a credit rating, and an account balance (perhaps balances for current, 30-, 60-, and 90-day periods). There may also be a salesman associated with the customer. In cases where a customer has several ship-to addresses (e.g., a company with several factories), there may be several salesmen, one for each ship-to address, in which case the salesman would be related directly to ship-to address and indirectly to customer.

Each customer generates one or more orders. If the customer has only one ship-to address, this is the only connection that needs to be made between the customer and an order. However, if there are several ship-to addresses, then each order needs to be related not only to the customer but also to a ship-to address.

Every customer order also has an order number, an order date, a total amount, and one or more line items. Each line item includes a part, a quantity, the unit price, and an extended price. Depending on how much a company wants to track and evaluate its operations, many dates can be associated with an order. There are at least two basic dates—the date the customer sent the order (ordered) and the date the company entered the order in its system. A customer making a query about an order knows only the date when it was sent. However, when a company is evaluating its performance in filling orders, the critical date is when the order was received and entered in the system. Another date is the date on which the order was filled (i.e., the material was shipped to the customer). This date is essential if the company wants to track how long it is taking to fill orders. In some cases the customer may be promised delivery on or by a certain date.
(i.e., the material was shipped to the customer). This date is essential if the company wants to track how long it is taking to fill orders. In some cases the customer may be promised delivery on or by a certain date.

When the order is being processed, two additional documents are created—a picking slip and an invoice. The picking slip is used for actually pulling the parts and packing them for shipment. The items on the picking slip may even be ordered to minimize routing through the warehouse. The picking slip may be produced physically and then used by the person who manually pulls the items from inventory. With an automated warehouse the picking slip may be transmitted electronically and used to instruct the material handling system.

The invoice is simply the bill to be sent to the customer. A copy is usually included with the shipment, but the official copy to be paid is usually sent separately. This is definitely the case when the ship-to and bill-to addresses are different.

In some cases the order cannot be completely filled from inventory. Either some items are out of stock or the quantity ordered exceeds the quantity on hand. Either case results in a back order. Back orders are handled in several different ways depending on company policy. In some cases the entire order must be filled, or it is back-ordered in its entirety. However, in most cases, as much of the order as possible is filled, so that only individual line items are back-ordered. The model permits either option by linking back order to both order and line item. Depending on how the company operates, two dates can be associated with each back order. The first, the date the back order was filled, should always be in the model. Without this information a company cannot evaluate its performance with back orders except to count the number of back orders. Even if the number of back orders is declining, there is still a problem if the average time to fill them has gone from a few days to a month. Without this back-order-filled date, management cannot keep track of this type of performance. The second date for a back order is a promised-by date. Although many systems do not include a promised-by date, without it the only priority for filling back orders is simply the date of the original order.

Back orders normally occur only in companies that fill customer orders from an existing inventory. The concept does not really apply if a company schedules its production specifically to fill individual customer orders.

All of the above information model applies to every customer order, regardless of whether it is filled from inventory or specifically scheduled for production. The rest of this section describes the additional information that is needed in a job shop environment. Surprisingly, very little additional information is needed.

The most important additional information is that the customer order may be related to one or more manufacturing work orders (i.e., the orders that instruct the factory to make the specific parts the customer has ordered). The information model for the manufacturing work order is described later in the section on manufacturing orders. More precisely, these manufacturing orders may relate directly to specific parts in line items in the customer order.

Two additional dates are important: the date production is scheduled and the date production is actually completed. These dates are shown here because they need to be accessed through the customer order, as when a customer wants to know the status of an order. However, in reality these dates are related directly only to the manufacturing order and only indirectly (through the manufacturing order) to the customer order.

Parts/Products

Figure 13.3 shows various sections of the information model for parts. All parts have three types of data — part identification numbers and descriptions, product structure or bill of materials data, and inventory data.

The model shows four different relationships between part and inventory quantity. The first is the quantity actually on hand. However, some of these parts may already be committed for scheduled production, so the second is the quantity committed for production. If production is scheduled for specific customers, then this quantity committed may be further broken down into the quantity committed for each customer. The third relationship is the quantity available for use — i.e., the quantity on hand minus the quantity committed. This is the actual quantity that

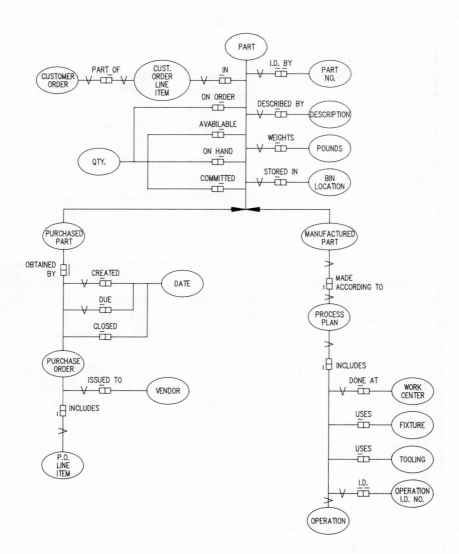

Figure 13.3   Information model for parts

can be shipped or committed for new production schedules. The fourth, from the purchasing function, is a quantity on order. This is the number of parts included in outstanding purchase orders. The model relating parts, vendors, and purchase orders shows how this quantity on order is further decomposed.

The product structure specifies where and how many parts of each type are used in other parts, assemblies, and products. The product structure was discussed in more detail in Chapter 9.

The above information model applies to all parts. However, there are two basic types of parts—those which the company buys and those which it manufactures. Furthermore, even manufactured parts may include other purchased parts and raw materials. Figure 13.3 also shows the information models for each of these subtypes—purchased parts and manufactured parts.

A purchased part is uniquely identified by the company's own part identification number. A part may be purchased from one or more vendors. Each vendor identifies the part with its own part number, which is normally unrelated to the manufacturing company's number.

For each vendor there is also a set of information similar to that for a customer. This includes a vendor identification number, a vendor name, and possibly two addresses, one where the purchase orders are sent and one where the payments are sent. There may also be summary totals of the amounts due the vendor and when the payments are due. For each purchase order there is a purchase order number, a date issued, and one or more line items. In some cases there may also be a date when the material is needed. Each line item specifies a part and a quantity. In the purchase order the part must be identified by the vendor's part number, but the manufacturer may also include its own part number to ease the processing in receiving. The unit price and extended price are usually also included so that a total amount can be determined for the purchase order. A complication not included in the model is that there is not a single unit price for a part. At a minimum the price depends on both the part and the vendor. Furthermore, for a single vendor the unit price may depend on the lot size.

Most companies evaluate the performance of their vendors. Examples of vendor performance criteria include average lead time and ability to meet specific delivery commitments in terms of date and quality. Summary performance criteria are related to the vendor. However, the detailed criteria relate to specific purchase orders or even line items. The company must decide how much vendor performance data to maintain and how to use it. For example, companies may drop a vendor who cannot deliver on schedule, especially if the company is trying to implement JIT inventory control. Similarly, a company may drop a vendor who is delivering poor-quality material.

The other type of parts are those which the company manufactures rather than purchases. The main additional information for this type is the process plans specifying how they are made. The information model relating parts, process plans,

205

and machine tools has been described in Chapter 12. All of this information also relates to the manufacturing orders, which are described below.

Manufacturing Orders

Manufacturing work orders are detailed orders to the factory specifying both what is to be made and which resources are to be used to make it. The master production scheduling application generates all of these work orders for the next production cycle. During the cycle these orders are released, and the work begins to flow through the factory.

Figure 13.4 shows the information model for the manufacturing work order. This model shows a direct link between the work order and the customer order. This is essential in many small operations, especially job shops. In larger companies where goods are produced to inventory rather than to order, this direct link does not exist. However, the rest of the information model would be the same.

The manufacturing work order is designated with an identification number, the name of a specific part or product, the date when it was created, and the specific production cycle or period. There may also be a specific date when the order must be completed and the product available. The work order also specifies the quantity to be produced.

Each manufacturing order includes a routing or process plan, which consists of one or more production operations. However, the process plan specifies only the type of machine tools, tools, and fixtures to be used. The manufacturing order is more detailed and includes exactly which machine tools, tools, and fixtures are to be used and the amount of time each will be used. The master scheduler uses the standard setup and unit run times from the process plan to calculate the estimated times on each machine tool for the quantity to be produced. Ideally, during the production the actual time used on each machine is added to the order. This allows exact manufacturing times and costs to be determined. If these exact times are significantly different from the standard times, then they can be used to either identify and correct a production problem or to update the standard times with more accurate values.

A manufacturing work order can also have two types of status information: a general status and a work progress status. In terms of general status, the order can be scheduled (the work has been scheduled but not yet started); released (work has actually begun and the order is in process); or completed (the work has been completed and the product is ready to be shipped or placed in inventory). In the case of products made to order, these status codes are related to the status codes for the customer order, which indicate that the customer order was received, is in process, is completed, was shipped, and is finally paid for. The work progress status simply specifies which of the steps in the process plan is currently being done.

The information model shows only a simple "requires" role between the process plan and raw materials. In reality this relationship may be much more complex. In their simplest form raw materials may be purchased parts to be assembled into

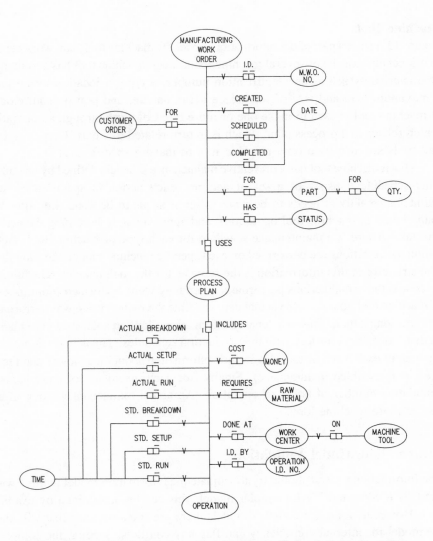

Figure 13.4 Information model for manufacturing work orders

a final product. In other cases it may be material such as tubing, sheet metal, or plastics to be cut, stamped, molded, or machined into parts. To support these cases the raw material object must be expanded into a more complex structure. Even more complexity arises if lot traceability is required.

Machine Tools

Figure 13.5 shows part of the information model for machine tools and work centers. Work centers consist of several machine tools. Each machine tool has certain basic characteristics such as an identification number, a type, a location in the plant, a maximum load and size of workpiece it can handle, and power requirements. A machine tool is used to make one or more types of parts through an operation, which relates to a process plan, which is in turn related to a part. Certain fixtures and tools are also used on a machine tool to make a specific part.

Each machine tool has a preventive maintenance schedule defined by its builder. This schedule consists of a set of actions. Each action is specified by what maintenance activity needs to be done, when it needs to be done (i.e. after how many hours of machine tool operation), and approximately how long the activity will take. There is a maintenance schedule for each type of machine tool. Actual maintenance actions are performed on each specific machine tool on the shop floor. The structure of this information is the same as for the maintenance schedule, but it records the actual actions performed, when they were performed (both in terms of machine tool hours and the actual date and time the maintenance was performed), and how long it took. This maintenance information allows maintenance to be planned so that it does not interfere with the production schedules. The actual maintenance records for each machine tool also include information about breakdowns and repairs (i.e., nonscheduled maintenance). Finally, for each machine tool there is also a cumulative number of hours of operation. An actual maintenance action affects one or more machine tools.

Information Model Validation

The information analyst should try to validate the information model in three ways. First, is it consistent? With simpler models this can be determined by examination. However, for more complex models there are software tools that will check the model for internal consistency and flag any conflicts. Second, the completed model should be reviewed by subject matter experts, preferably some or all of whom were not involved in its development.

Third, users need to exercise the model by posing the types of queries and updates that the applications using the model must process. Usually this is done by defining a prototype database from the information model (some software tools will create this schema automatically), populating it with a few records of each type, and allowing a group of users to work with it using a high-level query language

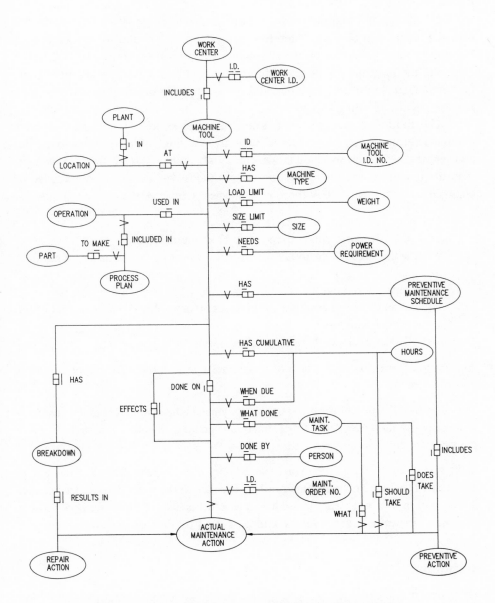

Figure 13.5   Information model for machine tools

and a report writer. The more queries and updates the model can process, the more confidence one has in its validity.

Of course, information model validity is not absolute. It is only relative to how the model will be used. Therefore, a model may be valid for one company, but not for another, or not even for the original company several years later. For example, the information model without the direct link between customer orders and manufacturing orders may be valid for a company building to inventory but not a company building to order.

The following example queries are intended as idea generators, not as a complete definitive set. The reader is encouraged to think of his or her own queries and see whether the information model can satisfy them. If it can, fine. If it cannot, then the reader should try to determine how the model needs to be extended or changed so that it can satisfy these new queries. Consider the following queries:

> List all of customer X's orders.
> List all customers who ordered part X in the past year.
> What is the status of customer X's order? If building to inventory? If building to order?
> What customers have back orders over 30 days old? For which parts?
> Which vendors have purchase orders over 30 days old? For which parts? Who are alternate vendors?
> List all customers with work in process.

As examples, processing for two of these queries using the information model is described below.

List all of customer X's orders. This only needs the simple fact that a customer issues a customer order. Once this connection is made, any other information about the order could also be provided.

List all of the customers who ordered part X in the past year. The basic path is from part to line item to customer order. The date of the order determines whether it was within the past year; if so, a single additional fact links the order to the customer. If desired, the results could be sorted by date or customer.

Summary

This chapter has explained an information model to support production planning and control. It identified five major functions (production scheduling, shop-floor control, materials management, maintenance, and costing and administration) and decomposed them. It then described an information model to support these functions. The model involves customers, parts, manufacturing orders, and machine tools. The chapter concluded with a discussion of model validation and showed how several typical queries would be processed using the information model.

Further Reading

Halevi, Gideon. *The Role of Computers in Manufacturing Processes.* New York: John Wiley and Sons, 1980.

Schultz, Terry R. *Business Requirements Planning: The Journey to Excellence.* Milwaukee: The Forum, 1984.

14

Computer-Aided Quality Control

Role of Quality on Manufacturing Strategy

Quality Control

Traditional Quality Control
Lot Traceability

Future Directions in Quality

Information Model for Quality Control

Summary

$\mathbf{T}$he computer can dramatically improve manufacturing quality. This chapter discusses manufacturing quality and how CIM applications can improve it. Quality is also a function of design, so any design and analysis applications that lead to a better design also support product quality, as described in other chapters. This chapter, however, focuses on manufacturing quality and the information model to support it.

213

Role of Quality on Manufacturing Strategy

Product quality is no longer simply an afterthought. It can be a significant competitive advantage. However, if a corporation opts to emphasize high quality rather than low cost in its competitive position, then it needs a compatible manufacturing strategy.

Quality is ultimately defined by the customer. Internal quality measurements are usually only proxy variables for what the customer explicitly values. Customers value quality because of the problems poor quality causes. In the extreme case poor quality can be life-threatening. In less extreme situations it is inconvenient and/or expensive.

For example, in aircraft and medical equipment poor quality can be life-threatening. It is usually difficult and expensive for the customer to test the product quality, especially if the product is already assembled. Therefore, for these types of products the image of the company and its concern for quality is often more important than cost. It is not like a flashlight or a battery, where a product failure has a low cost—a replacement for the customer. A failure of these critical products damages the company's image with quality-conscious customers and can dramatically reduce sales.

Where product failure is not life-threatening, it is still inconvenient and expensive for the customer. Even when repair and/or replacement is free, poor quality still creates problems for customers, especially business customers. For business customers poor product quality from their suppliers has ripple effects. Poor quality affects their schedules, damages their reputation with their customers, and incurs additional costs when they have to repair their product.

Many companies implicitly recognize the real cost of poor quality when their warranties carefully exclude consequential damages. They will only replace or repair their product. They will not attempt to make up for consequences or lost opportunities caused by the product failure.

A cost/benefit analysis usually shows that quality is a good investment. A dollar spent on improved quality often saves several dollars. Furthermore, most companies underestimate what they are currently spending on quality—or the lack of it.

First, there is the hidden cost of lost sales. Second, there is the warrantee cost in repairing or replacing failed parts or products that are returned. Additional quality costs are incurred throughout the manufacturing operation. The quality control and vendor evaluation in receiving is only the beginning. Inspection stations and quality control personnel throughout the plant are a cost, even if they do not find many problems. When problems are found, scrap and rework is also expensive.

In summary, most companies dramatically underestimate the cost of their quality control efforts. They usually also underestimate the potential savings of improved quality. This is important because quality control is essentially an overhead function. It does not "cut metal" or directly make products (i.e., it does not add value).

214

The above costs are only a partial list of the true cost of quality. Crosby provides a much more extensive list in terms of prevention, appraisal, and failure costs.[1] Prevention costs involve

- design reviews
- product qualification
- drawing checking
- engineering quality orientation
- quality programs
- supplier evaluations
- supplier quality seminars and programs
- specification reviews
- process capability studies
- tool control
- operation training
- quality orientation and training
- acceptance planning
- zero defects programs
- quality audits
- preventive maintenance

Appraisal costs include

- prototype inspection and testing
- production specification conformance analysis
- supplier surveillance
- receiving inspection and testing
- product acceptance testing
- process control acceptance
- package inspection
- status measuring and reporting
- statistical process control

Finally, direct failure costs include activities such as

- consumer affairs
- redesign
- engineering changes
- purchase order changes
- manufacturing order changes
- corrective action
- rework
- scrap
- warranty repairs
- service
- product liability

Quality Control

This section describes traditional quality control procedures and explains how the computer can aid these functions. It also describes the role of testing both to ensure the quality of the products that are shipped and to determine whether the manufacturing processes are in control. The last part of the section describes lot traceability.

Traditional Quality Control

The traditional quality control approach is to make the part and then inspect it. If it passes the inspection, it is good and can be shipped. If it fails the inspection, then it is bad and is sent to rework or scrap.

More precisely there are many inspections while the part or product is being made. The raw materials may be inspected when they are received before they are accepted. The process plan includes inspection points and test requirements along with the normal fabrication and assembly instructions. At any inspection the workpiece may be diverted for rework or scrap. However, in many cases, especially with large batches, each part may not be inspected. Only a small sample from each batch is usually tested. There are two problems with this traditional approach to quality control. First, it is reactive—it waits until a mistake has been made. Second, only small samples are tested.

The reactive approach is beginning to change with a process called adaptive control. With adaptive control the machine tool actually monitors the machining operation and adjusts it based on real-time feedback. However, this requires additional monitor capability and intelligence in the machine tool and its controller, so it is not being widely used today. Most production lines still have machine tools that fabricate the part and separate inspection stations to determine whether a mistake has been made.

There are also problems with testing only samples. With this approach, a manufacturer may ship bad parts because all parts are not tested. The objective of this type of quality control is to minimize the number of bad parts that are shipped and to minimize the quality control cost. But, in reality, this is only minimizing the cost of inspection, rework, and scrap, not the real cost of quality, as discussed earlier.

The trade-off implicit in sample testing is that the larger the sample, the fewer the bad parts that will be shipped, but the more expensive the inspection. The ultimate limit is 100 percent testing, which should find all bad parts before they are shipped. However, because testing is often hard, time-consuming, and expensive, there is a tendency to use the minimum sample size.

This testing really serves two purposes. In addition to the purely reactive concern to locate bad parts, there is an important proactive aspect: statistical quality control, which allows the company to determine whether the manufacturing process is in control before it deteriorates enough to produce bad parts.

A process is in control if two conditions are met. First, the parts must be within tolerance. Second, there must be no assignable variation from the target value (i.e., the variations are randomly distributed around the target value). Figure 14.1 shows two examples of out-of-control processes, although in neither case is the process yet producing bad parts.

In the first case the test results are not randomly distributed. There is a clear trend that will eventually exceed the tolerance. This could, for example, be the result of tool wear, which is getting worse the longer the tool is used. If the trend is spotted early enough, the problem can be diagnosed and corrected before any bad parts are produced. This is clearly a proactive approach to quality control.

In the second case all of the test results are randomly distributed and within tolerance. However, they are not randomly distributed around the target value but rather around a different value. Some bias has crept into the manufacturing process and is producing results with a constant offset from the target. The problem needs to be identified so this bias can be eliminated.

Statistical quality control involves monitoring the manufacturing process to determine whether it is in or out of control. Effective statistical quality control can determine that a process is out of control before it starts producing bad parts, thus reducing rework and scrap.

This type of statistical quality control can be done without a computer. In fact, it was being done for years before computers were available. However, computers can improve this type of quality control in two ways—through computer-aided testing and more detailed analysis.

Normally only small samples are tested. Assume that ten test results are needed to calculate a meaningful statistic. If only one in every ten parts is sampled, then 100 parts are produced before the statistic can be calculated, and statistics over several periods are needed to determine whether a process is out of control. Computer-aided testing makes testing much easier and cheaper so every part can be tested. This allows problems to be spotted much faster and reduces the amount of scrap and rework. In addition, 100 percent testing ensures (as much as possible) that only good parts are shipped.

One of the General Motors Truck and Bus Division plants provides a good example of this approach. All of the openings in sheetmetal parts are inspected by a machine vision system. Out-of-tolerance openings are marked, and the part is removed from the production line for rework or scrap. This avoids wasting any additional effort on a bad part until it has been reworked. If two consecutive parts have the same mistake, the process can be stopped and corrected before additional bad parts are produced. Assuming the system stores the actual measurements instead of simply indicating pass/fail, then it also has all of the data it needs to constantly monitor the process. Computers can assist in storing and analyzing these quality data even if computer-aided testing is not used, or even if the production line has no automation.

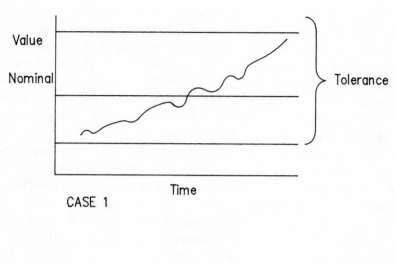

CASE 1

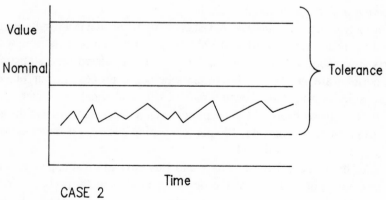

CASE 2

Figure 14.1   Statistical process control

Lot Traceability

The above discussion of sampling and statistical quality control applies for any parts. It could be considered as a minimum level of quality control. Even more sophisticated data collection and tracking can be done for critical parts, such as aerospace and medical parts. This approach is called lot traceability. In extreme cases, when tracking lots of one, it is called serial traceability.

Quality control as described above occurs during manufacturing (i.e., before the parts are shipped). Lot traceability is required to find potential problems in parts after they have been shipped. The reason for lot traceability is best shown by an example.

Assume you are building jet engines. They pass all of the required quality tests during maufacturing and are shipped. Later in the field several turbine blades fail in less than a third of their expected life. Further tests of the failed blades show a slight impurity in the metal, and you suspect that the same problem may affect all of the blades made from the same batch of raw material. Lot traceability will allow you to identify all of the turbine blades made from a specific shipment of raw material and all engines these blades were used in. This allows you to notify the customer so that all of the affected blades can be tested or replaced before they fail.

Lot traceability requires keeping much more detailed records about the actual production of the parts and where they are used. However, for critical parts this extra effort is worthwhile.

In some cases the Department of Defense requires serial traceability—i.e., each part has a unique serial number and all of the production information is stored for each part. In extreme cases this means recording not only the raw material batch but also the individual machine tool and operator used at each step in the manufacturing process. An information system is important for this level of tracking.

Future Directions in Quality

The previous section contained no surprises. Most companies are aware of the concepts described above, and many companies are doing some or all of these activities. However, in the future the concept of quality will change dramatically. Although the quality concepts described in this section are widely practiced in Japan, only a few U.S. manufacturers are aware of them, and even fewer are practicing them.[2] The main quality concept in Japan is called company-wide quality control (CWQC). Total quality control (TQC) as practiced in the United States is only part of CWQC.

CWQC is based on several assumptions. First, quality is defined as uniformity around a target—i.e., reduced variability in process outcome. This is different from the fundamental assumption of statistical process control, which assumes that high quality means that the process is in control—i.e., it is producing parts within a specified tolerance. The U.S. approach provides little incentive for improving a process if it is within tolerance. However, Taguchi's loss function (which is a part of CWQC) often shows a significant benefit in reducing variability even if a process is already in control.

Second, with the Taguchi method cost is the primary driver. It translates variability in product characteristics into a monetary value so various quality activities can be compared. With this method, when a decision is made to drive down the cost of production, a quality improvement is an automatic windfall benefit. This provides a major advantage because quality is no longer an intangible that is hard to justify.

Third, the emphasis is on continuous improvement. Many small, incremental improvements in the product and the processes for making it have a much greater cumulative effect than a few major improvements. Because of this, the analysis can often be "quick and dirty." Approximate results that can be implemented today are better than exact results next month or next year. Since the CWQC process is ongoing, today's approximate results can be defined tomorrow.

CWQC consists of seven stages:

- product orientation
- process orientation
- system orientation
- humanistic orientation
- societal orientation
- cost orientation
- consumer orientation

The traditional quality control approaches described in the previous section address only the first two or three of these stages. The product orientation inspects finished parts to find defective ones that need to be scrapped or reworked. The process approach goes a step further and determines how well the process is working, but this statistical process control focuses only on whether the process is in control, not on reducing process variability. The system-oriented approach attempts to drive quality consideration back to a number of functions, not just manufacturing. Design for manufacturability is one aspect of a systems approach to quality.

The last four stages of CWQC are found primarily in Japan, with only a few U.S. and European companies considering the issues they address. The humanistic stage focuses on education and training. Training is done simply to improve a person's skill. Education, however, is done to change a person's thought process and approach to the job. This improvement in personal capability is critical because it automatically generates improved process capability—i.e., product and process improvements. This education and training reduces manufacturing costs in two ways: through the resulting product and process improvements and by increasing the span of control. Better educated and trained workers can operate more autonomously with fewer levels of management control.

The societal stage really involves product and process design optimization. These product and process improvements will occur almost automatically with a well-educated, trained, and motivated workforce.

The cost stage concentrates on the real cost of quality. Taguchi's loss function allows companies to identify the costs of quality both to the company and to society at large. The cost savings identified by the Taguchi approach can be an order of magnitude greater that the benefits identified by the more traditional methods. The loss function helps a company concentrate on the improvements with the greatest payoff.

The final stage, quality function deployment (QFD), has a consumer focus. It identifies product characteristics important to the consumer and focuses attention on these quality issues throughout the product and process development process. It translates the customer requirements in the customer's own terms (i.e., the "voice of the customer") into the technical characteristics and process variables that must be controlled. Sullivan describes this approach in more detail.[3]

In the future there will be a much greater emphasis on these newer, broader concepts of quality. However, the information model described in the next section supports both the short-term traditional quality approach as well as this more rigorous, long-term approach. The type of production statistics collected for statistical process control are also the ones needed for CWQC. The real difference is in how the data are used. The traditional approach uses the data to determine whether a process is in control (i.e., producing within tolerance), while the newer approach uses the same data to process variability that needs to be reduced. Later stages of CWQC, specifically QFD, help identify more precisely the types of measurements that need to be captured and how they are related to specific customer requirements.

Information Model for Quality Control

Figure 14.2 shows the basic information model to support quality control. The two basic objects are the design and the part. The part is identified by a part number. The specific part is made according to a design. Every part is made according to some design. A specific part is identified by either a lot number or a serial number, depending on whether lot or serial traceability is required. Parts have geometric features and nongeometric requirements. (Note that geometric feature and nongeometric requirement are simply shorthand for potentially very complex quality control requirements—i.e., any measurement collected during inspection and testing.) The geometric feature has a design value and a maximum and minimum tolerance for that dimension. These three values relate to the design, not the specific part being produced. The specific part has a measured or tested value, which should lie within the tolerance range. Every specific part (or each part in the test sample) has a measure length on which statistics can be calculated. The nongeometric requirement has a similar structure—a name, a design value, maximum and minimum values, and a measured value.

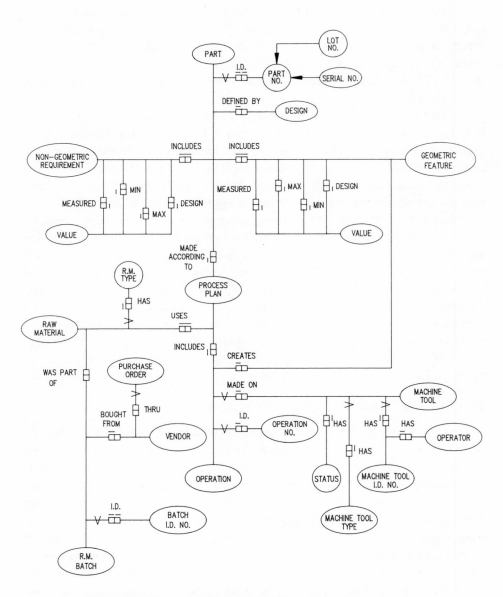

Figure 14.2   Information model for quality control

The part design is manufactured according to a process plan, which consists of operations. Each operation specifies a machine tool type and possibly a type of raw material. The raw material arrives in batches, with each batch having a batch identifier and a vendor. The raw material from a specific batch is used for a specific part, identified by either lot number of serial number.

Similarly, there are specific machine tools identified by a serial number for each machine tool type. A specific machine tool run by a specific operator is used to make a specific part. There is also a role linking a geometric feature with the process plan operation that created it. This provides the linkage between the test results and the process being monitored. If statistical analysis of this result shows that the process is out of control, there is a connection to the specific machine tool that must be fixed.

Many of the objects in this information model also appear in the models in other chapters. These are the points of integration between various information models and the functions they support.

Summary

This chapter described the role of quality in a company's strategy and how the cost of quality or the lack of it is frequently underestimated. It then described the traditional approach to quality control (i.e., sampling to ensure product quality and to determine whether the manufacturing processes are in or out of control). It also explained the importance of lot traceability for certain types of products. The chapter concluded by describing an information model to support quality control.

Notes

1. Philip B. Crosby, *Quality Is Free: The Art of Making Quality Certain* (New York: Mentor Books, 1979), pp. 105–106.
2. Much of what follows in this section is based on the work of Sullivan. See, for example, L. P. Sullvan, "The Seven Stages in Company-Wide Quality Control," *Quality Progress* 19 (May 1986): 77–83; L. P. Sullivan, "Reducing Variability: A New Approach to Quality," *Quality Progress* 17 (July 1984): 15–21; and L. P. Sullivan, "Quality Function Department," *Quality Progress* 19 (June 1986): 39–56.
3. Sullivan, "Quality Function Department."

Further Reading

Martin, John M. "Developing a Strategy for Quality." *Manufacturing Engineering* 99 (Aug. 1987): 40–45.
Wright, Roger N., and Don A. Lucca (eds.). *Product Design Engineering for Quality Improvement*. Dearborn, Mich.: SME, 1983.

15

Robotics

Definition and Use

Robotics Programming Languages and Issues

Information Model for Robotics

Summary

This chapter provides an introduction to robotics. It first defines what a robot is and describes how robots are being used. It then discusses some of the types of information needed to support robotics programming languages. The last section describes a high-level information model for robotics.

Definition and Use

Robots are a major topic in CIM today, but it is not always clear what is and is not a robot. A few people still consider simple pick-and-place machines to be robots. The growing consensus, however, is that a robot is a much more sophisticated device. The following two definitions emphasize this.

The Robotics Institute of America (RIA) defines a robot as "a reprogrammable, multifunctional manipulator designed to move material, parts, tools, or specialized devices, through variable programmed motions for the performance of a variety of tasks."[1]

VDI (Association of German Engineers) has a similar definition: "Industrial robots are universally applicable devices with several axes of motion, which may be freely programmed (i.e., altered without mechanical interference) with respect to their sequence of motion and angles or positions and may be guided by sensors—if applicable. They are equipped with grippers, tools, or other means of production and are able to perform manipulation and/or production tasks."[2]

Both of these definitions emphasize two points—flexibility and programmability. Flexibility is an obvious factor considering the wide range of tasks robots are currently performing. Typical tasks include painting, welding, applying adhesives, assembly, and material handling. While this list is impressive, it is even more dramatic to identify how robots are being used in some of the more automated factories.

General Motors has been modernizing truck production operations at one of its newer facilities.[3] Ninety-eight percent of the welding is done automatically by 117 robots. Sixty robots do 100 percent of the painting. Seventy percent of the sealant application is done by ten robots with vision systems for control. Additional robots are used for waterjet carpet cutting. This factory has already produced over 250,000 vehicles with record productivity and quality. This is just one of many examples of how robots can be effectively integrated into a total production system.

The two major benefits of robots are flexibility and quality. Although robots are not as flexible and adaptable as people, they are much more so than fixed automation systems. For this reason robots are often found in production lines producing small or medium lot sizes of many different products and/or models. Since flexibility is paid for in terms of speed and cost, robots (like flexible manufacturing systems) are not as effective for mass production. If this is true, why are there so many robots in the automotive industry? In the short term the automobile industry requires flexibility because a production line produces a mix of models and options, not a single unchanging product. In the long term robot flexibility eases the change-over between model years. It is much easier to load a different program than to replace fixed automation tooling.

Another factor for the automobile industry, or any robot user, is quality. Once they are programmed and tested, robots can deliver high-quality products consistently. This improved quality is one of the main reasons the Japanese are moving into robotics so quickly.

Unfortunately, many people see robots primarily as a labor-saving device. The problem with this perspective is that the direct labor component of many products is relatively minor—certainly nothing like it was several decades ago. The benefits of the improved flexibility and quality, although harder to measure, usually far outweigh the savings in direct labor.

The one place where robots are effectively replacing people, regardless of flexibility and quality issues, is in hazardous environments, such as paint spraying and loading and unloading hazardous machine tools.

Most robots are being installed in plants today as an integral part of the production process, not as isolated cases of replacing people. However, this often requires rationalizing the manufacturing process. A person cannot simply be moved out of the production line and replaced with a robot. Other parts of the production line have to change to interface with the robot effectively. The concept of design for manufacturing or design for assembly recognizes this. This concept, discussed in more detail in Chapter 16, recognizes that a good design includes considerations about how the product will be manufactured. Since robots are less flexible than people, many of the ambiguities that are acceptable today cannot be tolerated in a more automated environment.

Installing robots involves much more than just the robot itself. A company must consider the entire system within which the robot will be placed. The "total robot system" that must be considered includes the robot, the work area, the material handling system, the machine tool, and the human operator.

The robot itself has certain characteristics and limitations that determine how it interacts with its environment. The work area involves the placement of the robot, the machine tools it works with, and the accessibility of the workpieces, tools, and fixtures. For safety the work area must be isolated in such a way that movements of the robot do not endanger workers. The material handling system includes how the workpieces, tools, and fixtures are delivered to and removed from the work area as well as how they are moved within the area, such as how the robot loads and unloads one or more machine tools. Finally, design of the area must consider how humans will interact with the robot. These humans may include operators who are running the workcell, maintenance personnel who work on the robot and other equipment in the area, and "trainers" who must teach the robot what to do.

In effect, robotics requires a systems approach. It is not simply the installation of an isolated piece of equipment but rather an aspect of the entire production process. At a minimum you must determine how the robot affects all of the operations within the affected workcell.

The steps in selecting a robot are similar to those for selecting any other major automation component. First, you need to precisely define the requirements. Second, you need to talk to other users doing similar operations. The emphasis here is on similar operations. Someone else's experience with spray painting does not help if you are going to do material handling. You should focus on those robot characteristics that are critical to your operations and how other companies integrated their robots into the rest of the production process. Third, you should insist on a full-scale demonstration doing the type of operation you are considering. Seeing a robot in a relatively clean environment go through the motions required for spray painting is not the same as seeing one actually painting in a dirty environment and adjusting to changes in paint batches. Fourth, you need to analyze the data obtained during the selection process. These data include processing requirements, operating costs and benefits (both tangible and intangible), the impact of robotic systems on the rest of the production process, and the degree of flexibility needed. Finally, in selecting the robot vendor you should consider both short-term and long-term issues. You are not simply buying a piece of equipment and expecting the vendor to go away. You are taking another step toward a more automated and integrated production facility, which will continue to evolve over time. Therefore, you are beginning what should be a long-term relationship with the vendor. This perspective should be a significant factor in the selection decision.

There are several barriers to widespread use of robots. First, extensive time and costs may be required to redesign or modify an existing production facility so it can use robots effectively. Second, effective use of robots requires a more integrated and disciplined system than many companies have today. Third, there are still certain inherent limitations in many robots. While most robots have high repeatability (e.g., hundredths or thousandths of an inch), they are not capable of such precise movement to a specified point. This is not a major problem when you are manually teaching a robot by moving it through the desired motions. However, this is a very expensive way to create or modify a robot program because it ties up the robot and the associated equipment (sometimes even the production line) and is a more error-prone type of programming. The most effective approach involves off-line programming of the robot based on part and tooling data created elsewhere in a CIM system. However, this approach is most effective if you can precisely specify a point and have the robot go there. Research on robot arm calibration and position sensing is addressing this problem, but it has not yet been solved.

Two additional problems are the lack of trained personnel and the cost of the robot systems. Ignoring the system redesign cost identified above, just the direct cost of the robot can be significant. These costs include the robot itself, the associated tooling, the control system and software, and any additional sensors that are required for more control and flexibility.

Robotics Programming Languages and Issues

Although there are many programming languages for robotics, they all have certain elements in common.[4] They all must tell the robot how to operate within its environment. Some limited ones simply specify commands, independent of this environment. In this case the robot programmer must know everything about the environment, much as an assembly language programmer must know far more about the computer environment than the user of a higher-level programming language. Other higher-level robot programming languages capture more information about the robot's environment and can factor this information into the program.

This "world model" of the robot has many components. It includes the position and orientation of the workpiece as well as any gripping and fixturing points on the workpiece. With sophisticated feedback systems, such as vision and tactile sensing, the robot can still operate if this information is less precise or if a workpiece has been misoriented. However, the more precise this positioning information, the more effectively the robot can operate.

The robot also needs information about the physical characteristics of the workpiece, such as weight, surface condition, and stiffness. The workpiece weight along with movement and arm extension determine the inertia with which the robot and its control system must deal. Stiffness and surface condition can affect the gripping force with which the workpiece can be held.

A robot may have to deal with multiple workpieces or objects. For assembly a robot may get various parts from different places and connect them. Even if the robot is working with a single workpiece, it may still need to locate and move various tools and fixtures. This means that the robot must know not only know the absolute position and orientation of these objects but also their relative positions and orientations with respect to each other.

The robot world model must also know the positions of the various material handling components feeding and removing material from its workcell.

In addition to having this world model at a point in time, the system must also keep track of how the model changes over time. These changes may occur because the robot itself moves or moves an object or because other components in the material handling system move objects. In effect, the robot must keep track of how this world model is manipulated by the execution of the robot program.

Depending on the construction of the robot and the type of joints, it can use rectangular, cylinderical, or spherical coordinates. There are also various local and global coordinate systems for the robot and for its world model.

Depending on the type of robot, its movement can be either point-to-point or continuous path. More sophisticated robot languages allow the programmer to control the velocity and acceleration of the motion as well as its direction. In the simplest cases motion is simply programmed and executed exactly as programmed. More sophisticated systems and languages incorporate feedback from various sensors, usually either vision or tactile. This control, using real-time feedback, is similar to the NC research on adaptive control.

Most sensors have a fairly common set of operations, such as activating or disabling the sensor, reading sensor data, or checking the sensor status. There may also be sensor specific operations, such as setting various device parameters.

Most robot programming languages address all of the above issues to various degrees. However, one of the major problems with developing robotic applications today is the proliferation of programming languages, with none clearly emerging as an industry standard. There are certain commonalities across all of these languages, especially for similar robots, since they must deal with similar world models, types of movements, and control mechanisms. Examples of these languages include:

AL—   derived from ALGOL
SRL—   based on AL with PASCAL elements

PASRO — integrated into PASCAL, with geometric data
AML — related to PL/1
VAL — Unimation language developed for robotics
ROBEX — based on NC programming
RAIL — Automatix language for industrial robots
IRDATA — software interface developed by VDI

ROBEX, developed as an extension to APT (the NC programming language), includes a set of standard geometric objects (e.g., point, line, circle, pattern, plane, beam, cylinder, sphere, and cone). These geometric objects overlap the ones described earlier in the chapter on geometric design, so the same information model can support them. ROBEX also allows the programmer to define bodies as collections of these geometric primitives, similar to the features used in feature-based design. Parts are then defined as collections of bodies.

Some of these languages allow engineering data types, dimensions, and operations. For example, AL includes predefined dimensions for distance, velocity, angle, angular velocity, time, force, and torque. In addition, AL allows extensions to include new data types and dimensions.

VDI has developed IRDATA and is proposing its use as a basic language for all robots. This proposal is being sent to the International Standards Organization for consideration. IRDATA includes record types to describe robots, machine tools, sensors, work space, and frames. It also includes ways to specify motion, program control flow, computational operations, and I/O. In addition to the usual data types of Boolean, integer, real, character, string, pointer, and array, IRDATA has four new data types. Vector specifies an xyz coordinate. Orientation consists of three real numbers for angles orienting an object in space. World is a combination of a position vector and an orientation. Joint is a set of real numbers specifying the robot position and orientation.

Information Model for Robotics

This section describes a high-level information model of the concepts needed to support robotics. Some of the model summarizes the world model described earlier but with more explicit relationships. It also provides an information model like the models in the other chapters. This allows the reader to fit the robotics information into the context of the other data created and used by other CAD/CAM applications.

Figure 15.1 shows the robotics information model. The model distinguishes between a robot type and a specific robot. Some facts relate to a robot type. A robot type has a power requirement, speed and weight limits, and an envelope within which it can move. These facts apply to any specific robot of that type. A robot type also has a set of end effectors and sensors that can be attached, although all robots of a type may not have all of these optional components. A robot type also

230

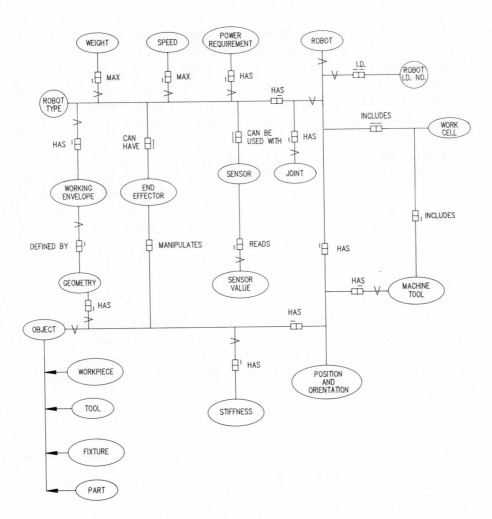

Figure 15.1   Information model for robotics

has a type of coordinate system and joints that can be moved over a certain range of motions.

Each specific robot has an additional set of facts. A specific robot has a position and orientation where it is located on the shop floor. Each joint and specific end effector that is attached also has a position and orientation. Similarly, the specific machine tools in the workcell have both positions and orientations. The various objects, such as workpieces and fixtures, with which the robot must deal also have positions and orientation. They also have their own geometric definition. Objects that the robot must grip or move also have weight and stiffness, which affect the acceptable gripping force. These objects may also have both a current position and orientation and a future position and orientation to which they should be moved. If the specific robot has sensors, they monitor certain data such as position, orientation, movement, or force.

In effect, this information model defines the capabilities of each type of robot and much of the world model for each specific robot. However, much of the information in the model also relates to other parts of the design and manufacturing process. Part geometry is created during the design process and may have many other attributes attached to it. The machine tool in this model ties it to all of the other models that include any machine tool information.

Summary

This chapter provided two definitions of a robot, both of which emphasized flexibility and programmability. It described how robots are being used and discussed the importance of taking an integrated, systemic approach to robotics. It then identified some of the characteristics of robot programming languages and described some of the data they require. Finally, the chapter provided a high-level information model to support robotics.

Notes

1. Joseph F. Engelberger, *Robotics in Practice: Management and Applications of Industrial Robots* (London: Kogan Page, 1980), p. 8.
2. Christian Blume and Wilfred Jakob, *Programming Languages for Industrial Robots* (New York: Springer-Verlag, 1986), p. 4.
3. Robert Booth, "MAP 2.1 Local Area Network for Computer-Integrated Manufacturing," presentation at Data and Knowledge Engineering for Manufacturing Conference, Hartford, Conn., Oct. 1987.
4. Much of the information in this section is from Blume and Jakob, *Programming Languages for Industrial Robots*.

Further Reading

Blume, Christian, and Wilfred Jakob. *Programming Languages for Industrial Robots.* New York: Springer-Verlag, 1986.

Design and Manufacturing Functions

Brody, Herb. "The Robot: Just Another Machine?" *High Technology* 6 (Oct. 1986): 31–35.

_____. "U.S. Robot Makers Try to Bounce Back." *High Technology Business,* Oct. 1987, 18–24.

Engelberger, Joseph F. *Robotics in Practice: Management and Applications of Industrial Robots.* London: Kogan Page, 1980.

Henderson, Dale L. "Off-Line Programming Cuts Costs, Saves Time." *Robotics Today* 8 (Aug. 1986): 23–24.

Hunt, V. Daniel. *Industrial Robotics Handbook.* New York: Industrial Press, 1983.

Stauffer, Robert N. "Justification of Robotic Systems." *Robotics Today* 8 (June 1986): 35–43.

Stoll, Henry W. "Design for Manufacture." *Manufacturing Engineering* 100 (Jan. 1988): 67–73.

Ullrich, Richard A. *The Robotics Primer: The What, Why, and How of Robots in the Workplace.* Englewood Cliffs, N.J.: Prentice-Hall, 1983.

16

Flexible Manufacturing Systems

The number of flexible manufacturing systems in the United States and Japan is steadily growing. These systems are a compromise between the traditional hard automation of mass production and the tremendous flexibility of small job shops. This chapter discusses this aspect of automation and describes the type of information model needed to support such systems.

The chapter first explains what a flexible manufacturing system (FMS) is and contrasts this approach with the job shop and hard automation. Second, it identifies the benefits of flexible manufacturing, both generically and specifically in terms of actual cases. Third, it describes some of the problems many companies encountered in implementing an FMS. Fourth, it identifies and describes the main components of an FMS. Finally, it provides an information model that captures the basic information needed to support the flexible manufacturing approach.

235

What Is a Flexible Manufacturing System?

A flexible manufacturing system is best described by identifying its components. An FMS consists of a set of machine tools, an automated material handling system linking them, and a computer system to control them.

In a typical FMS when a part is scheduled for production, the computerized control system determines which raw materials, tools, fixtures, and machine tools are needed. It schedules the production time on the machine tools. It then tells the automated material handling system (AMHS) where to get the raw material, tools, and fixtures and when they are needed where. The AMHS loads the material onto pallets, loads the pallets onto carts, and routes them to the appropriate machine tools or machining centers. At the machine tool or center, the pallet is unloaded from the cart, which can then go to its next stop. At the machine tool the pallet is unloaded, and the individual materials, tools, and/or fixtures are loaded onto the first machine tool. Once the processing on that machine tool is completed, the material is unloaded from the machine tool and moved to the next machine tool. Loading and unloading machine tools and passing workpieces between machine tools in the same workcell is usually done by a robot.

The flexibility of the FMS allows it to produce many different parts simply by loading different NC or robot programs. It also uses data from its database to determine which raw materials, tools, and fixtures need to be sent when to which machine tool to make a different part. The main physical limitations on these systems involve the size, shape, and weight of the part and the manufacturing processes and tolerances required to make the part. Cost can also be a major problem with an FMS.

A large, sophisticated FMS may include dozens of machine tools, robots, a material handling system, and several computers. Such a system may cost $10 to $20 million. On a more modest scale an FMS could consist of only a few machine tools, a robot to load and unload them, a simple material handling system, and a single computer. This low end is sometimes called a flexible machining cell, but regardless of the terminology the concepts are the same—the only difference is one of scale. Today a typical FMS integrates eight machine tools and the automated material handling system that supports them. Some flexible manufacturing systems produce only a few dozen parts, while a few may produce several hundred. An FMS at LTV Dallas was installed in 1984 to make over 500 different parts for the B-1B, and there are plans to add another 800 parts for commercial aircraft components.[1]

Although there are not many flexible manufacturing systems today, they represent large state-of-the-art operations in some major companies. In 1985 a Yankee Group study reported only 50 examples of a full-scale FMS in the United States and projected only 284 by 1990. However, on a smaller scale it found 250 flexible manufacturing cells and projected over 1,900 by 1990.[2]

There are more flexible manufacturing systems in Japan than in the United States. In a few cases these systems run entire factories in a "lights-out" mode — i.e., completely unmanned during normal operations. This type of lights-out operation is still relatively rare, but it is more common in Japan than in the United States.

Benefits of an FMS

An FMS is a compromise effective for moderate-volume production where flexibility is more important than high production rates. At one extreme there is the job shop with high flexibility but relatively low production volumes. At the other extreme there is the hard automation typical of mass production facilities, where any change creates a major problem.

An FMS supports many types of flexibility. One type of flexibility involves design changes. These changes may be minor design modifications or completely new parts. Another type of flexibility involves changes in the product mix. An FMS is designed to produce parts with a certain set of characteristics — either existing parts or possible future designs. In the short term the mix may change for seasonal demand, while in the long term the mix changes as new products are introduced and old products mature and then decline. Short runs for small orders can be inserted during longer production runs with little loss in efficiency, whereas in more conventional operations these scheduling changes could create major problems.

The two key direct benefits of an FMS are more scheduling flexibility and dramatically increased machine utilization. For example, with the LTV FMS mentioned earlier, machine tool utilization jumped from 15 to 80 percent, and such increases are not uncommon. As another example, GE installed an FMS to produce motor frames and gear boxes.[3] The savings in this case included a 240 percent improvement in employee productivity, improved part quality and consistency, reduced production cycle time from 16 days to 16 hours, and a 38 percent increase in capacity with 25 percent less floor space. In general, an FMS can provide the following benefits:

- easier design changes
- easier to introduce new products
- easy to change the product mix
- easy to quickly add special orders to production schedule
- less work in process inventory
- faster production cycle, requiring less inventory
- better machine tool/equipment utilization
- better production control and scheduling
- better quality and more consistency

How frequently are these benefits realized? A Frost and Sullivan study[4] of 20 flexible manufacturing systems in the United States found the following range of benefits in various areas:

237

1. Number of machine tools needed dropped 60 to 90 percent.
2. Direct labor savings increased from 50 to 88 percent.
3. Machine efficiency increased by 15 to 90 percent.
4. Processing cycle time dropped by 30 to 90 percent.
5. Floor space requirements dropped by 30 to 80 percent.
6. Product costs dropped by 25 to 75 percent.
7. Number of setups dropped by 10 to 75 percent.

Furthermore, these savings do not take into account the intangibles, such as improved quality and more rapid delivery. These benefits, however, are not without costs. The next section describes some of the common problems companies encounter when planning for and installing a flexible manufacturing system.

Implementation Problems with an FMS

A company can encounter many problems when attempting to implement an FMS. Some of these problems, such as how to justify an FMS, are the same for any CIM system. Other problems, however, arise because an FMS requires a higher level of integration and demands a more disciplined manufacturing environment. This section identifies some of these problems and suggest ways to deal with them.

There are several aspects to the justification problem. First, there is the biasing effect of current cost accounting procedures, which focus on reducing direct labor. Years ago when direct labor was a major cost component in most products and most overhead was attached to manhours, this was a reasonable approach. However, today the labor component in most products is relatively small. This creates problems in cost-justifying many systems. This does not mean that cost-justifications should not be done—only that they must be done more carefully and with some understanding of the underlying assumptions and their impact on the results.

A second justification problem is that many of the benefits of an FMS are intangible and hard to quantify. Machine utilization and work-in-process inventory can be quantified easily. But what are the monetary benefits of easier design and product changes, flexibility in terms of product mix, better control of the production schedule, and higher, more consistent quality? How does a company quantify the cost of a missed delivery?

A third problem with justification is that an FMS is not a stand-alone system. It has a major impact on the entire factory, and it is difficult to partition out the costs and benefits of the FMS from those of other activities that must also be carried out. For example, Lardner of Deere has estimated that "We could cut our capital investment for automation by 50 to 60 percent just by getting the design and manufacturing people together from the beginning."[5] In some cases these gains would be considered benefits of an FMS, when in reality they are simply the benefits of improved communications. They could be obtained without all the expense of an FMS.

Another implementation problem is poor shop floor management and planning. In the past this was tolerable because people on the shop floor could adjust to discrepancies. However, an FMS requires a more disciplined environment where everything has been precisely defined. This requires a level of planning and integration far beyond what most companies are used to. There are major problems when companies simply try to automate their current operations (especially with an FMS) without first rationalizing and organizing them. Lardner's comment above is one indication of this. In another comment he has suggested that in many cases we are computerizing utter confusion and inefficiency.[6]

Clearly, a company needs to get its manufacturing operations together before it implements an FMS. One of the key steps here can be "design for manufacturability" or "design for assembly." This approach provides the discipline that makes subsequent automation much easier. However, this discipline also makes non-automated manufacturing much easier.

Some of the principles of design for assembly include[7]:

1. Products should be built on a stable, easy-to-orient base.
2. Parts should be constructed of subassemblies.
3. Parts should be assembled from above in layers.
4. Guide pins should be used for alignment.
5. Parts should be inserted in straight-line motion.
6. Number of parts should be minimized.
7. Bolt and nut assembly should be avoided.
8. Once a part is inserted, it should not be possible to dislocate it.
9. Parts should be compliant and self-aligning.

Gerald Hock at GE has estimated that the design for assembly approach can lead to a 20 percent reduction in the number of parts in a product and a 40 percent reduction in assembly labor.

Another major problem arises from not knowing what level of flexibility is important—that is, what is required, what is desirable, and what is just bells and whistles. Flexibility is not free. An FMS buys its flexibility at the cost of lower production rates and volumes. If a company does not need flexibility, then an FMS is not the best solution—or even an appropriate one.

A recent Harvard Business School study of ninety-five FMS operations in the United States and Japan found that many U.S. companies are misusing the technology.[8] Japanese systems were producing more types of parts than their U.S. counterparts by an order of magnitude. In effect, many U.S. companies were paying for the flexibility but not using it effectively. In some cases the companies were still benefiting from the FMS approach but not nearly as much as they could have with better planning. The study also found that often in the United States the flexible manufacturing systems did not perform as well as the conventional technology they replaced. Therefore, it is essential that a company know what level of flexibility it needs and what it is willing to pay for that level.

Components of an FMS

An FMS has three basic components—workstations, an automated material handling system, and a computerized control system. The workstations are the machine tools or machining centers included in the FMS. The automated material handling system may include robots to load and unload the machine tools and a system to move pallets of parts, workpieces, tools, and fixtures through the factory. Finally, there is a computerized control system to keep track of the status of the system and all of the material flowing through it.

An effective FMS must balance the flexibility in all of its parts. For example, a very flexible control system buys nothing if the machine tools and the material handling system do not provide a comparable level of flexibility. A high precision machine tool may not be effective if the material handling system cannot place the workpieces with the required precision.

In many cases the control system software is what constrains the system's flexibility. The capability of the control system software should be a key factor in evaluating and designing an FMS. One of the problems is that most of these systems are customized one-of-a-kind products. Furthermore, the vendors of these systems are not system software houses specializing in integration.

Information Model for an FMS

Figures 16.1 and 16.2 show a basic information model for a flexible manufacturing system. The model includes two submodels—one for an automated material handling system and the other for machine tools. The FMS includes only one AMHS, but an AMHS could support multiple FMS operations in a factory. The FMS can include many machine tools, but each machine tool can belong only to a single FMS.

Figure 16.1 shows the submodel for the automated material handling system. An FMS can include multiple pallets, vehicles, and tracks. Each pallet has both a type and a unique identifier. A pallet has load limits in terms of both weight and dimensions. Finally, a pallet has a current load. The current load consists of one or more shipments. Each shipment consists of a tool, fixture, or workpiece and has both a weight and dimensions. Each shipment also has a source and destination place.

A place is also related to a track over which vehicles can move. The FMS includes multiple tracks. Each track consists of path segments, each of which starts and ends at a place. Place is also related to machine tools, which are located at a place, and to vehicles, which have a current position. Using these relationships involving place, a routing algorithm can determine how to move a shipment over the correct paths to get it from its source to its destination. When a request is made

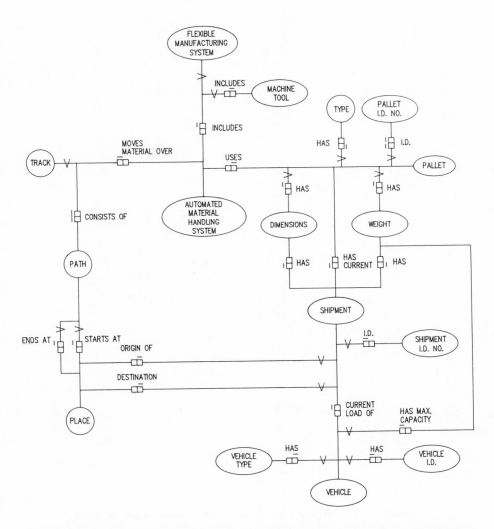

Figure 16.1 Information model for FMS—automated material handling system

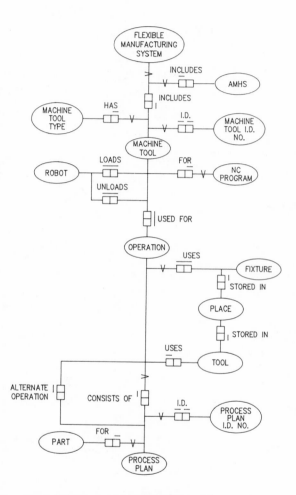

Figure 16.2   Information model for FMS—machine tool

for a vehicle to pick up a shipment with certain load characteristics, the control system can determine which of the vehicles with enough remaining capacity is the closest. It can then route the vehicle to make the necessary pick up.

As with a pallet, a vehicle has a type, a unique identifier, a load limit, and a current load. The main difference is that a pallet load consists of shipments whereas a vehicle load consists of pallets. A vehicle also has a current position, which is located on some path segment.

The other major submodel for an FMS involves machine tools and robots. This submodel is shown in Figure 16.2. Each machine tool has a type and a unique identifier. It is also located at a place. A machine tool is loaded and unloaded by one or more robots. Each machine tool is related to one or more parts through a process plan and operations in the process plan. Each operation in the process plan uses tools and fixtures, both of which are stored in places. These places can be sources and destinations of pallets and vehicles. An operation may also require an NC program.

The information model for a specific FMS would be more detailed, but this generic model indicates the type of information needed to control an FMS.

Summary

This chapter has provided an overview of flexible manufacturing systems. It explained what an FMS is and identified its components. It described both the benefits of an FMS and the problems encountered in implementing one. Finally, it provided an information model for a typical FMS.

Notes

1. Jeffrey Zygmont, "Flexible Manufacturing Systems: Curing the Cure-All," *High Technology* 6 (Oct. 1986): 22–27.
2. Ibid.
3. Rudy M. Tepsic, "How to Justify Your FMS," *Manufacturing Engineering* 91 (Sept. 1983): 50–52.
4. Diane Palframan, "FMS: Too Much, Too Soon," *Manufacturing Engineering* 98 (March 1987): 34–38.
5. Zygmont, "Flexible Manufacturing Systems."
6. Palframan, "FMS: Too Much, Too Soon."
7. Rita R. Schreiber, "Mechanical Assembly: Robots Carve Their Niche," *Robotics Today* 8 (Oct. 1986): 25–32.
8. Ramchandran Jaikumar, "Postindustrial Manufacturing," *Harvard Business Review* 64 (Nov.–Dec. 1986): 69–76.

Further Reading

Boothroyd, G., and P. Dewhurst. *Design for Assembly: A Designer's Handbook.* Amherst, Mass.: University of Massachusetts, 1983.
Burgam, Patrick. "FMS Control: Covering All the Angles." *CAD/CAM Technology,* Summer 1984, 11–14.

Design and Manufacturing Functions

Drozda, Thomas J. "Jumping on the FMS Bandwagon." *Manufacturing Engineering* 90 (March 1983): 4.

Hammond, Gary. *AGVS at Work: Automated Guided Vehicle System.* New York: Springer-Verlag, 1986.

Krauskopf, Bruce. "Defining FMS: The Concept, the Users, and the Builders." *Manufacturing Engineering* 92 (June 1984): 41.

Miller, Richard K. *Automated Guided Vehicles* Dearborn, Mich.: SME, 1987.

Palframan, Diane. "FMS: Too Much, Too Soon." *Manufacturing Engineering* 98 (Mar. 1987): 34–38.

Stauffer, Robert N. "Commentaries on FMS Control." *CAD/CAM Technology,* Summer 1984, 15–17.

Stroll, Henry W. "Design for Manufacture." *Manufacturing Engineering* 100 (Jan. 1988): 67–73.

Tepsic, Rudy M. "How to Justify Your FMS." *Manufacturing Engineering* 91 (Sept. 1983): 50–52.

Warnecke, H. J., and R. Steinhilper (eds.). *Flexible Manufacturing Systems.* New York: Springer-Verlag, 1985.

Zygmont, Jeffrey. "Flexible Manufacturing Systems: Curing the Cure-All." *High Technology* 6 (Oct. 1986): 22–27.

Part Four
Integration Issues

Part Three has explained various design and manufacturing functions and built generic information models to support each of them. The common objects in these models are the points of integration among these functions.

Part Four focuses on some of the broader integration issues. Chapter 17 describes where within the corporation CIM information systems are being developed and how these development groups relate to the more traditional corporate information organizations. It also relates the growth pattern for CIM to the pattern found in information systems when technology changes. Finally, it discusses several basic MIS control mechanisms—a master plan, a postimplementation audit, and a steering committee. Chapter 18 identifies two key groups in the CIM organization—the CIM Steering Committee and the CIM Task Force. It also describes the type of training needed by these groups. Chapter 19 focuses on system selection issues, including the importance of manufacturing strategy in the selection plan and the importance of building a long-term relationship with key vendors. It also identifies specific selection criteria for the DBMS because of the central importance of this software. Finally, Chapter 20 reviews the competitive environment and the factory of the future. It also discusses the impact of several technology trends on CIM.

17

Information Systems Management: Lessons for CIM

This chapter addresses several key aspects of information systems management. The first section discusses information systems planning in its broadest context, relates it to CIM information systems, and explains the long-term relationship between CIM and the corporation's more general information systems planning efforts. The second section describes some key lessons and tools from information systems management. These items include the information systems master plan, the postimplementation audit, and the Information Systems Steering Committee. The third section focuses on project management. It describes the portfolio approach to selecting information systems projects as well as the specific steps that should be included in a project plan and effective procedures for managing information systems projects.

Information Systems Planning

This section reviews some of the key concepts in information systems planning in relation to the location of and growth of the information systems function. It also relates them directly to CIM information systems. An underlying assumption in this chapter is that a key to CIM integration is information systems integration. Therefore, in the long term, the planning for CIM and business information systems should be coordinated.

For CIM information systems planning there are two key issues. First, where in the organization is the CIM information system function located? Second, what is its growth pattern and how does this growth pattern relate to the one exhibited by business information systems?

Location in the Organization

In most companies CIM information systems and traditional data processing or management information systems are located in different organizations. Management information systems (MIS) and engineering information systems (EIS or CIM) usually report up different management chains.

In some companies this was simply the continuation of the early distinction between the two groups, which occurred partly because early computers were not powerful enough to support both business and engineering groups. In companies with large engineering efforts these two groups may have never been merged. This dichotomy was further encouraged because of the different characteristics of engineering and business users, systems analysts, and application developers. When there were already two information systems groups, CIM clearly fell into the engineering area.

In other companies the business and engineering information systems groups may have been merged. However, this frequently occurred when the engineering effort was relatively small and could no longer justify its own computer system. In most of these cases business information systems became the dominant activity. However, the development of CIM systems, especially the early drafting-oriented ones, often led to a reemergence of engineering information systems. These systems were located in the engineering area because they were dedicated to that function and because the traditional business information systems groups had no interests or expertise in these systems, which were initially special-purpose, stand-alone systems.

Now the nature of CIM systems has changed. They are relatively powerful systems, most using conventional hardware (VAX, IBM, PRIME, CDC, etc.) rather than special-purpose hardware. Furthermore, they now support many engineering functions, some of which are closely linked (or should be) to the more traditional business functions, such as MRP. Finally, as the price of these single-function CIM systems has declined, they have proliferated into many departments within engineering. This pattern is similar to that of business information systems, with a central corporate system and many separate division or departmental systems and a proliferation of microcomputers.

In summary, regardless of whether or not there was already a separate engineering information systems group, CIM systems were usually located in the engineering rather than the traditional business information systems area. However, in many cases CIM or engineering information systems have become or are becoming simply another information systems department, facing many of the same issues that have plagued business information systems.

Growth Pattern

This section describes the growth pattern of business information systems and explains how the lessons we have learned there can be transferred to CIM information systems.

Stages of growth for information systems—Studies have shown a common information systems growth pattern in many companies regardless of size or industry. In 1974 Gibson and Nolan described four stages of growth in electronic data processing based on research at Harvard Business School.[1] The four stages are initiation, expansion, formalization, and maturity. These stages are shown in Figure 17.1. A stage is determined by three dimensions: the nature of the applications, the personnel specialization, and the management techniques and organization.

The first stage is initiation. When a company introduces data processing, it typically concentrates on a few relatively simple applications. These applications are primarily for cost reduction and involve automating a few well-defined clerical procedures (e.g., accounting and billing). The personnel specialization involves computer skills (i.e., the ability to translate the simple requirements into computer programs to efficiently use the new and expensive hardware). Management techniques are usually almost nonexistent because management perceives the area as being too complicated and technical to understand.

Today with the rapid decline in hardware costs, the emphasis on end-user computing with microcomputers, and standard-packaged applications, this initiation stage is changing somewhat. However, there is still an emphasis on simple stand-alone applications and management avoidence of the area.

In the expansion stage there is usually a rapid proliferation of applications in many areas. (A later article called this stage "contagion.") After seeing a few successes with simple applications, managers in many areas want their own applications. Most of these new applications are still relatively simple, but toward the

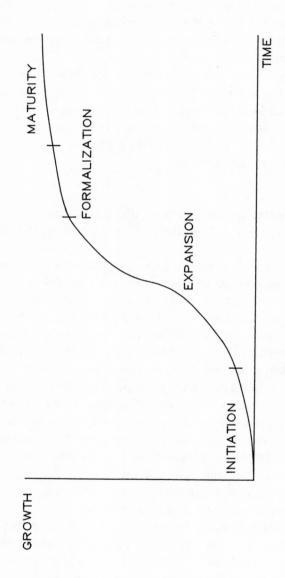

Figure 17.1 Stages of growth

end of this stage more complex applications are attempted. In some cases these applications involve new procedures that could not be done without the computer. To support this proliferation, the companies studied saw a rapid, uncontrolled growth in their data processing budgets and staff. Personnel specialization began to appear with systems analysts identifying requirements and doing the system design, programmers focusing on the detailed programming design and implementation, and operations personnel ensuring that the computer was used efficiently.

Usually there is still very little management control in this stage. Upper management still perceives the data processing area as being too complicated to manage. During this stage many information systems managers are often promoted into management because of their technical skills, not their management skills, so they have neither the skills nor the tools to effectively control this growth.

The transition between the expansion stage and the formalization stage occurs with the realization that data processing and the system development process are out of control. During the formalization stage there is often a dramatic decline, if not a moratorium, on new application development. Maintaining existing applications and in some cases linking them together takes most of the data processing development resources.

Personnel specialization becomes more important is this stage. People with expertise in formal methodologies and development tools are recruited. Formal requirements definitions with sign-offs by user management and more precise project plans become common. Management becomes much more interested in formal controls and evaluation mechanisms. Top management is more concerned with the costs and results of data processing, although they still avoid the technical details. However, these concerns tend to force information systems managers to concentrate on basic management controls rather than on the purely technical issues.

According to Gibson and Nolan, the maturity stage involves a resumption in the growth of new applications. However, these new applications tend to be more integrative, often involving data-driven development efforts more common to data management than to the earlier file-oriented development approaches. Many of these applications involve new activities and functions designed to provide the corporation with a competitive advantage rather than simply reduce its costs. New personnel specialization typically involves database management, data administration, and data communications. Finally, information systems managers begin to be perceived as senior managers in their own right, not simply technicans supervising other technicans.

Two changes have occurred since the original formulation of these four stages of growth over a decade ago. First, information systems technology has changed dramatically. In some ways this new technology has changed the characteristics of some of the stages, but in most cases it has simply allowed these stages to occur faster and in much smaller organizations, which are even less able to adjust to them. Second, to account for later developments in the companies, Nolan has revised the growth model to include six stages. However, there is another way to generalize the model without this type of revision.

Although the research on stages of growth looked at many companies in different industries, these companies were all large enough to set up computers and implement data processing relatively early—when the hardware and software start-up costs were high. Since then, however, technological developments have dramatically reduced these costs. Processing power and storage that in the early 1960s would have cost millions of dollars is available today for thousands or tens of thousands of dollars (and that is in current dollars—adjusted for inflation the change is even more dramatic). Similarly, applications that once took many man years to develop can now be bought off the shelf for a few thousand dollars or developed by end users in a few hours or days.

This change in the technology has two implications. First, much smaller companies, or even individual departments, can begin to use information systems. These companies have and can support much less personnel specialization. Therefore, end users and their managers frequently become involved in more technical issues than they can deal with, such as backup and recovery of critical data files.

Second, because so many standard applications are being marketed, a company can quickly acquire many incompatible applications, which will greatly complicate its operations. As the company begins to "fix" or tailor these applications to their specific needs, it discovers that a few of its key users are, in effect, becoming information systems people, but often without the necessary training. Finally, as users become more sophisticated and want to link their applications and pass data among them, they quickly run into a brick wall. Such "after-the-fact integration" of purchased software or user-written, single-function applications is impossible or extremely difficult and expensive. These end users have run into one of the key problems that caused the collapse of the expansion stage. They have neither the time nor the resources to shift end-user computing into the formalization stage.

Thus, with today's technology a small company can move through the first two stages too fast to identify the problems and figure out what needs to be done. Outrunning its learning curve makes the transition from expansion to formalization much more difficult. Unfortunately, such small organizations, whether companies or departments, frequently do not have the resources to cope with the resulting crises.

Generalizing the growth model—The-four stage growth model was developed in the early 1970s when the most advanced corporations were just entering the maturity stage. An obvious question is what has happened since. Is the model complete, or has new technology led to additional stages or a completely different growth path?

The researchers subsequently reexamined some of these companies to answer this question. At the time of the reexamination the key new technology was database management. The model was reformulated to include six stages: initiation, contagion (rapid expansion), control (formalization), integration, data administration, and maturity. These new stages explain what happens as database management and data administration evolve in the organization. However, this adjustment ignores the question of what happens when other new technologies (such as end-user computing and expert systems) emerge and begin to be adopted by companies.

An alternate way to generalize the growth model does not require changing the stages. Recall the general shape of the growth curve, which is similar to the classic learning curve or the innovation curve described by Foster.[2] Another way to generalize the curve is to say that it represents the growth of a certain technology within information systems, not the growth of information systems in general. With Foster's concept this basic growth curve applies to all technologies. Therefore, to generalize it, we need only to consider how the growth curves for various technologies are related; we do not have to change the basic growth model.

For example, in the information systems departments of large organizations there are several distinct technologies, each going through its own growth curve (see Figure 17.2). These technologies include the traditional application development approach (which the Gibson and Nolan study found), data management technology, data communications technology, end-user computing and workstation technology, expert systems technology, office automation technology, and others.

Two factors complicate how a company plans and implements these new technologies. First, a company may be at different stages for different technologies. For example, it may be in the formalization or maturity stage for traditional application development technology, in the expansion stage for data communications, and in the initiation or expansion stage for data management; it may not have started expert systems technology. These technologies impact each other. For example, the formal application development methodology and life-cycle approach used for traditional application development is not appropriate for effective data administration and data- driven development. However, it may be easier to modify one formalized approach into another formalized system—at least people are no longer arguing about whether there should be formal development procedures.

The second complication is that different parts of the organization may be at different stages with the same technology. In some large companies the business information systems department may be well into the growth curve for data management (e.g., at the formalization or even the maturity stage), while the engineering or CIM information systems group is at the initiation stage or even earlier. This can further aggravate the already tense relationship between these two groups. The business information systems group perceives the CIM group as being behind the times and using obsolete technology. On the other hand, the CIM group sees the business group as assuming that a dramatic change in the way they develop and relate applications is nothing more than another application.

Both perceptions are partly correct. However, they create needless conflict and hostility because neither group realizes that they are dealing with different

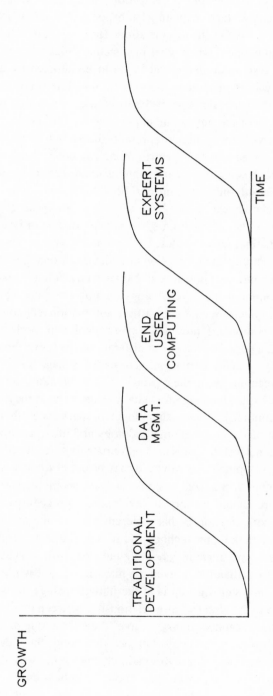

Figure 17.2 Multiple growth curves

technology curves. If the Not Invented Here syndrome can be overcome, each group can learn from the other and make faster progress along the technology curves.

In summary, the best approach is to use the four-stage growth curve but to focus on how the technologies blend with or replace each other. For example, data management technology changes the application development process. Similarly, end-user computing changes the traditional role of a central information systems department. However, it also impacts the application development process in two ways: by increasing the reliance on standard purchased application packages and by allowing some end users with little technical analysis background to begin to develop their own applications.

While end-user computing can be an effective way to deliver processing power and data to the user, application development by end users today is appropriate only for certain types of applications—small, relatively simple stand-alone applications and report definitions. However, in the future new development technology may remove this limitation.

Stages of growth for CIM information systems — The previous section has described the stages of growth as they apply to information systems in general. This section focuses more specifically on CIM applications and explains what these stages mean in this context. Remember that there is a distinction between the stage for a specific company and the stage for an industry (i.e., the most advanced companies).

The initiation stage involved single-function applications, such as drafting, NC programming, engineering analysis, and later solid modeling. Although these applications can be very complex from the CIM vendor's perspective, they are fairly simple from the engineering information systems department's perspective. They are simply purchased applications that need only to be selected and installed. However, many of the analysis programs may be developed internally for specific users. Thus for CIM this stage is almost identical to that for business information systems — single-function, single-department applications that simply automate a well-understood operation. The main difference is the greater reliance on purchased rather than internally developed applications.

Many companies are still going through this initiation stage, although the CIM industry as a whole is now in the late expansion or early formalization stage. The implication is that many small or unsophisticated companies think they are buying a product to satisfy a single function when in reality they are being locked into a set of functions as implemented and tied together by the CIM vendor.

Originally there was a significant difference between the initiation and the expansion stages. However, this is less true today because the major CIM vendors have a set of applications. Therefore, a company can buy and install a number of applications from the same vendor relatively quickly. The important point is that while these applications are provided by the same vendor and run on the same hardware, they are not usually integrated. They normally simply transfer files, so propagating changes and ensuring consistency is difficult or impossible. There are a few exceptions to this, but they usually involve start-up vendors with research and prototype systems rather than large critical production systems they can demonstrate.

For CIM the distinction between initiation and expansion may not relate to the number of applications or the rate at which they are installed. The critical factor seems to be the amount of internal development. Until a company begins to build its own applications on top of the vendor's products or tie applications together beyond what the vendor provides, the methodology and integration problems that lead to the formalization stages do not develop.

In fact, with CIM the first two stages could be renamed "purchased applications" and "internal development." The formalization stage occurs when the methodologies for internal development fail. There are two phases of the internal development stage. The traditional file-oriented development methodology is adequate as long as the development involves only single-function, stand-alone applications. It breaks down in the second phase when more integrated, multifunction (perhaps multidepartment) applications are attempted. The combination of these applications with inappropriate methodologies is what forces the shift to the formalization stage.

In most companies the business information systems area has already been through this problem because most of their applications were developed internally and the integration problem became a crisis earlier. Furthermore, many of the major purchased business applications today are built on an integrated data management technology. CIM informations systems can avoid many of these problems if the formal data-driven methodology developed or adopted by the business systems group becomes a corporate standard. But this is likely to happen only when there is a single information systems group, not separate business and engineering information systems groups.

For CIM the formalization stage may be more difficult because many departments are involved. This is especially true when each engineering area is doing its own information systems development. The problem is eased somewhat if there is an overall EIS group. However, even in this case there is usually a significant difference in methodology between the EIS and MIS groups when EIS starts the formalization phase. There may even be some difference at the end after EIS has adopted a data-driven approach. In the first case EIS and MIS are on different learning curves (i.e., for each methodology) whereas later, even if they are on the same curve, they are at different points. For purely engineering or purely business applications this may not matter. However, it can be a serious problem for bridging applications, such as going from an engineering to a manufacturing bill of materials or coordinating engineering and manufacturing change control.

Another problem during this transition stage is that users may feel "over-analyzed." Until a relatively complete, formal methodology is adopted, different developers, each with different objectives and approaches, meet with the users to understand their problems. From the users' immediate perspective there seems to be little payoff for this seemingly redundant effort. An obvious solution is a development moritorium until the methodology issues are resolved and an integrated methodology is approved. In the past this approach was sometimes used by business information systems. Since the users did not have their own information resources, they had to wait. Unfortunately, this is not feasible today because if someone does not solve the users' current problem in a global context, then the users will solve it themselves in a departmental context.

Consider a typical example of this overanalysis. A user is trying to design and analyze a specific type of part. One development group with a file-oriented approach interviews the user to get the requirements for the design applications. Another development team with the same methodology needs additional information to develop the analysis application. Some of their questions will be different, but there can be significant overlap. Then some developers with a data-driven approach need to interview the user to build a common information model that can be used by many future applications. From the user's perspective this information has already been provided to two other groups. Finally, an expert systems developer, again with his or her own methodology, wants to interview the user to build an expert system to automate more of the design process. Clearly, the user is not impressed with all of this activity. Unfortunately, it may be a frequent and unavoidable problem during the formalization stage.

The maturity stage is the point at which these problems have been resolved. A common data-driven methodology has been adopted so that, once requirements and design information have been captured from the user, any of it can be reused for subsequent applications. Furthermore, the methodology captures the information in enough detail to facilitate the necessary integration. Building the information model for the first few applications may be time-consuming, but for later applications the modeling is much faster because most of the information model already exists. Ideally, only minor application-specific additions are needed to the integrated information model.

As a final point, remember that these stages are stages on a technology learning curve. A company will go through a similar set of stages with any new technology. Although it has been through these stages with data management, a company will still go through a similar set of stages when it introduces artificial intelligence technology. The only consolation is that, by recognizing this process over time a company will learn how to more effectively manage the introduction of technology in general, not just a specific technology.

Given this stage model for information systems growth, the next section describes several management control mechanisms that were developed by many corporations as part of the formalization stage. These mechanisms, if used earlier, could ease or eliminate some of the transition problems between stages.

Management Control Mechanisms

Research has indicated that those companies with successful information systems functions have several things in common. First, they have a formal, written information systems master plan and have related it to the corporate strategy. Second, they do postimplementation audits (or postaudits) of their projects to learn how to improve their development process. Finally, they have an active Information Systems Steering Committee.

Information Systems Master Plan

Information systems management should be considered within the context of an overall information systems master plan. This master plan should have four components — strategy, technology forecast, inventory of current capabilities, and project plans.

First, there should be a section on corporate strategy to set the context. For a CIM information system this section should also include both manufacturing and CIM strategies. Ideally, the CIM information systems plan would be a subset of the overall corporate information system plan. However, if MIS and CIM report through different organizations, this may not be possible. If so, then the section should relate the CIM information system plan to the MIS plan.

The second section of the information systems master plan is a technology forecast, anticipating changes in information systems technology over the next five years. More importantly, this section should indicate how these changes can affect the corporation, especially in terms of new competitive opportunities, not just in terms of cost reductions.

The third section is a technology inventory. Given current and anticipated information system technologies, the master plan should determine what capabilities currently exist within the corporation for each technology. Some technologies may have been abandoned as obsolete or inappropriate. Other technologies will be the current state of the art for the company and represent the standard operating procedures. The company may be experimenting with and evaluating some of the newer technologies. Finally, the company may simply be tracking some of the newer technologies. Whereas section 2 of the plan provides an indication of where the industry (both the information system vendors and the company's competitors) is on the learning curve for new technologies, section 3 is an indication of where the company is on these learning curves. Some companies have a culture that makes them rapid adopters of new technologies, while others are content to use only proven, well-tested technologies.

The fourth section of the MIS plan includes a description of all current projects. At a minimum it must include a summary of all the approved and active projects. However, it may also include a description of major anticipated projects.

Postimplementation Audit

The second major management tool is the postimplementation audit. This audit is an attempt to determine whether the project was a success. Was it completed on time and within budget? Did the application meet its functional and performance specifications? Was the test phase relatively smooth, or were there many unanticipated problems? Was the conversion to operational status acceptable and were the users adequately trained?

The purpose of the postaudit is to improve the system development process, not find and correct problems with the project being examined. For example, a single late project may or may not be important. However, if it involved a new technology, then perhaps the estimating factors need to be lengthened until there is more experience with the technology. On the other hand, if most projects are late, then the estimating factors may be too low or more details may be needed in the specifications and the design before the estimates are made. The postaudit is simply an organizational mechanism for learning from and improving the system development and management process.

Information Systems Steering Committee

The Information Systems Steering Committee is the main mechanism by which top corporate management controls the information systems function. The previously mentioned survey by Harvard Business School showed that not only do most companies with successful information systems functions have a corporate-level steering committee, but that 90 percent also had divisional steering committees, and 80 percent had functional ones.

To be effective, the Steering Committee must include the senior corporate executives, such as the CEO and the VPs for manufacturing, marketing, finance, and information systems. The steering committee ensures top management's understanding of and support for the information systems function. Although its precise charter evolves over time and depends on the corporation's sophistication in terms of information systems, there are several basic oversight functions that must be included. These functions are as follows:

1. Set direction for information systems.
2. Set budgets and resource limits.
3. Resolve organizational structure issues.
4. Oversee major staffing and auditing decisions.

First, the Steering Committee sets the direction for information systems and ensures that the direction is consistent with the corporate strategy. It does this by setting objectives for information systems, by reviewing the long-range information sytems plan, and by ensuring that there is a mechanism for generating and updating a formal information system plan. Second, it rations or budgets the resources for information systems and ensures that a formal project selection process is in place and being used. Third, it addresses the organizational and structural issues relating to information systems. It is interested in the organizational context in which the information systems function relates to the rest of the corporation, not the internal structure of information systems. For example, in a manufacturing company the Information Systems Steering Committee would be involved in whether there should be a single information systems function or separate ones for business and engineering information systems and, if separate ones, how they should be coordinated. Finally, the committee would be involved in key staffing and management auditing decisions in information systems.

Although this Steering Committee was important in the past, it is becoming even more important in the future. Control is important because information has become a critical corporate resource and the total information systems budgets for most companies are growing rapidly. When all of the information systems activity was consolidated in one or two departments, it was relatively easy to control. Today with the trend to decentralization and distributed systems it is becoming much harder to control and coordinate information systems activity. A much smaller percentage of those dollars are directly visible and under the control of the information systems manager. Therefore, the Steering Committee becomes a key mechanism for coordinating this activity. The CIM Steering Committee is further described in Chapter 18.

Project Management

This section discusses project management as it applies to information systems projects. CIM information systems project management, as described in this section, is just one component of an overall manufacturing systems project in the broader context.

Project Selection: Portfolio Approach

Traditionally, project selection has been done in a very limited context. The benefits and costs for a single project are analyzed to decide whether it is worth doing. If the benefits outweigh the costs, if the resources are available, and if a user or group of users is willing to pay for it, then the project is scheduled. Various organizations use this method with different levels of sophistication—i.e., more or less accurately identifying all of the benefits and costs. For example, are intangible benefits identified? Is the personnel cost of training and any reorganization included? More sophisticated selection procedures would involve probabilities and expected ranges of benefit and cost values. Simple comparisons across projects could also be done to select those projects with the greatest expected net benefit. However, all of these variations still consist primarily of analyzing a single project in isolation until the final comparison step. Given certain resource limits the company does the top N projects.

A different level of sophistication suggests that projects should be selected not in isolation, but at least partly in terms of the resulting project mix. This is the portfolio approach to project selection.[3] This approach is much more appropriate for information systems management and especially for CIM information systems projects. Consider a stock portfolio. Clearly, you want to pick the best stocks. However, if you have several investment objectives, "best" is relative to a specific objective. Therefore, you make decisions not solely in terms of individual stocks but also in terms of balancing your portfolio with respect to all of your objectives.

Similarly, an information systems department has multiple objectives with its projects. Information systems should provide a net benefit to the company, just as investors want to make money on all their stocks. But this can be done with various types of projects. For example, some projects provide a modest benefit, but they involve few resources and relatively low risk. Risker projects may have potentially much greater benefits. In some cases the risk may occur because the project involves many parts of the organization. In other cases relatively small projects may involve high risk because they involve experimenting with a new technology. While it would be reckless to have only high-risk projects in a portfolio, it could be dangerously short-sighted to have only low-risk ones.

An information systems project with certain anticipated benefits is exposed to four types of risks. First, the project may not provide the planned benefits. This is an information systems problem if the system developed by the project does not meet the functional and performance requirements specified by the users. In some cases the system meets all of its requirements, but there are simply not the dollar benefits the users anticipated in such a system. While this is not really an information systems failure, the users and the information systems people may be able to identify more precise ways to specify the next system to minimize this risk.

The second type of risk involves overruns of either time or cost. This risk can affect the net benefit in two ways. Cost overruns directly reduce the net benefits. Schedule overruns affect the net benefit indirectly in two possible ways. The first and simplest way is that schedule overruns usually drive up the project costs. Second, schedule slippage reduces the benefits by delaying them and providing them over a shorter time. For example, a company may lose the first six months of anticipated cost savings; or, instead of having a competitive advantage for a year before a competitor develops a similar system, the company may be left with only a six-month lead time or possibly none at all.

The third and fourth risks involve more technical information systems factors: poor technical performance and incompatibilities among various hardware and software components of the system. These risks usually reduce the net benefit by driving up the costs because the solutions usually involve additional hardware or software development.

Although these risk exposures cannot be quantitified, there are ways to rank projects. This involves categorizing projects along three dimensions: project size, technology, and project structure. Figure 17.3 summarizes these dimensions and their factors.

Project size, the first dimension, has several components. How large is the project in terms of manhours? How long is the project in terms of its schedule length? How large is its scope in terms of the number of departments that are involved? Large, multiyear projects involving many departments are much riskier than small six-month projects involving a single user department. There is a practical limit to project size. Very large projects should be broken down and managed as smaller, less risky ones, even if the actual selection is done in terms of the larger original project.

The second dimension is technology. The components of this dimension essentially identify various learning curves. The lower the developer or user is on the greater number of learning curves, the greater the project risk. From the information systems side of the project the learning curves primarily involve new hardware and system software. The first workstation application or the first database application or the first expert system application is riskier than the second or third or tenth one in each area. Another factor is how well the information systems team knows the application area. Their first application in a new area is riskier than later ones because they have much more to learn and can be confounded by unanticipated problems.

A user aspect of this dimension involves the extent to which the user groups have been using applications and working with information systems people. The project will go much more easily if they have been through the process before and know what to expect during the development cycle. Note that if the information systems group formalizes or changes its development methodology and the way users participate in the development process, then the users (and probably the information systems people on the project) are now on a new learning curve and the project's risks are increased.

The third dimension is the project structure, which involves changes in organizational and task structure. Along this dimension the lowest-risk project is one that is simply building a replacement system for an already well-defined set of functions and procedures the users are now doing. However, these projects are relatively rare. The risks increase as more significant changes are required. The more the users' procedures must change, the greater the risks. More risk occurs if the user organization must change. A similar risk occurs if the information systems organization must change. Greater risks are involved if attitudinal changes are necessary. This is the reason the shift from the traditional data processing approach to the data management or information resource management approach is so difficult. It involves an attitudinal change on the part of both users and information systems people—from "its my data" to "its the organization's resource and whoever needs it can use it." Finally, projects that require changes from top management are very risky. However, this risk is moderated if top management is driving the

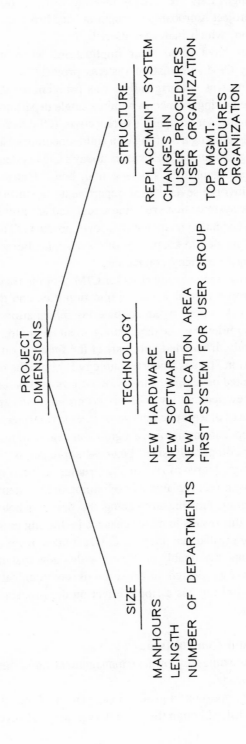

Figure 17.3   Project dimensions for portfolio management

project to support changes they are already making. Still, if top management is directly involved, the project is probably so important and broad that it affects many parts of the corporation, which increases its risk.

These dimensions have some clear implications when we consider the characteristics of many CIM information systems projects.

The size dimension was not originally a risk problem for CIM information systems. They automated a single function within a single department, so they were not large systems from the user company's perspective. (Of course, from the CIM vendor's perspective, developing a drafting or a solid modeling system was a major project and entailed a significant risk.) However, today's CIM systems involve much more risk from the user organization's perspective, both because they are larger and and because they involve several user departments. A further complication is that many of the basic systems that are being integrated are provided by turnkey vendors, who are independently enhancing their own products. The software configuration management needed to keep a set of CIM applications integrated over time is a new technology for many companies.

The technology area creates many risks for CIM. For the traditional business information systems people CIM is a new application area and therefore a high risk. However, if the work is done by an engineering information systems group, the application area is familiar, but the data management technology is new. Some CIM applications are truly distributed with part of the function on the mainframe and part on the workstation. This is a new technology for both the microcomputer- and the mainframe-oriented developer. Finally, expert-system-based CIM applications are still another new technology. CIM is progressing so rapidly that most projects are at the bottom of at least one (and sometimes several) technology curves. Therefore, most CIM applications involve a significant degree of technology risk— much more so than for comparably sized business applications.

They also have a high degree of risk on the structure dimension. At this time very few systems involve direct replacement of comparable systems. Perhaps the simplest case is automating drafting—replacing the drawing boards with CAD workstations. However, this results in major changes in drafting procedures. While most drafters who are interested can adapt to CAD, it takes from three to twelve months before they become reasonably proficient with a new system. Since drawings are still the basic way design information is communicated throughout companies, automating drafting has a ripple effect on the procedures within and among many departments.

Project Management and Control Issues

This section summarizes some key project management and control issues for information systems projects.

Three concepts are important in project management. First, there is a set of roles that someone must fill, although the same person may fill several roles. The three key roles are sponsor, acceptor, and project manager. The sponsor is the key manager or executive who is supporting the project—i.e., its advocate within the organization. If there is not a sponsor or advocate, then the project may have serious problems and its chances of success are reduced. The acceptor is the person who approves the system when the project is completed. The acceptor could be the sponsor, but this function is usually delegated to someone else, frequently a key user manager. The project manager is the person responsible for the actual management of the project (i.e., identifying and structuring the tasks, scheduling them, and managing the people working on the project). Each of these roles has a clear set of responsibilities. Major problems can arise if these responsibilities are blurred—for example, if the acceptor begins to get involved in project management or if the project manager begins to try to affect the test and acceptance process.

The second key point is that when a project begins we know the least about what needs to be done, the resources that will be needed, and the schedule. However, there is a tendency to make many critical decisions very early. An alternative is to try to defer as many decisions as possible until they must be made. This is not an attempt to avoid decisions, only to defer them if possible until more information becomes available.

The best example of this technique involves approving only the next phase of a project, not the entire project. The implication when you start a project is that you will finish it, but that assumes you know what you are approving. In the early stages of large projects estimates are only approximations. However, you know a great deal more about what is involved in the next step, so your estimates for that are very good. Therefore, you approve the next step and reevaluate the project at the end of that step. In reality, there are probably time and cost estimates for the entire project, but these should be updated at each point where a new project phase is approved.

Finally, to effectively manage projects, there should be a project plan that includes a specific set of steps, each with a defined set of outputs. This allows you to determine whether you have enough information to begin a step and whether you know exactly what needs to be done. It is also easier to estimate the resources required for the next step than for the entire project.

For an information system project these steps include:

1. Definition of project's scope
2. Definition of the system requirements
3. Preliminary/conceptual design
4. Detailed design
5. Implementation
6. Start-up/conversion
7. Operations
8. Maintenance/enhancement

In the past we have hurried through the initial steps to get to the "real work" — i.e., implementation. However, we have now learned that more time spent in these early steps, especially in defining the scope and requirements, can result in faster overall development and in far fewer problems during implementation, start-up, and operations. This is important because it is much more expensive to correct a problem found in these later steps than in the earlier ones.

The project management methodology described by Paul Thompson in *CAD/CAM Information Engineering*[4] builds on these lessons. It emphasizes enterprise modeling and requirements analysis. Enterprise modeling sets the overall context for corporate information systems and helps in setting priorities. The requirements analysis expands selected portions of the enterprise model with more detailed functional and information analysis. These analyses lead to a prototype system that the users can exercise to ensure that their requirements have been correctly identified. Once this prototyping has been done and the requirements definition approved, then the development project can proceed using any of several widely available data driven design methodologies.

Summary

This chapter has identified some of the major lessons that information systems management provides for CIM. First, it provided a four-stage framework for understanding and managing changing information systems technology. These stages included initiation, expansion, formalization, and maturity. Second, it described three key management mechanisms — the information systems plan, the postimplementation audit, and the Information Systems Steering Committee. Finally, for project management it described a portfolio approach to project selection and identified the key steps in a data-driven information system development project.

Notes

1. Cyrus F. Gibson and Richard L. Nolan, "Managing the Four Stages of EDP Growth," *Harvard Business Review* 52 (Jan.–Feb.): 76–88.
2. Richard N. Foster, *Innovation: The Attacker's Advantage* (New York: Summit Books, 1986).
3. F. Warren McFarlan, "Portfolio Approach to Information Systems," *Harvard Business Review* 59 (Sept.–Oct. 1981): 142–150.
4. Paul Thompson, *CIM: The Information Engineering Methodology.* (Boston: Digital Press, forthcoming).

Further Reading

Buss, Martin D. J. "How to Rank Computer Projects." In *Catching Up with the Computer Revolution,* ed. Lynn M. Salerno. Cambridge, Mass: Harvard University Press, 1984.

Gibson, Cyrus F., and Richard L. Nolan. "Managing the Four Stages of EDP Growth." *Harvard Business Review* 52 (Jan.–Feb. 1974): 76–88.

Head, Robert V. *Planning Techniques for Systems Management.* Wellesley, Mass.: QED Information Sciences, 1984.

McFarlan, F. Warren. "Problems in Planning the Information System." In *Catching Up with the Computer Revolution,* ed. Lynn M. Salerno. Cambridge, Mass.: Harvard University Press, 1984.

McFarlan, F. Warren. "Portfolio Approach to Information Systems." *Harvard Business Review* 59 (Sept.–Oct. 1981): 142–150.

Nolan, Richard L. "Managing the Crises in Data Processing." *Catching Up with the Computer Revolution,* ed. Lynn M. Salerno. Cambridge, Mass.: Harvard University Press, 1984.

Synnott, William R., and William H. Gruber. *Information Resource Management: Opportunities and Strategies for the 1980s.* New York: John Wiley and Sons, 1981.

Withington, Frederick G. "Coping with Computer Proliferation." *Harvard Business Review* 58 (May–June 1980): 152–164.

18

CIM Organization

CIM Steering Committee

Committee Functions
Committee Membership

CIM Task Force

Task Force Membership
Task Force Functions
Task Force Training

- Corporate strategy, operations, and CIM technology
- Communications
- Group process
- Managing change and innovation

Summary

This chapter describes some of the organizational changes that a commitment to CIM implies. It identifies two levels of CIM groups – the CIM Steering Committee and the CIM Task Force. It explains why these organizations are important, who should be on them, and what their functions are. The chapter also discusses the types of training needed by the CIM Task Force. The training on communications, group process, and managing change and innovation is included because of the complexity and importance of CIM. This is a complex area requiring the cooperation and understanding of experts from many disciplines and departments. The ease with which these people can communicate and the effectiveness with which they work together in small groups will have a major impact on how well the corporation can identify its needs and implement the necessary systems. Research has consistently shown that the effectiveness of work groups and the quality of their outcomes are critically dependent on the preparation and training of the groups and their leaders. Since many of the technical and management people who will be involved in these groups have not received this type of training, this training section reviews some of the basic concepts.

CIM Steering Committee

The CIM Steering Committee (CSC) is a high-level group of senior executives who must set the direction and provide the oversight for the CIM development and implementation from the overall corporate perspective. There are many similarities between this group and the Information Systems Steering Committee, which was discussed in Chapter 17. In fact, there will be much overlap in the membership of these two committees.

The CIM Steering Committee's function and emphasis will evolve as the corporation's automation work progresses. Some of these changes are a logical part of the learning process, while others may reflect the background and interests of the CSC members. However, throughout its life the CSC has two types of functions—leadership and management. Eventually some of the management functions may be delegated, but senior management cannot delegate the leadership functions, and during the initial period the leadership functions are the most critical.

The leadership functions are linking the critical strategies and providing internal support for the CIM efforts. In the early phases the CSC must be the real driver behind the CIM efforts. If the commitment is not there at this level, then the rest of the corporation can and will assume that CIM is simply a lot of talk and continue business as usual. Obviously, this reaction would be a disaster for the CIM development effort.

Committee Functions

The specific functions of the CIM Steering Committee are as follows:

1. Linking strategies
2. Internal marketing
3. Developing/reviewing CIM framework
4. Setting priorities
5. Project selection
6. Project management and postimplementation audits

The first function of the CSC is linking the various types of strategies. Chapter 1 discussed manufacturing strategy and how it must be consistent with the overall corporate strategy. Inconsistencies can create many serious problems. For example, a corporate strategy emphasizing quality and service combined with a manufacturing strategy concentrating on being the low-cost producer will not work. Therefore, the senior executives on the CSC must ensure that both a corporate strategy and a manufacturing strategy are in place and that they are consistent. Similarly, the manufacturing strategy must drive the CIM strategy, which the CSC must develop and approve. This CIM strategy identifies the critical factors and types of systems that are necessary to support the manufacturing strategy.

Finally, the CSC must also ensure that the information system strategy and plan are also consistent with the CIM strategy. This last linkage is important because a major part of the CIM strategy involves information systems, even though it is in the context of factory automation rather than traditional business-oriented information systems. Establishing this linkage with the information system strategy is complicated in some large companies because two completely separate information systems organizations may have evolved, one for business and one for engineering, as we noted earlier. This linking of strategies may be the first attempt to formally coordinate these two departments.

This function of linking related strategies must be done by senior corporate management. Unless they are committed to doing it, it simply will not be done. This function cannot be done by middle or lower level management because they have neither the perspective nor the authority. Although there are many issues demanding the time and attention of senior management, the importance of CIM to the company's competitiveness and survival should ensure their participation in the CIM Steering Committee.

Internal marketing is a second key leadership function. The CSC must be the driving force pushing the corporation into automation, especially in the early phases. This leadership function is critical because for most companies CIM involves a major change in the way they do business. This is especially true for integrated CIM. For example, using a CAD system to automate drafting may not be a major change, but integrating manufacturing guidelines and cost trade-offs in the design process will be a major change. Only senior management can overcome the organizational inertia because ultimately it may require changes in the organizational culture, procedures, and even the organizational structure. Some of this work can and should be begun even before all of the strategies are linked together. The CSC can begin to prepare the organization for the necessary changes even before all of the details are worked out. This parallelism is important because both of these steps can be very time consuming.

There may be various people (e.g., technical staff as well as some middle- and lower-level managers) advocating CIM efforts. But initially they are simply individuals and cannot drive the organization in this new direction. However,

271

they can be an important resource for the CSC. First, they are probably the most knowledgeable about these new technologies. Second, once the CSC has set the direction they will be even stronger advocates and others will pay more attention to what they are saying. Finally, some of these people will become the nucleus of the CIM Task Force, which must oversee the development, implementation, and management of the corporation's new CIM system.

The remaining four functions involve more management than leadership. Therefore, the actual work may be delegated, although the CSC is still responsible for it, must ensure that it is done, and must approve it.

Each corporation should develop a CIM framework or architecture that is appropriate for its own requirements. The initial strategies will set the scope for this framework. However, as the framework is developed, the learning process will make it possible to clarify some of the strategies, so there will be an iterative process.

The strategies define where the corporation is going and which factors are critical for moving it in that direction. The framework or architecture must then identify the functions and the interfaces that are necessary to support those strategies. This must be done at two levels: in terms of the business functions and interfaces and in terms of the information systems and databases. At the second level the framework simply identifies major systems and their high-level requirements and the general types of objects in each database. The framework is not a detailed requirements definition or implementation plan.

Finally, since developing the framework is a learning process and helps to clarify the strategies, the CSC should receive periodic (monthly or quarterly) reviews of the framework as it is developed, not simply be presented with a final, completed framework to approve at the end of the process. Ideally, the CSC should want these reviews, but if for some reason they do not, then the staff developing the framework should encourage them.

Once the framework has been developed and linked to the strategies it will be much easier to communicate to the rest of the corporation where things are going and the types of changes that will be necessary.

Depending on the strategies and the corporation's current strengths and weaknesses, another function of the CSC is to identify a set of priorities in terms of business functions or factors. Do we need to improve product reliability or service? Are manufacturing or inventory costs out of control? Is the development cycle too long? Do we keep redesigning the same products?

These priorities identify which parts of the framework should be attacked first. In addition to identifying key areas the CSC should also explicitly identify the criteria for setting priorities. This will help rank various projects in the same areas.

The CSC has two functions in project selection, but their direct involvement will depend on the size and importance of the specific project. For the largest and most important projects the CSC will want to make the actual selection and provide the final approval. It is critical to realize that importance is not simply a question of dollars. For example, the CSC may set a $200,000 budget threshold to review and approve all projects over that limit. However, there may be some $50,000 projects that are so important that they will also want to review and approve them. These small but important projects are those that commit the CIM development effort to a specific path. Decisions eliminating many otherwise viable options or decisions that would be very expensive to change later should be reviewed in terms of the commitments being made, not as if they were small independent projects. Obviously, the CSC must rely on the CIM Task Force to bring these projects to their attention because their size could allow them to be missed.

For smaller, less important projects the CSC simply needs to ensure that a formal project selection mechanism is in place and is being used. Middle management and the CIM Task Force managers can select and approve the projects based on the priorities and criteria that were set in the above function. For these projects the CSC would be exercising control mainly through the budget process—i.e., "here is the budget; go do the most important projects." The CSC would rarely change the priorities for these projects. Too many changes at this level would indicate a problem with the way the CSC had defined or communicated its priorities.

The CSC role with the project management and postaudits function is similar to its role with project selection. For major projects the CSC will want to review their status, track them, and check the postimplementation audits. However, in most cases their main role is simply to ensure that adequate project management and postaudit procedures are in place and are being used.

Committee Membership

From the functions described above it is clear that the CSC members must consist of senior corporate management. In fact, many of them will also be members of the Information Systems Steering Committee. At a minimum the CSC should include the CEO and the vice-presidents for engineering, manufacturing, marketing, finance, and information systems. Depending on how the corporation is organized, other executives may also be included. For example, if the corporation is structured by product rather than function, then the VPs for the major product divisions should be included, especially if each division does its own engineering and manufacturing. Furthermore, if the company has a major engineering information system function, the senior manager of this function should be included, even though it probably is part of the engineering or manufacturing organization. Finally, the senior manager of the CIM Task Force should also be a member of the CSC.

Staff support for the CSC comes from two sources. First, the members will have personal staff support from their own areas. Second, once the CIM Task Force is established, part of its resources will also provide support for the CSC.

This section has discussed the CIM Steering Committee, a high-level strategy and management committee to control and coordinate CIM development from the overall corporate perspective. The next section describes the lower-level working group that actually manages the CIM projects and in many cases does the actual work.

CIM Task Force

The CIM Task Force is a lower-level working group made up of people from all parts of the corporation. As a group, the CTF should have a relatively complete understanding of how the company does design and manufacturing and what the critical operational problems are. However, these people should be open-minded and interested in how systems and procedures should be changed and improved. In fact, some of them may have been pushing the company in that direction even before the CIM Steering Committee was established. These people either know in great detail how their areas operate or they have a network of contacts so they can find out quickly. The key point is that these people should be receptive to rather than resistant to change.

Task Force Membership

Members of the CTF are drawn from many areas, such as design engineering, drafting, product development, manufacturing engineering, the shop floor, and information systems (both the business and the engineering groups). If there are significantly different product lines or manufacturing technologies within the company, then there should be people from each of these areas. This is true even if the initial effort will affect only one product line or pilot plant.

Obviously, the people on the CTF are valuable to their current departments. However, their value to their departments should not override their long-term value to the corporation as a whole. This issue must be addressed directly because the CTF should include some of the company's top people in these areas. A part-time CTF is a compromise some companies have used. The members remain in their original departments, but some of their time is freed up and allocated to the CTF. The risk with this approach is that over time their normal workload will build back up and the CTF will only get the leftover time. This can be a disaster.

The safer approach is to establish a full-time CTF, even if it is only a core group with the others provided on a part-time, as-needed basis. For this strategy to work, the key people should be assured that a move to the CTF represents a significant career step. If the normal progression comes through functional departments instead of staff positions (and to a certain extent the CTF is a staff operation), then some of the key people may not be willing to make the move, particularly if they think it will slow down their careers. In reality, working on the CTF should be a significant benefit to a person's career, but senior management must make this clear.

Task Force Functions

The CIM Task Force performs several types of functions. At a high level the CTF will help refine the CIM strategy and define the overall systems architecture. At another level the CTF will actually manage many of the CIM projects, especially those which integrate multiple functions. Depending on the size and scope of the CTF, its members may be active participants or consultants on various project teams. CTF members will be particularly active in enterprise modeling, requirements analysis (i.e., functional analysis and information analysis), and definition of the system architecture.

Although the focus of this book is CIM information systems, the CTF will also be involved in the broader context of manufacturing technology and equipment selection. Because of the CTF's role in tracking CIM technology, some of its members will be internal consultants helping various departments select, install, and integrate products from a variety of vendors. These could range from MRP systems to robots to MAP-based communications systems.

Task Force Training

Task Force members need both technical and nontechnical training. The technical training involves corporate strategy, operations, and CIM technology. The nontechnical training involves communications (i.e., presentation and writing), group process, and managing change and innovation. Since many Task Force members will have come out of technical areas, these skills are often ignored. However, for a major integrating activity like CIM these skills are essential. Furthermore, research has repeatedly shown that the quality of any group's output can be dramatically improved with training in this area.

Corporate strategy, operations, and CIM technology — First, they need to know the various strategies — the corporate strategy, the manufacturing strategy, and the CIM strategy to the extent that it has been developed. However, the CTF will play a major role in refining and planning the implementation of the CIM strategy.

Second, everyone on the CTF needs at least a minimum understanding of how the company operates. Each person is an expert in one or more areas, but none of them knows every area. Some training will be needed to provide the members with some minimum level of understanding of all the functions. It is hard to integrate a complex set of functions if one does not understand enough about them to talk to the people doing them. This training can be provided by having members of the CTF do presentations explaining their area. A book like this one can also be used to build up a common level of understanding of the various design and manufacturing functions and the information required to integrate them.

Third, the CTF needs some background in current CIM technology. They must know the current state of the art to determine reasonable objectives and system architectures. Many of these people were probably already tracking developments in certain areas before they joined the CTF. However, CTF management should make sure that all of the critical technologies are being tracked in an organized way.

Communications—The ability to communicate is critical for the CIM Task Force members. First, they are dealing with a complex area where it is as easy to confuse as to clarify issues. Second, they are dealing with a diverse group of experts and users who are knowledgeable in only a few of the relevant areas. Therefore, effective written and oral communication skills are essential. Unfortunately, many technical people are not trained in this area. They can communicate effectively primarily with other experts in their own disciplines.

This section summarizes two key concepts—a presentation formula and audience analysis—that can improve these communication skills.

There is a widely quoted formula for technical communications that applies to both written and oral communications—Tell them what you are going to tell them. Tell them. Then tell them what you told them. This simple but effective formula is based on the way most people learn things, especially complex things. We do not remember a list of details. Instead we remember specific details in an organized framework. The better the new ideas fit within a framework, the easier they are to remember. In the first step, telling them what you are going to tell them, you provide your audience with a framework. This framework relates to things they already know, but more importantly it gives them a way to organize what you are going to tell them. In the second step, telling them, they get the details as part of a second look at the framework. However, they now have a context in which to organize and remember them. The last step, telling them what you told them, serves two purposes. It is a third review of the framework—which will help them remember it. It is also a last chance for you to reinforce the key points you wanted to make. A good reader or listener also uses this review as a check to ensure that they identified the key points you wanted to make. If these steps are missing, your reader/listener may still identify and remember your key points, but they have to work harder to do it. Furthermore, the more complex or unfamiliar the area, the more difficult it becomes for the reader/listener to do this without the help this formula provides.

The second important factor for the presenter or writer is audience analysis. Who is in the audience? What do they need or want to know and why? What level of detail are they interested in? Ideally, the audience is homogeneous—they have the same background information and want the same thing from the presentation. Unfortunately, this is rarely the case, especially with most CIM presentations. If the anticipated audience is too diverse, it is more effective to break it down and do several different presentations. Although this takes more time, the results are much more effective.

It is important to know the level of detail the audience needs. This can depend on their expertise, their level of interest in the topic, and their confidence in the presenter. People who are experts or are interested in the topic will want more details. If the audience has confidence in the presenter, they will settle for less detail. In one case they may simply want the recommendation, while other presenters may have to carefully reconstruct their analysis.

One effective technique is to anticipate the key questions and plan a two- or three-minute mini-presentation to answer them. Use the mini-presentation only if the question is asked. This same approach can be used in writing by carefully labeling the more technical sections, which can be skipped without losing the flow of the document. This approach is also effective in dealing with levels of technical details. Let the questions control the level of detail. Finally, realize that a person asks a question in terms of their own background and understanding of the topic. Therefore, you need to be careful to answer the question they wanted to ask, not necessarily the one they actually asked. For example, if an information systems person asks about a programming task, that is probably what they want to know about. However, to a manager or an engineer, programming may be the same thing as application development (i.e., the overall process of telling the computer what to do), so even though they are using the same words, they may be trying to ask a much more general question. An answer about programming details may not be what they are looking for.

Group process—Group process is another important area that can dramatically affect the quality of the CTF's work. Research has shown that groups and leaders who have be trained in these methods produce much better results than groups that are simply thrown together to sink or swim. Ideally, both the group and the group leader should be trained. This helps the group members understand what the leader is trying to do, and it gives them a chance to practice these new skills in a learning environment that is less threatening than their normal work environment.

There are essentially two types of meetings—communications meetings and problem-solving meetings. The purpose of a communications meeting is either to convey information or to build up support or morale for something. The problem-solving meeting is the focus of this section. The purpose of a specific problem-solving meeting may be to identify a problem, identify alternative solutions, evaluate alternatives, or make a decision.

Four leader skills are important:

1. The leader must be able to effectively state the problem without implying a solution. Such an implied solution biases the analysis. And solutions suggested by the group leader, either directly or indirectly, are not evaluated fairly by the group. There is usually a strong bias either for or against the solution. The leader should limit himself or herself to a short initial problem statement and let the group refine it until there is agreement. The leader should also clearly state the scope within which the group must operate. This keeps the group from wasting time and effort on an unacceptable solution.

2. The leader must be able to introduce information as it is needed during

the discussion. Since the initial problem statement should be short and concise, additional information must be introduced during the discussion. A long problem statement initially reduces the group involvement.

3. The leader should be able to draw out people in the group and get more information without creating defensiveness.

4. The leader should be able to identify and summarize at key points.

Brainstorming is a popular method for generating alternatives. The purpose of brainstorming is to encourage the generation of ideas. This is done by separating the idea generation and evaluation steps. During the actual brainstorming phase ideas are only suggested, and these ideas may or may not build on previously suggested ideas. Any attempt to immediately evaluate an idea tends to cut off the flow of new ideas because it makes people defensive and hesitant to suggest things. In the second phase of the meeting the ideas are then organized so that the group can begin to evaluate them. This deferred evaluation is difficult for many technical people who tend to immediately start analyzing things.

Maier has suggested a set of screening rules to improve the quality of a group decision.[1] These rules help eliminate two types of errors. One error involves overgeneralizing from previous experience: "This problem is like the one yesterday, so here is the answer." However, the problem may be like yesterday's problem in three ways and unlike in ten more important ways. The other type of error occurs when we fail to use the facts that are known. Maier's rules help eliminate personal bias in selecting a solution, avoid conflict over questionable facts and conflicting interpretations, and minimize personal conflict in the problem solving process.

The first rule is to reject solutions transferred from other situations. Only when the facts show a clear and strong similarity should a transferred solution be seriously considered. Second, solutions should be rejected if they are based on facts or interpretations of facts that are challenged by members of the group. Third solutions supported by unchallenged facts and interpretation should be further evaluated. Fourth, solutions based on a trend should be further considered if any exceptions to the trend can be adequately explained.

Managing change and innovation – The CIM Task Force is a major force for change within the corporation. Therefore, its members and managers, as well as other managers throughout the company, need to know how to manage change and innovation. Change is essential for manufacturing today, and will determine whether it is to remain competitive or to regain lost ground. Therefore, any discussion of CIM implementation must consider how to manage change.

There are always technical problems in designing and implementing CIM systems. However, the most serious problems, the ones that ultimately determine success or failure, are almost always people problems, not technical ones. In spite of this premise, which is widely accepted, few managers are trained to recognize and deal with the impact of change on people. Any training that is provided usually has an organizational perspective and focuses on planning—i.e., determining the objectives, identifying the resource requirements, getting the resources, training employees, and implementing the change. If people were always rational and unemotional, this would be an excellent way to deal with change. However, people are not like that, especially when they are being forced to change.

Managers must be trained to realize that change affects people personally and emotionally, sometimes in unpredictable ways. They need to be trained to identify symptoms and diagnose how their people are responding to the change. Managers need techniques for dealing with these responses, so they can help people work through their problems. Finally, managers are also people and have these same reactions to change. Before they can effectively lead people, they must resolve their own reactions to the change.

This type of training is difficult because it involves not simply understanding intellectually what needs to be done. It also requires an emotional commitment from the manager that this is an effective way to manage change. It also requires practice and coaching because this type of interpersonal skill can be developed only through practice.

This section describes a framework for understanding how change impacts people and how managers can help themselves and others understand and accept change. The information here is based on Wilson Learning Corporation's seminar Managing in a Changing Environment.[2]

Change can occur in either of two ways. Ideally, the people affected can participate in deciding what the change will be and how it will be implemented. This participative style of management usually results in much better decisions and is typical of the Japanese management style. Unfortunately, U.S. manufacturing companies usually exhibit the second approach to change. This is change that is imposed on people by outside forces. These outside forces may be upper management, changing customer tastes, or new technology that gives a competitor a significant advantage. Whatever the reason for the change, managers determine its success or failure by how well they manage themselves and lead their employees.

Change occurs in three phases—endings, transitions, and beginnings. During the ending phase people are concerned with how the change will affect them. In the transition phase they start making connections between where they are now and where the change is leading them. Finally, a person accepts the change and starts to focus on how to implement the new beginnings determined by the change.

A problem is that, once most managers accept the change, they start planning how to implement it (i.e., the beginnings phase). This leaves their people adrift to work out their own endings and transitions. This adjustment can be difficult, and without any formal organizational support people will rely on informal support groups, which may or may not support the change.

An effective manager must determine how his or her people are responding to the change and then help them adjust. To do this, the manager needs a diagnostic tool to understand how his or her people are responding to the change. The manager also needs a set of strategies to deal with each person's response – and with the way that response changes over time.

The diagnostic tool is a change scale from 0 to 10. This change scale simply indicates whether a person is moving toward the change (10) or away from it (0). There are two important points about this scale. First, the scale is a diagnostic tool for an individual, not for a group or a department. A department does not accept or reject a change – only the people within the department can do that. Therefore, the diagnostic tool should be applied only to individuals. Second, where a person is on the scale is not important – rather, the person's movement over time is the critical issue. A person who started out at 1 and is now at 5 is making more progress than someone who started out at 6 and a month later is still at 6.

The change scale is a relatively subjective measurement. However, there are some criteria to help locate someone on it. These criteria involve three independent dimensions:

- victim/owner
- loss/gain
- rigidity/resilience

The victim/owner dimension indicates whether the person is accepting some responibility for what is happening. A person acting as a victim usually regards change as something bad. The victim is passive and does not try to control the direction of the change and its impact. On the other hand, a person can take ownership of a change and begin to affect how the change will impact him or her. Taking ownership of the change does not mean you like it or will benefit from it, only that you are beginning to adjust and respond to it so that you have some control over what is happening to you. For example, a victim will complain about being laid off, but an owner may get additional training so he or she can be recalled earlier or shift into a less vulnerable job.

The loss/gain dimension is subjective because it depends on the person's *perception* of loss or gain – not the *reality* of loss or gain. Objectively, a transfer may involve many gains for a person, but subjectively it may be perceived as a loss because it involves losing many valued contacts and informal relationships.

Rigidity/resilience involves how a person's job behavior changes in response to the change. Some people will rigidly try to maintain their old behaviors and working arrangements. Other people are less concerned with the form and can easily adapt to new procedures and tasks needed to accomplish perhaps the same purpose, although doing it in a different way.

To place a person on the change scale, the manager uses these three dimensions as a guideline and identifies the specific behaviors and comments that places a person somewhere on each of these dimensions. Periodically the manager must reevaluate a person's position on the change scale. A person's behaviors and comments of two weeks ago say nothing about where the person is this week. A manager has to evaluate recent behaviors and comments to determine the person's current position on the change scale. Although this change scale is a valuable tool, it does not by itself tell a manager how to deal with a person. This is determined by identifying how the person is responding to the change.

There are four common responses to change — disengagement, disidentification, disorientation, and disenchantment.

1. *Disengagement* ("Quit and stay") — The person continues to come to work and go through the motions but is totally uninvolved in what is happening.

2. *Disidentification* ("I used to be somebody") — In this case the person feels that the change has taken away some aspect of his or her identity. The expert on a machine tool or procedure that is replaced may feel, despite twenty years of experience, as green and unimportant as the new hire who knows nothing about the procedures. In fact, research has shown that changing as little as 15 or 20 percent of a person's job can cause a sense of loss and confusion.

3. *Disorientation* ("Where do I fit in?") — This person is floundering not because of resistance to the change but simply because he or she does not know what to do to support the change. This is perhaps the easiest response to deal with, but if it is ignored, it may become one the more serious ones, such as disengagement or disidentification.

4. *Disenchantment* ("Ain't it awful?") — The person with this response is usually very vocal, which can lead to several problems. First, if a group is left to themselves without effective leadership, they will look to each other for support. Because the disenchanted person is more vocal, he or she can have a tremendous influence on such a leaderless group. Second, because this person is so vocal, unless a manager is careful to diagnose each person individually, this person can unduly influence how the entire group is perceived. This can become a self-fulfilling prophecy — the group is perceived as negative and so is treated negatively, which confirms their negative perception. Disenchantment often masks one of the other responses. For example, a less vocal and self-confident person may become disengaged rather than disenchanted.

Once a person has worked through his or her response to the change (i.e., gotten through the ending phase), it is time for the transition phase. Different people will be ready for the transition phase at different times. How long it takes a person to get there depends on the specific change and its effects on the person. There is a common set of activities during the transition phase: clarify, share, and engage.

Clarification is the first step. This concentrates on the employee's concerns, values, and perception of how the changes affect him or her. The manager can clarify by actively listening to the employee's concerns and the emotions behind those concerns. The manager can also help the employee focus on and understand his or her real concerns. (For example, "I know you were upset by all three of those incidents. Was the problem the same in all three cases?") Often the person has not made a connection and may never make the connection unless someone focuses his or her attention on it. Another way to clarify is to restate the employee's concerns once they have been clarified and focused. This indicates to the person that the manager has really listened, even if the manager cannot solve all the problems.

As the second step the manager shares with the person, revealing what he or she knows of the change and its effects. If the manager does not know what is happening in certain areas, he or she should be willing to say that. It is much easier to accept the fact that a manager does not have an answer than to think the manager has the answer but is not going to share it. That perception can destroy the basis for future communications.

The third step is to engage the person in the change and get them involved. This means shifting the person from a passive victim role to a more active owner role.

In addition, managers must realize that they are not immune to change. They respond to change just like everyone else. Depending on how the change affects them, they will also exhibit one of the reponses described above. Ideally, their managers will help them work through the change, but they cannot rely on this. Therefore, managers should be prepared to manage themselves through the change process. (Ideally, all employees should also be prepared to work their own way through the change because their managers may not help them through the process.[3])

During this self-management process managers should consciously listen to and evaluate what they are telling themselves about the change. This involves asking four questions: What am I telling myself about the change? Is it true? What do I want from the change? What is the first step I should take to get what I want from the change? These simple questions force the manager to take active ownership of the change, consider it in terms of the gains rather than the losses, and exhibit resilience in terms of different behaviors that are necessary to get the potential gains from the change.

Only then are the manager and employee ready to address the new beginnings. This is a clear contrast with our usual concerns when a change occurs: What are my new objectives? What tasks are necessary? What resources do I have? What is the plan for meeting these new objectives with the new resources? These activities all involve new beginnings, and we jump to them immediately, usually ignoring the necessary preparation of the ending and transition phases.

New beginnings have two distinct components. First, there must be a vision of where we want to be. Without such a vision people have nothing to commit to and work toward. A vision provides them with something to identify with and work toward. The second component, a plan, is simply a mechanism for accomplishing something. People may work hard to accomplish a plan, but only because they are committed to the vision that the plan is trying to achieve. Consider the difference between a blueprint and an artist's sketch. People do not become committed and emotionally involved in a new house when the architect shows them a blueprint. In most cases they can't even read it. The sketch is what provides the vision that they become committed to. Without the vision there is no commitment.

Major industry figures and people who have succeeded with major automation projects are leaders with a vision. They can quickly and emotionally explain where they are going and what they want to accomplish. They also have a plan to get them there (or a staff that can develop such a plan for them). But if they are successful, it is because people buy into the vision, not the plan.

Summary

This chapter has discussed several key CIM organizational issues. It described the importance and role of the CIM Steering Committee and the CIM Task Force. It also described three important but often-ignored areas of training for the CTF: technical communications, group process, and change management.

Notes

1. Norman R. F. Maier, *Problem-Solving Discussions and Conferences: Leadership Methods and Skills* (New York: McGraw-Hill, 1963).
2. Managing in a Changing Environment, a seminar developed by the Wilson Learning Corporation, Eden Prairie, Minn.
3. Working in a Changing Environment is a new Wilson Learning Corporation seminar designed to help employees do this.

Further Reading

Chiantella, Nathan A. (ed.). *Management Guide for CIM*. Dearborn, Mich.: CASA/SME, 1986.

Ferraro, Richard A., Terry E. Hunley, and Orry Y. Shackney. "Banishing Management Barriers to Automation." *Manufacturing Engineering* 100 (Jan. 1988): 44–48.

Foster, Richard N. *Innovation: The Attacker's Advantage*. New York: Summit Books, 1986.

Kanter, Rosabeth Moss. *The Change Masters: Innovation for Productivity in the American Corporation*. New York: Simon and Schuster, 1983.

Knox, Charles S. *CAD/CAM Systems: Planning and Implementation*. New York: Marcel Dekker, 1983.

Maier, Norman R. F. *Problem-Solving Discussions and Conferences: Leadership Methods and Skills*. New York: McGraw-Hill, 1963.

Nolan, Richard L. "Managing Information Systems by Committee." *Harvard Business Review* 60 (July–Aug. 1982): 72–79.

Woodward, Harry, and Steve Buchholz. *After-Shock: Helping People through Corporate Change*. New York: John Wiley and Sons, 1987.

19

System Selection

**Importance of Manufacturing Strategy and
Selection Plan**

Importance of Vendor Selection

Requirements Definition

DBMS Selection

Users
System Usage
Data

Summary

This chapter discusses several critical issues in selecting CIM systems. The focus
is on the major issues that are the keys to integration.

The first section explains the importance of an overall maufacturing strategy
and a plan to drive the entire selection process. (Many of the project selection issues
discussed in Chapter 17 also apply to system selection.) The second section explains
the importance of vendor selection as opposed to simply product selection. The
third section discusses requirements definition. Detailed requirements definition
and selection procedures for each application area, however, are beyond the scope
of this book. The fourth section provides a more detailed discussion of DBMS selection criteria because of the importance of DBMS to the entire integration effort.

Importance of Manufacturing Strategy and Selection Plan

With a major system as complex as CIM it is important to identify at the outset the long-term system requirements, although the system will be implemented in a series of steps. Without an overall framework and an implementation plan there is no guarantee that the pieces will fit together later as they are acquired and implemented.

CIM selection decisions should be driven from the context of an overall manufacturing strategy rather than from an individual departmental perspective. Without this overall framework and effective control of the selection process, suboptimization can become a major problem. The ultimate goal of CIM is to improve the corporation's competitiveness by improving its design and manufacturing operations as a whole, not simply by making independent improvements in each department—even though some of these independent improvements may provide significant benefits. If they do not fit within the plan or within a revised plan, they may be risky. This risk relates to another problem: with poor planning, an early application in a relatively minor area can seriously impact a later decision about a more important system. For example, a decision about a drafting system or a solid modeling system may impact later decisions about NC programming and process planning.

Importance of Vendor Selection

Traditionally information systems selection emphasizes the application package. The selection team defines the requirements, sees demonstrations, evaluates systems, perhaps does benchmarks of the top contenders, and makes a decision. Except in extreme cases the characteristics of the vendor play a relatively minor role.

With CIM, however, selection of the vendor or vendors is critical. The company is not just buying their application but also their architecture and their long-term direction. This means a long-term system commitment. CIM is not like a reporting system that is relatively easy to change later. Over time these systems become an integral part of day-to-day design and manufacturing operations. Later changes will impact the entire corporation, not just one or two departments.

It is important to ask not only whether the vendor's current product is acceptable but also whether the vendor is on the right track and moving in the right direction. Is the vendor seriously concerned with integrating a variety of applications, especially those from other vendors, or is the vendor concerned only with a narrow set of products or its own product line? Is the vendor primarily emphasizing mainframe, minicomputer, or workstation systems, or does the vendor realize that in a major CIM architecture all of these systems have a role? In summary, is the vendor's direction consistent with the company's manufacturing strategy and the types of applications needed to support it?

Is the vendor's technology proven and widely used, or is it new and as yet unproven? A new and unproven technology should not necessarily be ruled out.

Starting early on the learning curve may improve the company's long-term competitive advantage. However, a new technology does mean a higher risk, more resources, and usually a closer working relationship with the vendor, all of which a company must be willing to accept.

As an indication of this growing vendor importance, many large companies are developing approved vendor lists. Selecting products from vendors on this list is made relatively easy, and there is corporate support for them. It is extremely difficult, although not impossible, to use vendors not on the approved list. An approved vendor list is an important tool to discipline the CIM selection process. Furthermore, vendors on the approved list must be able to work together effectively because no single vendor will have all of the answers.

Requirements Definition

In spite of the importance of the vendor, a company buys specific products. Therefore, requirements definition is still important.

The requirements should be defined within the context of the overall manufacturing strategy. Important application areas (i.e., those critical to the manufacturing strategy) should be defined in some detail. Even if you do not know all of the details of your long-term architecture, what you do know today should provide an umbrella under which current selection is done. Over time these requirements will become more precise as you learn more and the architecture evolves.

The requirements definition should distinguish between absolute requirements (i.e., mandatory features) and desirable features, with weights assigned for their importance. In most cases requirements should involve results rather than how something is done internally.

Finally, requirements should be structured from the top down, but they should be done down to a very low level. For example, it is not enough to specify a solid modeler. You should identify the types of geometry (e.g., specific primitives) that must be included, the types of operations you want to do on them, and the applications with which the solid modeler must interface. Without this level of detail too many things can fall through the cracks. Ideally, a requirements definition should be done as if the product were going to be built internally. Then you can make a buy or build decision based on how close existing products are to your requirements.

One of the major requirements areas is the interface among applications and the way data is managed and shared. Most CIM systems today are still not DBMS-oriented, although many of the new ones are. If you select a non-DBMS-oriented system, the specific interfaces and translators are critical. The vendor should provide the critical ones such as IGES and, in the future, PDES. However, you should also be able to devise and implement translators if necessary for applications that the vendor does not support. Normally this could be done from a standard format, such as IGES, rather than directly from the vendor's internal format.

When you consider a DBMS-based system, you should evaluate the DBMS as if you were considering buying it as a separate package. Important DBMS evaluation criteria are identified in the next section. However, you should consider several additional questions. The vendor has defined a specific database for its applications. Can you extend this database for your own requirements? Can you add new record types or relations to the database? Can you add new attributes or domains? These issues will be critical later when you want to build internal applications on top of the vendor-supplied system. Is the vendor willing to release its database definition so third parties can integrate their applications to it? This open architecture will provide you with much greater flexibility in the future.

The emphasis so far has been on relatively high-level issues. The next section is a more detailed focus on DBMS selection. This additional detail is provided because of the importance of the DBMS in integrating CIM. Without effective data management you simply have a collection of applications, not a real CIM system.

DBMS Selection

This section is essentially a summary of the key DBMS selection factors described in the 1975 CODASYL Systems Committee report *Selection and Acquisition of a Data Base Management System*,[1] adapted for CIM.

The database administrator (DBA) must identify data management requirements and assign them priorities. This analysis must consider both current and future applications as identified by the corporate and the manufacturing strategy. The main characteristics for evaluating the DBMS involve the types of users, ways in which the system will be used, and the data.

Users
Many types of people will use a CIM system and therefore the DBMS that supports it. A partial list includes:

- design engineers
- draftsmen
- design analysts
- engineering managers
- process planners
- production schedulers
- expeditors
- foremen
- machine tool operators
- maintenance personnel
- inventory and stockroom personnel
- clerks
- salesmen
- programmers
- systems analysts

Today many of these users may deal with the database only indirectly (i.e., through an application program). However, in some cases today and in many more cases in the future these users will directly query and update the database. Therefore, the ease of use of the DBMS is important.

Additional questions involve the number of users, their level of training and expertise, and the way in which they use the system to do specific functions.

The number of users on the system is an important factor. For some applications, such as engineering change control, there will be only a few users, especially users who are allowed to change any of the data. For other applications, such as inventory control, there may be many users. System load depends on the number of users, what they are trying to do, and whether their demand peaks or is spread out more uniformly.

User experience and training with a DBMS are also important. If the users have little training on a DBMS and do not use it enough to become experienced, then a friendly user interface, such as menus with many prompts and explanations, will be important. However, such features can become a major aggravation to well-trained and experienced users. With most systems today this difference in user experience is less of a problem than it used to be. Most systems provide different interfaces for the experienced and the novice user. The novice can select items from a menu and fill out a form on the terminal to tell the DBMS what to do, while the experienced user can enter short, concise commands. Furthermore, the user can usually decide at any point which option to use. Therefore, the DBMS should have both types of interface and be easy to learn and use. A user should be able to begin using the system after learning only a small part of it.

The third consideration is the type of operations the users perform. At one extreme there are the parametric users, who essentially fill in the blanks for a fairly limited set of requests. For example, in the traditional work scheduling or shop-floor control system the user may be a worker on the shop floor who queries the system to select the next job or to enter job status. (If the DBMS interface is too complicated, an application can sit between the DBMS and the user. However, whenever this has to be done, it increases the load on the application developers and increases the costs of using the system.) At the other extreme there are the application programmers and ultimately the DBA, who have extensive knowledge of and experience with the DBMS and can easily use its more complicated command language.

System Usage

System usage characteristics include the usage mode, access methods, the amount of data sharing, and the degree of planned versus unplanned use of the system.

The usage mode refers to whether the application is batch or interactive and, if interactive, its response time requirements. The response time requirements will be different for different applications and even for different operations within the same application.

Data access method refers to how the data are being accessed and for what purpose. Does an application only retrieve data or does it also do updating? Does the application access the data sequentially or randomly? If the data access is random, how many access paths and keys are needed and are they all known when the database is designed?

The third characteristic is the degree of data sharing the DBMS must support. In the traditional database environment multiple users share the data concurrently — for example, several users may want to get at the inventory data at the same time. This requires access controls that lock data at the individual record or item level. However, for other types of applications, such as design, drafting, or analysis, file-level locking may provide adequate access control. This is especially true when the applications share data on a sequential rather than a concurrent basis. In this case the next user can get the data only after a previous user has finished certain processing. For example, you do not want someone to begin analyzing a design while someone else is actually working on it and changing it.

The fourth system characteristic involves the degree of planned versus unplanned or unanticipated use of the system. Planned versus unplanned refers to the functions that the system must perform, not to the timing. Those functions requiring relatively few, well-planned activities are the ones for which it is possible to develop parameterized applications that require relatively little user training and experience. At the other extreme are the unplanned and unanticipated requests. For example, if you are replacing machine tool X, you may want to request a list of the parts whose process plan includes this machine tool.

Data

The key data characteristics that affect DBMS selection include volume, growth rate, volatility, structural complexity, distribution, and importance.

Most DBMSs's today do not have problems with the volume and growth rate of the data. However, all of the large databases today are centralized on large mainframes. The problem will be more complicated with CIM databases because they will be distributed across many computers — multiple mainframes as well as workstations and shop-floor systems, especially as factory operations become more automated. Therefore, data volume and distribution issues are related. All of the standard business-oriented requirements for distributed database management will also apply to CIM.[2] But there will be additional requirements, such as check-out/check-in mechanisms to support sequential rather than concurrent data sharing. The appropriate engineering-oriented mechanisms will need to be built on top of existing DBMSs.

Both network and relational DBMSs can support the level of structural complexity needed for most engineering databases. The questions are really how easy they are to use and how well they perform with these very complex structures. The ideal solution is to benchmark the one or two alternatives, but benchmarks of complex database applications are difficult and expensive.

For the major alternatives—network and relational DBMSs—there are some general guidelines. A network DBMS will probably provide better performance, especially with large complex databases. A relational DBMS will be easier to learn and use for both users and programmers. The integrity and security of a network DBMS are much greater than for current relational systems. Therefore, the development time and cost differences are less dramatic when you include all of the integrity and security that must be built into the relational applications but which is automatically provided a network DBMS.

In the future many of these integrity and security problems with the relational system will be solved, but you should consider the capability of both types of systems before making a decision today.

Integrity and security involve the final data characteristic. Data quality and security involve cost and performance trade-offs. How current must the data be? Overnight updating is adequate for some applications, but process control and flexible manufacturing need real-time data. How much data integrity are you willing to pay for in performance and cost? Finally, how long can you afford to be without your data? Backup and recovery procedures involve a trade-off. More time spent backing up each operation means much faster recovery when there is a problem.

To evaluate a DBMS, you should consider all of these factors: user characteristics, system usage characteristics, and data characteristics. In many cases you may decide that no single DBMS can adequately meet your needs. Different systems to meet different requirements may not be an unreasonable solution in some cases. However, this alternative complicates data sharing and should be considered only as a last resort. If you take this approach, be sure that there are mechanisms to pass data effectively between the different systems.

Summary

This chapter has described the importance of the manufacturing strategy and long-term selection plan for CAD/CAM/CIM system selection. It also explained the importance of selecting the vendor and developing a long-term relationship with the vendor. It described some requirements definition issues and discussed in detail some of the evaluation criteria for selecting a DBMS.

Notes

1. CODASYL Systems Committee, *Selection and Acquisition of Data Base Management Systems* (New York: Association for Computing Machinery, 1976).
2. Olin H. Bray, *Distributed Database Management Systems* (Lexington, Mass.: Lexington Books, 1982).

Further Reading

CODASYL Systems Committee. *Selection and Acquisition of Data Base Management Systems.* New York: Association for Computing Machinery, 1976.

Stauffer, Robert N. "Justification of Robotic Systems." *Robotics Today* 8 (June 1986): 35–43.

Tepsic, Rudy M. "How to Justifiy Your FMS." *Manufacturing Engineering* 91 (Sept. 1983): 50–52.

20

Conclusions

The Competitive Environment

The Factory of the Future

New Technologies

Hardware
Database Management Systems
Expert Systems

Summary

This chapter summarizes the main points of the book and identifies some of the key trends that will affect the future of manufacturing and CIM technology.

The Competitive Environment

Manufacturing has become more competitive. Consumer and industrial customers want more complex products, more product tailoring to their specific needs, and greater product quality and reliability, and they want it all at low cost. Shorter product life cycles and a lack of skilled labor further complicate the situation. Finally, international trade increases the competition because different technologies and trade policies benefit some countries more than others.

To survive in this competitive environment, manufacturing companies must adapt to many changes, especially technological changes. These changes are occurring in product technology, manufacturing process technology, and information systems technology, which has been emphasized in this book. New materials and process technologies are clearly important and subject to extensive research. However, information systems technology is equally important because in the future how a company manages and processes its information will be as important as how it manages and processes materials.

Information technology is subject to many of the same trade-offs as process technology. A machine tool better able to hold tighter tolerances will reduce the amount of scrap and rework. Similarly, an application that tracks and monitors test results in real time identifies problems immediately rather than later, when the rework will be more expensive or additional work has been done on a part that will have to be scrapped. A better planning and control system will allow the same level of production with less inventory. Finally, a more integrated CIM system can speed up the product development cycle and reduce both design and manufacturing costs.

To realize the potential benefits of CIM, companies need a different type of employee. First, the development and implementation of these systems require people with a broad corporate perspective, not simply a departmental one. A narrow perspective may suboptimize too much and miss many opportunities for improvements.

Second, companies need people with a vision of what is possible and where the company should be going. This technology is moving too fast to wait for someone else to solve all of the problems before you commit to something new. If you wait, you will be too far behind on the learning curve.

Third, people must be willing to take *reasonable* risks. New technologies must be learned, and learning involves mistakes. Clearly, you do not want to "bet the company" on a new, unproven technology. But you may be willing to bet a small prototype project. If it works, you have progressed up the learning curve and can now use that technology on a major project with much lower risks. If the project fails, the results are not catastrophic and you have still progressed along the learning curve. You are now in a better position to decide whether to use that technology.

Finally, during these turbulent times manufacturers need people who can effectively manage change and innovation. This involves recognizing how changes affect themselves and the people who work for them.

The Factory of the Future

The "factory of the future" is a popular concept today. However, the factory of the future does not exist and never will. It is essentially a goal or a vision a company can work toward. Today the factory of the future may include A, B, and C, but gradually the factory of the future concept will evolve to include X, Y, and Z.

Before automating, a company should rethink its operations to better organize and rationalize them. Without this first step there is the serious risk of automating obsolete production technology and confusion. Not only is this a waste of effort, but it is also very hard to automate an unorganized operation.

This problem shows up clearly in the different way in which many U.S. and Japanese companies approach manufacturing problems. Given a product family that requires fifty tools on a machine tool, the U.S. approach is to build a tool holder for all fifty tools. The Japanese approach is to reanalyze the process plans to determine whether all fifty tools are really needed or whether a smaller number of common tools could be used. By simplifying the production requirements, they can then build a smaller, simpler tool holder.

Another critical difference between the U.S. and Japanese perspectives on manufacturing is in production efficiency. In the United States efficiency is usually considered in terms of long production runs, so a long setup overhead can be amortized over many units. On the other hand, the Japanese emphasize rapid setup time so they can economically produce small batches.

Manufacturing must be evaluated on many dimensions, not just one. These dimensions include cost, quality, product flexibility, volume flexibility, rapid delivery, and accurate delivery commitments. Depending on how a company chooses to compete, its manufacturing strategy will emphasize different dimensions. Different strategies will correspondingly lead to different types of factories of the future. Therefore, the ideal factory of the future will differ among industries and companies within an industry.

New Technologies

Although this book has emphasized one technology—information systems technology—manufacturing is facing rapid changes in many areas. For example, new materials allow products that were not possible a few years ago. These new materials are sometimes major competitors with existing materials (e.g., plastics and composites are replacing sheet metal in cars and aircraft). In addition, new production technologies permit cheaper and more precise operations on both new and old materials. Finally, information systems technologies and CIM impact all areas of design and manufacturing.

Although information systems technology is undergoing many changes, three of these changes will impact manufacturing dramatically. These three areas are hardware (specifically workstations), database management, and expert systems.

Hardware

Technology is rapidly improving the power and the cost/performance of computer hardware. This applies to processing power, memory, and secondary storage. These improvements are especially obvious with workstations. Engineering workstations are already in the multi-MIPS and multi-megabyte range, with no limit in sight. Communication systems allow these workstations to be linked into networks and to mainframes.

This means that CIM technology that a few years ago was limited to a few large companies is now available to much smaller companies. For the larger companies it allows CIM support to be spread throughout the company, not restricted to only a few key departments or people.

However, workstations are not the complete answer for CIM, except for a few very small companies. In spite of their growing power, workstations today and in the foreseeable future will support only isolated islands of automation. They cannot provide a way to integrate design and manufacturing data the way it needs to be done. It is very effective to download individual designs and applications and run them on a workstation. But each of these applications is an island of automation. Workstations by themselves do not have the power to store multigigabyte databases and allow many users throughout the company to share them.

This type of data sharing requires larger systems. Depending on the size of the company and the level of integration, this must be done on minicomputers, superminis, or mainframes. The key requirement is the power of the system and the DBMS it supports for managing the data.

For the future supercomputers are a potential integration tool, but this is only a potential.[1] Today supercomputers are used only for special number-crunching analysis and numerical prototypes. They are just another island of automation. However, with the DBMS approach, supercomputers could become a key to integrating large complex manufacturing operations. Without a DBMS to effectively manage the engineering and manufacturing data, they will not realize this potential.

Database Management Systems

Database management systems have benefited business in many ways. Today they are beginning to provide the same types of benefits for engineering and manufacturing. However, these benefits will be even greater in the future because of current research and development in several areas — engineering oriented database management systems, object oriented database management systems, and expert systems.

Virtually all of the database management systems today were designed for business. This does not mean they are useless for engineering, but they are not as useful as they could be. Engineering and manufacturing have some specialized requirements that a current business-oriented DMBS cannot meet. These functions must today be done within the application program. In the future engineering oriented DBMSs will have more of these features. Examples of these features include engineering data types (such as complex, vector, and matrix), engineering objects, version control, check-out/check-in procedures for distributing engineering data, and extended engineering data integrity.

These engineering-oriented systems may be developed from scratch, or they may evolve from the enhancement of existing business-oriented systems, but in the next few years these systems will begin to appear.

The other significant development in the database area will be the development of object-oriented systems, which will make it even easier to share data and develop applications. Although this is a new technology, it is important because these object-oriented systems will be the tool on which engineering-oriented DBMSs will be built.

The final DBMS development will be the merging of database management and expert systems and artificial intelligence technologies.

Expert Systems

Expert systems will dramatically improve CIM technology. Some design and manufacturing applications are really complex sets of rules, rather than a set procedure, such as is normally implemented in a traditional computer program. Rule-based expert systems will allow these applications to be developed in their more natural form.

Areas where expert systems are already being used include configuring complex products with many options, diagnosing equipment problems, and specifying the needed repairs. They are also used in systems in advanced robotics as well as in generative process planning.

Today most expert systems are relatively small and address limited problems. They are also stand-alone applications—i.e., islands of automation that are not integrated with the rest of a company's operations. In the future these systems will be larger and directly integrated with the corporate database. In fact, over time the combination of database management and expert systems will lead to knowledge-based systems capable of not only retrieving stored facts but also deriving and inferring data that were not explicitly stored.

Summary

This book has explained the importance of CIM in a competitive manufacturing environment. It has explained that the effective use of this technology requires database management and integration of many individual islands of automation. It has also identified some of the lessons from the management information systems area that can ease a company's transition to CIM.

For many companies this book can help during the first critical phase of integration. It does this in two ways. First, it explains the concepts of data management and the critical role played by database management in integration. Second, it provides an overview of the major design and manufacturing functions that must be integrated and describes a basic information model that can be used as starting point. Almost any manufacturer can use the information models in this book to begin to tailor them for the company's specific design and manufacturing operations. Ideally, this book will help many companies better understand and implement CIM technology.

Note

1. Olin Bray, "Engineering Data Management." In *Supercomputer Applications: Vol. 2. Industrial and Commercial* (Minneapolis: Consortium for Supercomputer Research, 1987).

Further Reading

Bray, Olin. "Engineering Data Management." In *Supercomputer Applications: Volume 2. Industrial and Commercial.* Minneapolis: Consortium for Supercomputer Research, 1987.

Feigenbaum, Edward A., and Pamela McCorduck. *The Fifth Generation: Artificial Intelligence and the Japanese Computer Challenge to the World.* Reading, Mass.: Addison-Wesley, 1983.

Harmon, Paul, and David King. *Expert Systems: Artificial Intelligence in Business.* New York: John Wiley and Sons, 1985.

Martin, John M. "CIM: What the Future Holds." *Manufacturing Engineering* 100 (Jan. 1988): 36–42.

Martin, R. Lee. "CAD/CAM—An Even Fuller Menu Ahead." *Manufacturing Engineering* 99 (Dec. 1987): 43–49.

Weiss, Sholom M., and Casimir A. Kulikowski. *A Practical Guide to Designing Expert Systems.* Totowa, N.J.: Rowman and Allanheld, 1984.

Winston, Patrick H. *Artificial Intelligence.* 2nd ed. Reading, Mass.: Addison-Wesley, 1984.

Glossary

abstracted model See IDEALIZED MODEL.

access path In database management the access path (logical and physical) refers to the way data are related in the data structure. For example, there may be two access paths between departments and projects—one relating projects to the departments that are responsible for them and another through employees (i.e., relating departments to their employees to the projects to which those employees are assigned regardless of which department is responsible for the project). The logical access path is the path through the information model (i.e., the real-world model) independent of how it is physically implemented. The physical access path is the implementation-dependent path through the database and includes mechanisms such as indexing, hashing, pointer chains, and joins.

adaptive process planning See PROCESS PLANNING.

AMHS (automated material handling system) An integrated system to move material through the factory and/or warehouse. An AMHS consists of both the mechanisms to move the material (such as conveyers, stacking mechanisms, and guided vehicles) and a control system to determine and control the routing of that material. There must also be a scheduling component that determines what material is needed where and when. However, this scheduling component is not usually considered to be part of the AMHS. Instead the output of this scheduler is the input to the AMHS.

AMRF (Automated Manufacturing Research Facility) The AMRF is a research program within the National Bureau of Standards. Its purpose is to determine how to interface clusters of machines in workcells with the necessary robots and material handling systems to provide integrated manufacturing operations. A number of companies were associated with this project. The facility is now available for companies to use to learn how to deal with these integration problems.

application program Software to do a business, engineering, or manufacturing function the users need. This is in contrast to system software, which directly controls the computer resources such a processors, storage, data, and communications. Application programs call or use system software to perform these direct control functions, which are transparent to the user. The main types of system software are operating systems, database management systems, communications systems, and graphics systems.

APT (automatially programmable tools) APT was the initial numerical control programming language developed in the late 1950s.

artificial intelligence The use of a computer to mimic intelligent behavior or decision making. This usually involves heuristic rather than traditional algorithmic methods. Some of the topics usually included in AI are expert systems, natural language processing, vision, and some aspects of robotics programming.

assembly An assembly is an organized collection of component parts and/or subassemblies. An assembly is a high-level entity within a bill of material or product structure that is combined with other assemblies to create a higher-level assembly or a product. A subassembly is a term sometimes used for a lower-level assembly, but there is no firm distinction between an assembly and a subassembly except their place in a bill of material.

assembly operation An assembly operation is one that combines several component parts, assemblies, of subassemblies. The operation may result in a permanent (welding or gluing objects together) or nonpermanent (using nuts and bolts or screw-on or snap-on connections) assembly.

attribute A characteristic of an entity or object that either identifies or describes it. These attributes can be organized into relations or record types and stored in a database. Grouping attributes with the appropriate entity types they describe and identifying how some attributes provide the link between two or more entity types is the key to information modeling and logical database design.

automated guided vehicle (AGV) A cart or discrete mechanism (as opposed to a conveyor in a hard automation system) for moving materials (parts, workpieces, or tooling) to various points within a factory or warehouse. These vehicles are computer controlled and can move throughout a plant along fixed guideways. AGVs are included in many large flexible manufacturing systems, but they can also be used in many less automated operations.

bill of materials (BOM) See PRODUCT STRUCTURE.

boundary representation Boundary representation (B-rep) is one of the basic ways to define solid geometry in a CAD system. With this approach, the boundaries of the solid are explicitly defined as various types of surfaces, whose boundaries are in turn defined as curves. The solid itself is only implicitly defined by its boundaries. Solids defined using CSG (constructive solid geometry) primitives can also be translated into a boundary representation, but the reverse is not always possible because the B-rep approach allows more irregular solids. Since the bounding surfaces and curves are defined explicitly, additional data about these geometric objects can easily be added to the geometric database.

CAD (computer-aided design) Earlier in a more limited context CAD referred to computer-aided drafting, but today it has a much broader meaning, including such functions as solid modeling, analysis, and drafting.

CADD Computer-aided design drafting.

CAE Computer-aided engineering.

CAM (computer-aided manufacturing) Earlier in a more limited context CAM referred to computer-aided machining (essentially numerical control activity), but today it has a much broader meaning including such functions as process planning, numerical control, robotics, and automated material handling systems.

CAM-I Computer-Aided Manufacturing—International is a cooperative research consortium. It funds projects that address several key manufacturing issues such as geometric modeling, computer-aided process planning, cost management systems, and the computer-integrated enterprise.

CAPP Computer-aided process planning. See also PROCESS PLANNING.

CAT Computer-aided testing.

CIM (computer integrated manufacturing) CIM is an umbrella term that covers the integration of all of the various design and manufacturing functions. It emphasizes integration rather than specific functions, which was the focus of many of the earlier terms such as CAD, CAE, CAM, and CAT.

CIM Steering Committee The high-level management group that is responsible for and controls the corporation's CIM effort. Specific functions of the CIM Steering Committee include linking corporate, manufacturing, and information systems strategies; internally marketing the CIM concept; developing and/or reviewing the CIM framework; setting priorities; selecting projects and/or ensuring that a formal project selection mechanism is in place; and ensuring that project management and postimplementation audit mechanisms are in place and being used.

CIM Task Force The lower-level working group that actually does much of the detailed CIM development and implementation. The CIM Task Force may include all of the people working on CIM, or it may include a smaller group of project managers and core technical experts, with most of the developers temporarily assigned to the Task Force from other areas. The basic functions of the CIM Task Force are to work with the CIM Steering Committee to develop a manufacturing strategy and the CIM framework; to manage and integrate the various CIM projects; and, depending on the way it is organized, to actually implement many of the CIM development projects.

CL program The cutter centerline form of an NC program is a neutral format for the set of machine tool instructions. It includes all of the geometric commands and generic machine tool commands such as coolant on/off. A postprocessor for a specific type of machine tool converts the CL program into the instruction that can actually be executed to do the machining. Since a part may need to be processed on several NC machine tools and each NC program is specific to a machine tool type, a part can have many NC programs.

CNC Computer numerical control uses a computer to control an NC machine tool. The NC program is stored in a computer and passed down to the machine tool in electronic form rather than as a punch tape. This results in better control of the NC programs, allows quicker updating of the programs, and eliminates the cost of paper tape, which for some large NC operations can be substantial.

CODASYL DBMS A CODASYL DBMS is based on a network data model and provides the type of functions identified in the 1971 CODASYL Systems Committee report *Feature Analysis of Generalized Data Base Management Systems*. In this type of DBMS different types of entities are represented by different record types. Relationships among object types are represented by sets with one record type as the owner and another record type as members of the set. The physical connections between the owners and members of sets and among the members of sets are implemented using embedded pointers.

configuration management/change control Configuration management is the process of controlling and keeping track of all of the engineering and manufacturing documentation for a part or product and keeping track of which versions of parts are used in which versions of assemblies and products. Change control is part of this process because once some design or manufacturing data have been released and are being used by other parts of the company, any changes must be formally approved by a Change Control Board after all of the consequences of the change have been identified and dealt with.

constraint In NIAM, constraints (or integrity constraints) are rules that are identified as part of the information model that must be enforced by the DBMS or the application programs which use the database. Examples of types of constraints include uniqueness, total, subset, and equality. Some DBMSs can enforce more of these constraints than other DBMSs. However, if the DBMS cannot enforce

them, they must be enforced by the applications programs or not enforced at all, which risks contaminating the database.

constructive solid geometry (CSG) In this approach the solid geometric objects are defined explicitly in terms of a set of solid primitives (e.g., box, cylinder, sphere) and combinations of these primitives. The boundaries of the solids are implicit. This representation allows attributes (such as material type and weight) to be easily attached to the solid itself, not to its boundaries.

CWQC (company-wide quality control) CWQC is a quality approach being used by many Japanese companies. It is a method for focusing on customer requirements and ensuring that quality is a major consideration in all functional areas. It defines quality as reducing the variability in a product, not simply meeting a set of product requirements. It uses statistics developed by Taguchi (a 1960 Deming Award winner) to define a loss function, which helps a company decide where to focus its efforts.

data administration (DA) Data administration, when compared with database administration, is the higher-level organizational function that allows the organization to more effectively manage its data. The two key components of data administration are strategic data planning, which identifies data-sharing opportunities, and standardization.

database administration (DBA) Database administration is the more technical function that directly involves the database management system rather than the higher-level organizational issues. The functions included under database administration are selecting and acquiring a DBMS, designing and defining the database, controlling access to the database, providing tools to make the database more accessible, and providing backup and recovery procedures.

database design Database design (logical and physical) is the process of identifying the types of entities, their attributes, and the relationships among entity types that should be modeled in the database. This logical database design is done using a formal design methodology (NIAM is the methodology used in this book). Once an information model and a logical database design are determined, physical database design is done by making performance trade-offs in the relative frequency with which the various access paths will by used by query and update operations.

database management system (DBMS) A database management system is the set of system software that manages and controls access to the data. Today almost all major DBMSs are based on either the network or the relational data model.

data dictionary/directory system (DD/DS) The DD/DS is one of the key tools the DBA uses to support development and management in a database environment. In addition to a complete logical and physical definition of the database, it also includes information about which applications and program modules use which data items. It also generates and stores the data definition parts of applications (e.g., COBOL data divisions). The earliest

DD/DSs were passive in that they simply stored information for documentation purposes but were independent of the actual operations of the DBMS. Therefore, there was little incentive to keep them up to date. Today many DD/DSs are active—i.e., a common data definition is used by both the DD/DS and the DBMS for all of its operations.

data independence Data independence (logical and physical) allows the data structures in the database to be changed without impacting the applications currently using the database. This greatly reduces the maintenance associated with changing the database. Physical data independence allows the physical data structures and access paths to be changed without impacting the applications. Logical data independence permits changes to the logical structures.

data model In the generic sense a data model is the fundamental model on which a DBMS is based. The two most common data models today are the network and relational. A data model includes both a data structure and operations on that data structure. The term *data model* is sometimes used in the narrower context as the specific model for a specific database (e.g., the data model for the manufacturing database). In this context it is the results of grouping the information model into logical record types or relations that can be implemented in a database. This grouped data model is sometimes called a *neutral data model*.

data structure One of the generic ways in which data are organized in a data model. The most common data structures are hierarchical, network, and relational.

DBMS independence DBMSs have always provided a degree of data independence. A newer extension of this concept is DBMS independence, which allows one DBMS to be replaced by a different DBMS without drastically affecting the applications. This is an ideal that can only be approached, not actually accomplished. The use of SQL as a standard DBMS interface is a move in this direction.

D-Class One of the commercially available classification and coding systems for group technology.

design for manufacturability The basic concept in design for manufacturability is that manufacturing factors must be considered during the design phase of product development. This is in contrast to the traditional approach, which has design engineers design the product and manufacturing engineers then determine how to make it. Design for manufacturability, as proposed by Boothroyd and others, identifies sets of manufacturing rules that can be factored into the design process to ensure that the design can be manufactured effectively. Some systems have automated these rules so the designer can quickly evaluate various design alternatives.

design retrieval This function allows a designer to quickly check to determine whether a part or assembly already exists that will satisfy the designer's requirements. Based on a classification and coding scheme, a design retrieval system can find all the similar parts so they can be reused as is or with slight modification. Design re-

trieval can save significant costs and time.

direct numerical control (DNC) This approach drives the machine tool directly from the computer rather than downloading the NC program to a paper tape or programmable controller.

dispatching This is the function on the factory floor that assigns specific tasks to specific work centers and machine tools. A dispatch list is one of the outputs of an MRP system.

distributed database management system A distributed DBMS allows a single database to be partitioned into subsets or fragments, with each fragment then located at one of more nodes in the distributed DBMS network. However, this distribution should be transparent to the users because the distributed DBMS should handle all of the complexity caused by distributing the database.

domain In relational databases a domain is an attribute or characteristic of an entity (i.e., a column in a relation or table). The term can also mean the set of data values that an attribute can assume—for example, the domain of all telephone numbers or employee numbers or dates. An integrity constraint is that only attributes with common domains of value can be joined. One can join a start date and a finish date since they are both from the domain date. However, one cannot join employee number and telephone number because they have different value domains and the result would be meaningless. Today DBMSs do not provide for the concept of value domains.

drawing The basic way to pass engineering data, especially part geometry, is with an engineering drawing. The traditional engineering drawing is a set of two-dimensional representations of the part geometry, with additional dimensioning and annotation. There are also other types of drawings, such as assembly drawings that show how a part is to be machined or how an assembly is to be put together. In the past these drawings were all in hardcopy form, but now with CAD systems they are sometimes created, passed, and used primarily in electronic form. In the long term these drawings may be replaced by annotated solid models in electronic form.

ENALIM (Evolving NAtural Language Information Model) An ENALIM is the basic diagram used in NIAM. It consists of objects (represented by circles), roles (rectangles), and various types of constraints (e.g., uniqueness, subset, equality, and subtypes) that are identified in the information model.

engineering database An engineering database is the overall corporate database that includes the geometric and nongeometric data required to support the various design and manufacturing functions. Logically there is a single engineering database, but physically it will probably be implemented as many smaller, separate databases, possibly even on different computers at different locations and using different DBMSs. Today almost all companies have only small subsets of this type of engineering database.

engineering data types These are the additional data types needed by most engineering applications but not yet supported by most DBMSs. At a minimum they include double precision, complex, vector, and matrix.

engineering DBMS An engineering DBMS is a DBMS design to satisfy many of the specialized needs of engineering applications. Conventional DBMSs, which were developed for the business environment, can provide much of the support needed by engineering applications. However, an engineering DBMS would also support some more specialized engineering requirements, such as engineering data types, version control, a checkout/check-in mechanism, and complex engineering integrity constraints.

engineering information system A generic term for the information systems department and/or the computers on the engineering and manufacturing side of the corporation. EIS is often completely separate from the comparable MIS (management information systems) group on the business side.

engineering objects In an object-oriented DBMS these are the common objects engineers use. Examples include geometric objects that are used to build models of parts and features, such as holes and slots, which combine both geometry and manufacturing operations.

enterprise model An enterprise model is a high-level functional model of what the corporation is trying to accomplish and how it operates. It identifies the basic business functions and decomposes them through several levels. It also specifies the information flow among these functions. It provides much of the information needed to define the requirements for information systems and can be used to rationalize the organization structure.

entity An entity is an object or thing about which the organization is interested. Records or relations in a database store data about various types of entities.

entity-relationship model This is a data modeling approach in which the key concepts are entity types and the relationships among them. An ER model, which is similar to but less detailed than a NIAM information model, is also used to create a logical database design.

equality constraint In NIAM an equality constraint relates two roles by specifying that an object instance in one role must also be in the other role. For example, every employee who has an employee number must also work in a department—an employee cannot be in one role without the other.

expediting A shop floor function used to speed up production when a manufacturing order is bottlenecked because some resources are missing. For example, if an order is being held up because certain raw materials are not available at the machine tool, the expeditor will find the necessary raw materials and get them to the machine tool. These raw materials may come from the inventory or somewhere else on the shop floor. While expediting is common and even essential in some cases, it creates a vicious cycle because, to speed up one order, the expeditor may take material already allocated for another order—thus shifting rather than solving the problem.

expert system An expert system mimics the decision-making capability of a human expert. Ideally, it includes both a set of rules, defined by a knowledge engineer and a subject matter expert, and an inference engine that uses those rules. Typical expert system applications today include medical diagnostics, equipment troubleshooting and repair, the configuration of complex equipment, and process planning. Today there are several expert system tools that allow designers to quickly build expert systems, although there is still a lack of tools and formal methodologies to help design the expert system.

fact The basic modeling concept in NIAM is a fact, which is defined precisely as an object-role-object combination. A part is made according to a process plan. Facts relating two real objects (called NOLOTs) are ideas. Bridges are facts relating a real object and a data object (called a LOT).

factory of the future The factory of the future is a concept or ideal goal of what a manufacturing company will be like in the future when currently anticipated technology is in place. As an ideal, it is a moving target that constantly changes as new technology is developed. Currently, the factory of the future ideal includes an automated, computer-integrated and computer-controlled factory floor, linked electronically to upstream computer-aided design and process planning systems. For a specific company the factory of the future ideal depends on both the industry and the company strategy.

feature-based design With feature-based design the engineer defines a part in terms of its features, such as holes, threads, slots, and fillets. This is much easier than the traditional approach whereby the designer must explicitly define the part in terms of its geometry. Since each feature has a predefined set of geometric parameters, all the designer needs to do is locate the feature on the part and specify its parameter values. The CAD system can then automatically generate all of the detailed geometry. This approach also simplifies downstream functions such as process planning. Physically features are created by manufacturing operations. If they are explicitly defined in design, the process planning is simplified because it does not have to aggregate a set of geometric objects and try to determine what feature it represents.

file A file is simply a collection of data read and/or written by a program. Information about the file structure and format is buried within the applications using the file. Many file-oriented applications are now being replaced by database-oriented applications.

finished goods Completed products that are ready to be shipped to customers or distributors. Finished goods, work-in-process, and raw materials are the three types of inventory tracked and controlled by manufacturing companies.

finite element analysis A type of analysis in which a large and/or complex object or geometry is broken up into small pieces (finite elements) that can be analyzed individually. The elements interact with each other through boundary conditions defined by the analyst.

fixed automation Fixed automation is designed to produce a specific product or very narrow set of products. Slight modification of the product can require major replacement of production equipment. This approach is used to mass-produce standard products because, if the production volume is high enough, this approach is the most cost effective.

fixture A fixture is a device to clamp or hold the workpiece on a machine tool while it is being processed.

flexible automation Flexible automation (in contrast to fixed automation) is designed to produce a wide range of products. New products can often be produced by the same production line simply by changing the NC programs for the machine tools and robots. Although a flexible production line is not as fast or efficient as a fixed line, with small or medium-size batches its flexibility makes it much more effective. Studies have shown that most manufacturing is done in lots of fifty or less.

flexible manufacturing systems (FMS) A set of automated manufacturing resources usually combining machine tools, robots to load and unload them, and an automated material handling system to move material, workpieces, and tools among them.

functional analysis An information systems methodology that identifies the functions a system must perform and the information flows among the functions. A functional analysis consists of a structure chart showing a hierarchical decomposition of the functions and a function flow model showing the information flows.

307

generative process planning See PROCESS PLANNING.

graphics The storage, processing, and display of geometry and figures by the computer. Graphics is important in CAD/CAM because geometry is a basic component of most part and manufacturing data.

group process techniques A set of human relations techniques that make it easy for small groups of people to work together effectively. Brainstorming is one of the best known techniques, but there are many others. These techniques are important in CIM because its complexity requires the expertise of many people.

group technology An approach developed to improve the effectiveness of producing similar parts in small batches. A classification and coding scheme is used to identify parts that are manufactured using similar procedures and machine tools. These machine tools can be clustered together and all of the parts can be scheduled together. A group technology classification and coding scheme also allows easy retrieval of similar process plans, an essential step for variant computer-aided process planning.

ICAM (Integrated Computer-Aided Manufacturing) A major U.S. Air Force program to improve the manufacturing technology in the aerospace industry. The program consists of many individual projects, each focusing on one aspect of computer-aided manufacturing, but all of the projects are organized under a common architecture. Many of the projects have produced public-domain software.

The ICAM program is run from Wright-Patterson AFB, Ohio.

idealized model An idealized or abstracted model is a simplified version of the detailed model of a part. For complex parts idealized models are analyzed because analysis of the detailed model would be too time-consuming and expensive. This is acceptable because many details do not affect the part's structural integrity or performance. Experience and judgment are required to determine which details can be eliminated without affecting the validity of the analysis.

IGES (Initial Graphics Exchange Specification) This is a program begun in 1980 by several large manufacturing companies and the National Bureau of Standards to facilitate the transfer of data among various CAD systems. The IGES standard, initially released in 1981, has been through several revisions. The current focus of IGES is the PDES (Product Definition Exchange Specification) effort, which is trying to define a comparable type of exchange specification for all of the data needed by manufacturing.

information analysis A formal approach for identifying the information model required to support a set of applications or for a database design. There are several IA methodologies, but the one used in this book is specifically NIAM (Nijssen Information Analysis Methodology).

information analysis relationships— binary The basic information model created by NIAM is a binary model. Roles relating objects (either real or data objects) are binary in that they can relate only two object types. There may be many relationships or roles between the same two object types, but each role can relate only two object types.

information model The set of objects, roles, and constraints developed using information analysis. The information model is independent of the DBMS on which the database will eventually be implemented.

inheritance Inheritance is used in object-oriented systems and artificial intelligence to relate data and operations on subtypes and supertypes. Any data and operations on a supertype is automatically inherited and applies to all of the subtypes. For example, everything that applies to the supertype part also applies to its subtypes — component part and assembly. However, each subtype has data and operations that do not apply to the supertype. The NIAM information model supports subtypes so it can support the data aspect of inheritance, but it does not include operations on the data. Today's DBMSs do not support the inheritance mechanism, but in the future object-oriented DBMSs will provide such support.

instance a single occurrence of an object type, record type, or a tuple in a relation.

integrity constraint One of the set of rules captured during information analysis which the DBMS must enforce to assure that the data stored in the database are valid and consistent.

inventory control The function to manage a company's inventory. This includes managing, controlling, and recording the material flows into and

out of the inventory. Inventory control usually includes raw materials, work-in-process, and finished goods.

IPAD (Integrated Program for Aerospace Vehicle Design) This program was a major NASA research program from the mid-1970s to the mid-1980s. It developed the prototype for several information system technologies. The only product to come out of the program was RIM, but some commonly accepted concepts (such as storing geometry in a database) were first tested in this program.

IPIP (IPAD Information Processor) IPIP was the major corporate-level engineering database management system that was developed by the IPAD program. A more limited relational DBMS called RIM (initially for a single user) was also developed by the project. IPIP was never widely used outside of the IPAD research project.

join Join is one of the three basic relational operations. It combines tuples from different relations that have a common domain.

Just-in-Time JIT is an approach that minimizes inventory by producing only enough parts for current needs. More precisely, it is a way of managing manufacturing operations, not simply an inventory control approach. If manufacturing operations are well planned and controlled, then a company needs to produce only the number of parts that are needed when they are needed. Large buffer stocks and inventory are not necessary. JIT can dramatically reduce working capital requirements. However, it requires a close working relationship with reliable suppliers; because the factory has at most a few days of inventory, a delayed shipment from a supplier can shut down the factory.

LOT (lexical object type) In NIAM a LOT is a data object that is actually stored in the information system. It either describes or identifies a real object (i.e., a NOLOT or nonlexical object). See also OBJECT.

machine tool The machines used to manufacture parts and that actually cut and shape material. The robots and material handling systems are not considered machine tools. Machine tools may be operated either manually or by a computer using an NC program.

management information systems (MIS) A term that refers to the information systems department responsible for business applications and systems. The term may also refer to the actual business information systems.

manufacturing order A manufacturing order is the specific order sent to the shop floor to make a specific part or product. In some cases the product is for a specific customer, while in other cases it is being made for inventory.

manufacturing strategy The objectives and plans required to ensure that a corporation's manufacturing facilities can effectively support its overall strategy. A manufacturing strategy is important in determining the types of CIM systems a company needs and the priorities.

MAP (Manufacturing Automation Protocol) MAP is the communica-tions protocol developed by General Motors and several other large manufacturing companies and being proposed as a standard. The use of a standard protocol makes it easier to connect computers and other equipment on the factory floor because products of many vendors are usually involved.

MC/DG (manufacturing cost/design guideline) This is one of the specific projects in the ICAM program. It includes a database of manufacturing costs for various design options so the designer can evaluate the costs of various design alternatives before selecting one. This is an attempt to remove the traditional barrier between design and manufacturing, which results in designs that cannot be manufactured or that are too expensive.

MIS plan The MIS plan, or master plan, specifies both what the information systems department is trying to accomplish and how it is going to accomplish it. The plan should consist of four parts: strategy, technology forecast, inventory of current capabilities, and project plans.

member A member of a set in a CODASYL DBMS. Sets are used to link owner record types to member record types. Cf. OWNER.

MI-Class One of the commercially available classification and coding systems for group technology.

model A model is simply a representation of something else. The model can be studied, analyzed, and/or manipulated to get a better understanding of the thing it is representing. There can be information models, functional models, solid geometric models, etc.

monocode A coding scheme in which the entire code has a single meaning. Any part of the code is meaningless of itself. Monocodes are often hierarchical: each digit or set of digits expands on the meaning of the previous digit (e.g., the fourth digit can have completely different meaning depending on the value of the third digit). Cf. POLYCODE.

MRP (Material Requirements Planning) MRP is one of the modules in Manufacturing Resource Planning or MRP II. The complete set of functions includes Customer Order Entry, Master Production Scheduling, Material Requirements Planning, Purchasing, Inventory, Shop Floor Control, and Costing. Originally, this entire set of functions was also referred to as MRP, which led to confusion. To avoid this, today the entire set is referred to as MRP II.

MRP II (Manufacturing Requirements Planning) See MRP.

mutual exclusion One of the subtype integrity constraints that can be specified in NIAM. If the subtypes of a supertype are mutually exclusive, then a specific object can be in only one subtype.

network DBMS See CODASYL DBMS.

NIAM (Nijssen Information Analysis Methodology) The fact-based information modeling methodology used throughout this book. See also INFORMATION ANALYSIS.

NOLOT (nonlexical object type) In NIAM a NOLOT is a real object type that exists in the real world. Examples include employees, customers, parts,

machine tools, and process plans. NOLOTs are related to each other by ideas and are related to LOTs by bridges. See also OBJECT.

normalization A database design procedure for relational databases. If the database is in third normal form, then certain update anomalies are eliminated. In third normal form all of the domains in a relation are functionally dependent only on the key domain.

numerical control (NC) Numerical control uses the computer to generate the commands to run a machine tool rather than relying on the operator. NC machine tools provide more accurate and more consistent quality parts than can be generated when an operator directly controls the machine tool. Originally the NC program was fed to the machine tool on paper tape, but today these programs are often transferred electronically.

object An object is one of the basic concepts used to build an information model. In NIAM objects can be real or data objects (NOLOT and LOT). Objects are related by roles. In artificial intelligence and object-oriented DBMSs an object has a more precise definition. In these contexts, an object is the combination of a data structure and a set of operations on that structure. There is a distinction between a logical object (i.e., the logical data structure and the logical operations on that structure) and the physical implementation of the object. The physical implementation should be transparent to the user.

object-oriented Object-oriented DBMSs and programming languages are based on the concept of an object, which has both a data structure and a set of operations. These operations are defined once and can be reused whenever the object is used. This approach also distinguishes between logical data structures and operations and physical ones. The application needs to deal only with the logical object because its physical implementation is hidden. The object-oriented approach makes application development and maintenance much easier.

off-line programming A term used in robot programming. In the past, robots were taught by manually walking them through the required motions. Today the more effective approach is to create the robot program using the models created in a CAD system. This is called off-line programming because the robot does not need to be used to generate the program. It is used only during a final check of the program. Current work with solid modeling is even trying to eliminate this expensive check-out step.

operating system The operating system is the system software (program) that directly controls the computer resources, such as processor time, memory, disk space, and terminals, and allocates these resources to applications as they are needed.

owner In a CODASYL DBMS the owner of a set is one of the two types of records related by the set. For example, "department" is the owner record type of the "works-for" set, and "employee" is the member record type. Cf. MEMBER.

parameterized design An approach to designing parts in a part family. A generic design for the part family exists in the system, but with variables instead of actual data values. In parameterized design the designer or an application simply specifies the parameter values and a specific design is created automatically.

part A part is simply a generic term for what is being manufactured or assembled. Parts are combined in a product structure or bill of material. There are two types of parts. Piece parts (or components parts) are the lowest-level parts and are made from machined or processed raw material. Assemblies (and subassemblies) are organized collections of parts that are put together and then treated as a single part.

PDDI (Product Data Definition Interface) PDDI, one of the ICAM projects, was an intermediate step between IGES and PDES.

PDES (Product Definition Exchange Specification) See IGES.

piece part See PART.

population table In NIAM a population table showing specific examples of objects in a role. It is used to clarify the uniqueness constraints.

postimplementation audit A study of an information systems development project, usually done once the application has been completed and is operational. The purpose of the audit is to evaluate the overall development process, not the individual application. For example, are the estimated procedures appropriate? Is a more detailed specification needed before the user sign-off on the design? Are better development tools needed to increase analyst and programmer productivity?

postprocessor The computer program that converts the CL file format of an NC program into an executable program for a specific machine tool. There are postprocessors for each type of machine tool.

polycode A coding scheme in which several independent codes are concatenated together. Each part of the code always means the same thing. For example, one set of digits may specify the material type and the next set the type of geometry. Cf. MONOCODE.

PRIDE (PRototype Integrated DEsign) system A NASA prototype design retrieval system.

process planning (adaptive and generative) Once a design has been completed and released, a manufacturing engineer must decide how to make it using the machine tools and resources the company has. (Sometimes new machine tools will be required, but this is not normally part of process planning.) This means determining manufacturing processes, their sequence, machine tools for each process, and the raw material to start with. The complete set of instructions explaining how to make and inspect the part is called a *process plan*. CAPP (computer-aided process planning) systems are being developed using two approaches. Adaptive or variant process planning finds similar process plans (like design retrieval) and lets the manufacturing engineer create a new process plan by making minor modifications to an existing one. Generative process planning takes the part information and the manufacturing capabilities of the company and creates a new process plan from scratch.

production scheduling This function takes the required output (the product mix and the time periods in which it is required), combines it with information about the factory capacity and resource requirements for each product, and determines when to produce how many of which products.

product structure The product structure (sometimes called a bill of material) specifies how parts are related in higher structures such as subassemblies, assemblies, and subsystems. The product structure can have many levels, depending on the complexity of the final product. Many companies have both an engineering bill of material (i.e., the way the product was designed) and a manufacturing bill of material (i.e., the way it is made). Reconciling these two different product structures is sometimes a serious problem.

program A set of instructions for a computer or an NC machine tool. A program may be either an application program or part of the system software.

project One of the basic operations in the relational data model. It specifies which columns or domains to extract from a relation.

QFD (quality function deployment) QFD is a quality method for translating requirements from a customer specification back through the various design and manufacturing functions and relating these requirements to specific product and process characteristics to be monitored.

real-time shop-floor control This involves monitoring activities on the shop floor directly. This approach is different from the traditional shop floor control in most MRP II systems, which require a separate data entry operation, often in batch mode. The level of integration needed by the factory of the future requires this type of real-time shop floor control.

record Data about a single occurrence of a type of entity or object. A record consists of individual data items. A record is part of a file.

record type In a CODASYL DBMS a record type contains data fields about a single type of entity. Different record types are connected by sets with owner and member record types. It is comparable to a relation in a relational DBMS.

relation In a relational DBMS a relation is simply a table of data that contains data about only one entity type. Data about different entity types are connected using the join operation. A relation is comparable to a record type in a CODASYL DBMS.

relational DBMS A relational DBMS is one based on the relational data model. It stores data in tables (called relations) consisting of rows (tuples) and columns (domains). The basic operations of a relational DBMS are selection, projection, and join.

relational operations Select, project, and join are the three basic operations for the relational data model and are used by relational DBMSs. The select operation extracts certain rows from the table. Project extracts the specified columns. Both select and project are operations on a single table (relation). The join operation is used to combine data from two or more relations based on common domains.

requirements analysis A requirements analysis is one of the key initial steps in developing an information system. It identifies precisely what the system must be able to do. It consists of three parts—functional analysis, information analysis, and process analysis.

RIM (Relational Information Manager) One of the DBMSs developed as part of the NASA IPAD program. One version of this software is in the public domain, so it is widely used by university research projects.

robot The Robot Institute of America defines *robot* as a reprogrammable, multifunctional manipulator designed to move material, parts, tools, or specialized devices through variable programmed motions for the performance of a variety of tasks.

role In NIAM a role is what relates two object types.

routing A routing is the set of instructions that specifies how to make a specific part. A process plan specifies generically how to make parts of a certain type. When a work order is sent to the shop floor to make fifteen parts of type X, the routing is the specific set of instructions for making those fifteen parts. One of the differences is that for an operation the process plan will specify a machine tool of a certain type, while the routing is more specific and will specify exactly which machine tool (by serial number) to use.

SQL (Structured Query Language) SQL is the relational query language

314

developed by IBM and now accepted as the standard language for relational systems.

schema A schema (conceptual, internal, or external) is the database definition. The complete schema includes the complete logical and physical definition of the database. However, current DBMS architecture calls for the schema to have three distinct components. The conceptual schema defines the logical structure of the complete database. The internal schema specifies how the data are physically stored and accessed. A database also has one or more external schemas, which describe how the applications and/or users expect to see the data. The use of three separate schemas provides greater data independence. The DBMS does all of the necessary conversion and translation among these three schemas.

select Select is one of the basic operations in a relational database management system. The select operation identifies or selects one or more tuples or rows in a relation. The selection expression (or Boolean selection expression) specifies the attribute values or ranges of values that determine which rows to select.

set In a CODASYL DBMS a set provides the connection between different record types. Each set has one owner record type and one or more member record types.

shop-floor control Generically, shop floor control is the function that controls operations on the shop floor. However, in a more confined context it is one of the traditional modules in an MRP II system. In this context it dispatches work orders to the shop floor and tracks their progress by having shop floor operators enter data when an operation is begun and completed.

software engineering A disciplined approach to software development that attempts to shift it from an art to a more precise engineering discipline.

solid model A solid model is the solid geometry created to represent an object (e.g., part, assembly, or machine tool). A solid model can be built using solid primitives in a CSG (constructive solid geometry) system or by combining more basic geometric objects using a boundary representation (B-rep) approach.

solid primitives Solid primitives are the objects used by constructive solid geometry (CSG) systems to create complex solid objects. Examples of solid primitives include box, cylinder, sphere, and cone. These solid primitives are combined using union, subtraction, and intersection operations to build more complex part and assembly geometry.

subassembly See ASSEMBLY.

subset One of the types of integrity constraints used in NIAM to relate two roles. For example, a part is designed by an employee, and an employee has an ID number. A subset constraint relates these two facts because the employee who designs a part must be a subset of the employees with ID numbers—in other words, the employee must work for the company.

supercomputer A supercomputer is a very powerful computer capable of several hundred to several thousand megaflops (million floating-point operations per second). These computers, made primarily by Cray and ETA (Control Data) and several Japanese companies, are used for complex scientific and engineering calculations that are beyond the capability of conventional computers. Although supercomputers are expensive (starting at several million dollars), they are so powerful that their cost performance is significantly better than most conventional computers. A number of new vendors have developed small, powerful (often parallel) processors with much lower costs but comparable cost performance. These systems are being called *minisupercomputers.*

Taguchi method A statistical method developed by Taguchi in the late 1950s. It relates quality to a reduction in variability rather than a fixed tolerance limit. It uses a loss function to identify the potential cost savings for specific quality improvements.

tool The tool, as opposed to the machine tool, is the consumable material that is actually in contact with the workpiece and cuts the metal or does the operation. For example, the machine tool is the grinder or the drill whereas the tool is the grinding wheel or the drill bit.

TQC (total quality control) In the United States the term TQF is used to describe the overall quality program, which usually focuses on product inspection and statistical process control. However, in Japan TQF is a specific technical subset of CWQC. In this case TQF addresses only product, process, and system quality issues.

tuple In relational databases a tuple is a single row in a relation. It consists of all of the domain values for one entity as defined in the relation.

uniqueness constraint In NIAM the uniqueness constraint determines whether an object type can participate in several instances of the same role. For example, an employee can work in only one department, so this role has a uniqueness constraint. On the other hand, an employee can work on many projects, so only the combination of employee and project is unique — neither role is unique by itself.

validation In information modeling validation is the process of reviewing a model with users to ensure that it correctly represents the real-world relationships. Model validation is always in terms of a certain set of functions. Whenever a new function is to be added to the system, the information model must be revalidated if any additional information is needed by the new function.

variant process planning See PROCESS PLANNING.

version Version is a concept used in configuration management to identify and keep track of how a design is modified over time. Depending on its impact, a design change may result in a new part with a new part number or just a new version of the previous part. If the revised design results in a part that is not interchangeable with the old part, then the part number changes. If the new part is interchangeable with the old one, then only the version number changes — the part number remains the same.

workcell A workcell is a collection of machine tools used to produce one or more families of parts. Traditionally, a part may have to be moved all over the factory to get to the ten machine tools that are needed to produce it. Using group technology, families of related parts are identified and all of the machine tools needed are clustered together in a workcell. This usually speeds up production and reduces movement of parts and workpieces during the manufacturing process.

work-in-process Work-in-process simply means material somewhere in the manufacturing process. Traditionally, there are three types of inventory— raw material inventory, finished goods inventory, and work-in-process inventory.

workpiece The generic term for the material to be processed on a machine tool or at a work center. Depending on where it is in the manufacturing process, a workpiece may be a piece of unprocessed raw material (before the first step in the process) or a finished part or product (after the last step in the process).

Bibliography

Abrial, J. R. "Data Semantics." In *Data Base Management*, ed. J. W. Klimbie and K. L. Koffeman, pp. 1–59. New York: North-Holland, 1974.

Ang, Chen Leong. "Planning Factory Data Communications Systems." *CIM Technology*, August 1987, 39–44.

Bairstow, Jeffrey. "GM's Automation Protocol: Helping Machines Communicate." *High Technology* 6 (Oct. 1986): 38–42.

Berbakov, Paul J. "Using Analytical Techniques to Create Part Programs." *Robotics Today* 8 (Oct. 1986): 19–20.

Bergstrom, Robin P. "Managing Intellectual Capital." *Manufacturing Engineering* 98 (Mar. 1987): 7.

Blume, Christian, and Wilfred Jakob. *Programming Languages for Industrial Robots*. New York: Springer-Verlag, 1986.

Bo, K., and F. M. Lillehagen (eds.). *CAD Systems Framework*. New York: North-Holland, 1983.

Boothroyd, G., and P. Dewhurst. *Design for Assembly: A Designer's Handbook*. Amherst, Mass.: University of Massachusetts, 1983.

Bray, Olin. "CAD/CAM Data Management." In *Proceedings of NASA Conference on Computer-Aided Geometric Modeling*. Washington, D.C.: NASA, 1983.

_____. *Distributed Database Management Systems*. Lexington, Mass.: Lexington Books, 1982.

_____. "Engineering Data Management." In *Supercomputer Applications: Volume 2. Industrial and Commercial*. Minneapolis: Consortium for Supercomputer Research, 1987.

Bray, Olin H., and Harvey A. Freeman. *Data Base Computers*. Lexington, Mass.: Lexington Books, 1979.

Brody, Herb. "The Robot: Just Another Machine?" *High Technology* 6 (Oct. 1986): 31–35.

_____. "U.S. Robot Makers Try to Bounce Back." *High Technology Business*, Oct. 1987, 18–24.

Buffa, Elwood S. *Meeting the Competitive Challenge: Manufacturing Strategies for U.S. Companies*. Homewood, Ill.: Dow Jones–Irwin, 1984.

Bibliography

Burgam, Patrick. "FMS Control: Covering All the Angles." *CAD/CAM Technology*, Summer 1984.

Buss, Martin D. J. "How to Rank Computer Projects." In *Catching Up with the Computer Revolution*, ed. Lynn M. Salerno. Cambridge, Mass.: Harvard University Press, 1984.

Chiantella, Nathan A. (ed.). *Management Guide for CIM*. Dearborn, Mich.: CASA/SME, 1986.

CODASYL Systems Committee. *Selection and Acquisition of Data Base Management Systems*. New York: Association for Computing Machinery, 1976.

CODASYL Systems Committee. *A Framework for Distributed Database Systems: Distribution Alternatives and Generic Architectures*. New York: Association for Computing Machinery, 1981.

Crowby, Philip B. *Quality Is Free: The Act of Making Quality Certain*. New York: Mentor Books, 1979.

Date, C. J. *Introduction to Database Systems*. 3rd ed. Vol. 1. New York: Addison-Wesley, 1981.

Daugherty, Tim. "Machine-Tending Robot Succeeds with Careful Planning, Design." *Robotics Today* 8 (June 1986): 15–16.

Drozda, Thomas J. "Jumping on the FMS Bandwagon." *Manufacturing Engineering* 90 (Mar. 1983): 4.

Drucker, Peter. *The Effective Executive*. New York: Harper and Row, 1966.

Durell, William R. *Data Administration: A Practical Guide to Successful Data Management*. New York: McGraw-Hill, 1985.

ElMaraghy, H. A., and N. C. Ho. "A Flexible System for Computer Control of Manufacturing." *Computers in Mechanical Engineering* 1 (Aug. 1982): 16–23.

Encarnacao, J., and F. L. Krause. *File Structures and Data Bases for CAD*. New York: North-Holland, 1982.

Encarnacao, J., and E. G. Schlechtendahl. *Computer-Aided Design: Fundamentals and System Architectures*. New York: Springer-Verlag, 1983.

Enderle, G., K. Kansy, and G. Pfaff. *Computer Graphics Programming*. New York: Springer-Verlag, 1984.

Engelberger, Joseph F. *Robotics in Practice: Management and Applications of Industrial Robots*. London: Kogan Page, 1980.

Farnum, Gregory T. "Made in America." *Manufacturing Engineering* 99 (Aug. 1987): 47–48.

Feigenbaum, Edward A., and Pamela McCorduck. *The Fifth Generation: Artificial Intelligence and the Japanese Computer Challenge to the World*. Reading, Mass.: Addison-Wesley, 1983.

Ferraro, Richard A., Terry E. Hunley, and Orry Y. Shackney. "Banishing Management Barriers to Automation." *Manufacturing Engineering* 100 (Jan. 1988): 44–48.

Foster, Richard N. *Innovation: The Attacker's Advantage*. New York: Summit Books, 1986.

Fulton, Robert E. (ed.). *Managing Engineering Data: The Competitive Edge*. Proceedings of the 1987 ASME International Computers in Engineering Conference. New York: ASME, 1987.

Gardiner, Keith M. *Systems and Technology for Advanced Manufacturing*. Dearborn, Mich.: SME, 1983.

Gerwin, Donald. "Dos and Don'ts of Computerized Manufacturing." *Harvard Business Review* 60 (Mar.–Apr. 1982): 107–116.

Gibson, Cyrus F., and Richard L. Nolan. "Managing the Four Stages of EDP Growth." *Harvard Business Review* 52 (Jan.–Feb. 1974): 76–88.

Groover, Mikell P. *Automation, Production Systems, and Computer-Aided Manufacturing*. Englewood Cliffs, N.J.: Prentice-Hall, 1980.

Groover, Mikell P., and Emory W. Zimmers, Jr. *CAD/CAM: Computer-Aided Design and Manufacturing*. Englewood Cliffs, N.J.: Prentice-Hall, 1984.

Gunn, Thomas G. *Manufacturing for Competitive Advantage: Becoming a World-Class Manufacturer*. Cambridge, Mass.: Ballinger Publishing Co., 1987.

Hales, H. Lee. "Producibility and Integration: A Winning Combination." *CIM Technology*, August 1987, 14–18.

Halevi, Gideon. *The Role of Computers in Manufacturing Processes*. New York: John Wiley & Sons, 1980.

Hammond, Gary. *AGVS at Work: Automated Guided Vehicle Systems*. New York: Springer-Verlag, 1986.

Harmon, Paul, and David King. *Expert Systems: Artificial Intelligence in Business*. New York: John Wiley & Sons, 1985.

Harrison, J. P., and Rakesh Mahajan. "The IGRIP Approach to Off-line Programming and Workcell Design." *Robotics Today* 8 (Aug. 1986): 25–26.

Bibliography

Head, Robert V. *Planning Techniques for Systems Management.* Wellesley, Mass.: QED Information Sciences, 1984.

Henderson, Dale L. "Off-Line Programming Cuts Costs, Saves Time." *Robotics Today* 8 (Aug. 1986): 23–24.

Higgins, William J. "Integration and Control of AGV Systems." *Robotics Today* 9 (Apr. 1987): 59–61.

Hitchens, Max W. "Simulation: The Key to Automation Without Risk." *CAD/CAM Technology,* Fall 1984, 15–17.

Holland, John M. "Small Robots for Tooling and Material Handling." *Robotics Today* 8 (Feb. 1986): 21–23.

Hopkins, Albert L., Jr. "Fault Tolerance — How Much Is Enough?" *Manufacturing Engineering* 99 (Aug. 1987): 58–61.

Hopwood, Norman W., Jr. "Managing Information as a Resource." *CIM Technology,* Aug. 1987, 33–36.

Hunt, V. Daniel. *Industrial Robotics Handbook.* New York: Industrial Press, 1983.

Hyde, William F. *Improving Productivity by Classification, Coding, and Data Base Standardization: The Key to Maximizing CAD/CAM and Group Technology.* New York: Marcel Dekker, 1981.

Hyer, Nancy Lea (ed.). *Group Technology at Work.* Dearborn, Mich.: SME, 1984.

IPAD II: *Advances in Distributed Data Base Management for CAD/CAM.* Washington, D.C.: NASA, 1984.

Jaikumar, Ramchandran. "Postindustrial Manufacturing." *Harvard Business Review* 64 (Nov.–Dec. 1986): 69–76.

Jeffery, Jay. "Expansions in Control Systems Technology." *Robotics Today* 8 (Apr. 1986): 47–48.

Kalra, Tilak R. "Robots Meet Criteria for Automating Three Workcells." *Robotics Today* 8 (June 1986): 27–28.

Kanter, Rosabeth Moss. *The Change Masters: Innovation for Productivity in the American Corporation.* New York: Simon and Schuster, 1983.

Kent, William. "A Simple Guide to Five Normal Forms in Relational Database Theory." *Communications of ACM* (Association for Computing Machinery) 26 (Feb. 1983): 120–125.

Knox, Charles S. *Engineering Documentation Flow.* New York: Marcel Dekker, 1984.

Knox, Charles S. *CAD/CAM Systems: Planning and Implementation*. New York: Marcel Dekker, 1983.

Krauskopf, Bruce. "Defining FMS: The Concept, the Users, and the Builders." *Manufacturing Engineering* 92 (June 1984): 41.

Leong-Hong, Belkis W., and Bernard K. Plagman. *Data Dictionary/Directory Systems: Administration, Implementation, and Usage*. New York: John Wiley & Sons, 1982.

Logan, James C., and Steven L. Cohron. "Palletizing and Packaging Robots Help Automate Packout System." *Robotics Today* 8 (Apr. 1986): 65–67.

Maier, Norman R. F. *Problem-Solving Discussions and Conferences: Leadership Methods and Skills*. New York: McGraw-Hill, 1963.

Mark, L. "What Is the Binary Relationship Approach?" In *Entity-Relationship Approach to Software Engineering,* ed. G. G. Davis. New York: North-Holland, 1983.

Martin, James. *Application Development without Programmers*. Englewood Cliffs, N.J.: Prentice-Hall, 1982.

_____. *Managing the Database Environment*. Englewood Cliffs, N.J.: Prentice-Hall, 1983.

_____. *Principles of Data Base Management*. Englewood Cliffs, N.J.: Prentice-Hall, 1976.

_____. *Strategic Data Planning Methodologies*. Englewood Cliffs, N.J.: Prentice-Hall, 1982.

Martin, John M. "CIM: What the Future Holds." *Manufacturing Engineering* 100 (Jan. 1988): 36–42.

_____. "Developing a Strategy for Quality." *Manufacturing Engineering* 99 (Aug. 1987): 40–45.

Martin, R. Lee. "CAD/CAM—An Even Fuller Menu Ahead." *Manufacturing Engineering* 99 (Dec. 1987): 43–49.

McFarlan, F. Warren. "Problems in Planning the Information System." In *Catching Up with the Computer Revolution*, ed. Lynn M. Salerno. Cambridge, Mass.: Harvard University Press, 1984.

_____. "Portfolio Approach to Information Systems." *Harvard Business Review* 59 (Sept.–Oct. 1981): 142–150.

McLean, Charles R., and Peter F. Brown. "Process Planning in the AMRF." *CIM Technology*, Aug. 1987, 23–26.

Miller, Richard K. *Automated Guided Vehicles*. Dearborn, Mich.: SME, 1987.

Munson, George E. "Robotics in Perspective." *Robotics Today* 8 (Apr. 1986): 29.

Musselman, Kenneth J. "Computer Simulation: A Design Tool for FMS." *Manufacturing Engineering* 93 (Sept. 1984): 117–120.

Nagy, Bence. "Planned Automation Enhances Efficiency." *Manufacturing Engineering* 99 (Aug. 1987): 55–56.

Nijssen, G. M. "Current Issues in Conceptual Schema Concept." In *Architecture and Models in Data Base Management Systems,* ed. G. M. Nijssen. New York: North-Holland, 1977.

Nolan, Richard L. "Managing Information Systems by Committee." *Harvard Business Review* 60 (July–Aug. 1982): 72–79.

————. "Managing the Crises in Data Processing." In *Catching Up with the Computer Revolution,* ed. Lynn M. Salerno. Cambridge, Mass.: Harvard University Press, 1984.

Ohmae, Kenichi. *The Mind of the Strategist: Business Planning for Competitive Advantage*. New York: McGraw-Hill, 1982.

Palframan, Diane. "FMS: Too Much, Too Soon." *Manufacturing Engineering* 93 (Mar. 1987): 34–38.

Porter, Michael E. *Competitive Strategy: Techniques for Analyzing Industries and Competitors*. New York: The Free Press, 1980.

Richardson, Douglas. "Implementing MAP for Factory Control." *Manufacturing Engineering* 100 (Jan. 1988): 79–82.

Ross, Ronald G. *Data Dictionaries and Data Administration: Concepts and Practices for Data Resource Management*. New York: AMACON, 1981.

Sach, Charles F., Jr. "Computer-Managed Process Planning: A Bridge between CAD and CAM." In *Proceedings of Auto Fact IV*, pp. 7-15–7-31. Dearborn, Mich.: SME, 1982.

Schaffer, George H. "Implementing CIM." *American Machinist* 125 (Aug. 1981): 151–174.

Schmidt, Thomas D. "Successfully Packaging the Painting Robot." *Robotics Today* 8 (June 1986): 31–34.

Schreiber, Rita R. "Mechanical Assembly: Robots Carve Their Niche." *Robotics Today* 8 (Oct. 1986): 25–32.

Schultz, Terry R. *Business Requirements Planning: The Journey to Excellence.* Milwaukee: The Forum Ltd., 1984.

Schumaker, Gerald. "Digital Product Models: A Must for CIM." *CIM Technology*, Aug. 1987, 27–30.

Skinner, Wickham. *Manufacturing: The Formidable Competitive Weapon.* New York: John Wiley & Sons, 1985.

Smith, J. M., and D. Smith. "Database Abstractions: Aggregation and Generalizations." *ACM Transactions in Database Systems* 2 (June 1977): 105–133.

Stauffer, Robert N. "Commentaries on FMS Control." *CAD/CAM Technology*, Summer 1984.

————. "Gantry Robots Facilitate Handling in In-Line Workcells." *Robotics Today* 8 (June 1986): 21–22.

————. "Graphics Simulation Answers Preproduction Questions." *CAD/CAM Technology*, Fall 1984, 11–13.

————. "Justification of Robotic Systems." *Robotics Today* 8 (June 1986): 35–43.

————. "Pallet Handling System Solves Dunnage Problem." *Robotics Today* 8 (Apr. 1986): 69–70.

————. "Tool Handling Advancements." *Robotics Today* 8 (Feb. 1986): 25–27.

Stoll, Henry W. "Design for Manufacturing." *Manufacturing Engineering* 100 (Jan. 1988): 67–73.

Stover, Richard. *An Analysis of CAD/CAM Applications with an Introduction to CIM.* Englewood Cliffs, N.J.: Prentice-Hall, 1984.

Sullivan, L. P. "Quality Function Deployment." *Quality Progress* 19 (June 1986): 39–56.

————. "Reducing Variability: A New Approach to Quality." *Quality Progress* 17 (July 1984): 15–21.

————. "The Seven Stages in Company-wide Quality Control." *Quality Progress* 19 (May 1986): 77–83.

Synnott, William R., and William H. Gruber. *Information Resource Management: Opportunities and Strategies for the 1980s.* New York: John Wiley & Sons, 1981.

Bibliography

Thompson, Paul. *CIM: The Information Engineering Methodology*. Boston: Digital Press, forthcoming.

Tepsic, Rudy M. "How to Justify Your FMS." *Manufacturing Engineering* 91 (Sept. 1983): 50–52.

Tulkoff, Joseph. "Process Planning in the New Information Age." *CIM Technology*, August 1987, 19–22.

Ullrich, Richard A. *The Robotics Primer: The What, Why, and How of Robots in the Workplace*. Englewood Cliffs, N.J.: Prentice-Hall, 1983.

Verheijen, G. M. A., and J. Van Bekkam. "NIAM: An Information Analysis Method." In *Information Systems Design Methodologies: A Comparative Review*, ed. T. W. Olle, H. G. Sol, and A. A. Verrijn-Stuart. New York: North-Holland, 1982.

Warnecke, H. J., and R. Steinhilper (eds.). *Flexible Manufacturing Systems*. New York: Springer-Verlag, 1985.

Weiss, Sholom M., and Casimir A. Kulikowski. *A Practical Guide to Designing Expert Systems*. Totowa, N.J.: Rowman and Allanheld, 1984.

Winston, Patrick H., and Karen A. Prendergast (eds.). *The AI Business: Commercial Uses of Artificial Intelligence*. Cambridge, Mass.: MIT Press, 1984.

Winston, Patrick H. *Artificial Intelligence*. 2nd ed. Reading, Mass.: Addison-Wesley, 1984.

Withington, Frederick G. "Coping with Computer Proliferation." *Harvard Business Review* 58 (May–June 1980): 152–164.

Woodward, Harry, and Steve Buchholz. *After-Shock: Helping People through Corporate Change*. New York: John Wiley and Sons, 1987.

Wright, Roger N., and Don A. Lucca (eds.). *Product Design Engineering for Quality Improvement*. Dearborn, Mich.: SME, 1983.

Yeomans, R. W., A. Choudry, and P. J. W. ten Hagen. *Design Rules for a CIM System*. New York: North-Holland, 1985.

Zygmont, Jeffrey. "Flexible Manufacturing Systems: Curing the Cure-All." *High Technology* 6 (Oct. 1986): 22–27.

Index

Page numbers in italics refer to illustrations.

Author

Olin Bray has twenty-five years of experience in information systems design and management, the last ten years in engineering data management and CAD/CAM integration. He has worked for and consulted with various companies, including Combustion Engineering, Control Data, Microelectronics and Computer Technology Corporation (MCC), Sperry (now UNISYS), and Boeing. He is currently with Combustion Engineering developing information models and integration strategies for engineering and manufacturing.

In the early 1980s he managed a large database design project using NIAM to build an information model for the geometry to support solid modeling, drafting, finite element analysis, process planning, and numerical control. He spent a year at MCC researching the engineering data management requirements to support VLSI CAD. Since then he has completed several papers and reports on engineering data management requirements for a distributed environment. He has conducted tutorials on engineering data management at both the ASME Computers in Engineering Conference and at NCGA.

Prior to becoming involved in engineering and manufacturing systems, he spent three years in Sperry's Advanced Systems Department working on distributed database management and database computer architecture. During this period he was an ACM National Lecturer on both areas and co-authored the first book on database computers (*Data Base Computers*, 1979, Lexington Books). He is also the author of *Distributed Database Management Systems* (1982, Lexington Books). He has delivered numerous papers at conferences such as AutoFact, COMPCON, the Hawaii International Conference on System Science, and several NASA workshops. He is currently a Senior Member of CASA/SME and a member of ACM and the IEEE Computer Society. He was also a member of the CODASYL Systems Committee while it was doing its distributed database management systems report.

Earlier Mr. Bray was the information systems manager for a large health center and the manager of a personnel research project. In the 1960s he did applications and systems programming for Boeing and Control Data. He has a B.S. in physics from the University of Alabama and an M.B.A. from the University of Minnesota.